MATCH
OF THE DAY
QUIZ BOOK

Foreword by

Gary Lineker

BOOKS

7 9 10 8

Published in 2013 by BBC Books, an imprint of Ebury Publishing.
A Random House Group Company.

Main text by Phil Bigwood
Copyright © Woodlands Books Ltd 2013

The Random House Group Limited Reg. No. 954009

Addresses for companies within the Random House Group can be found
at www.randomhouse.co.uk

A CIP catalogue record for this book is available from the British Library.

ISBN: 978 1 849 90672 2

Penguin Random House is committed to a sustainable future for
our business, our readers and our planet. This book is made from
Forest Stewardship Council® certified paper.

Commissioning editor: Albert DePetrillo
Managing editor: Joe Cottington
Project editor: Steve Tribe
Production: Phil Spencer

To buy books by your favourite authors and register for offers
visit www.randomhouse.co.uk

Printed and bound in Great Britain by Clays Ltd, St Ives plc

Contents

Foreword
by
Gary Lineker

I t is amazing to think that this is the 50th season that *Match of the Day* has been on the BBC in some form – and during that time we must have brought you thousands of goals, saves and talking points.

Don't worry, there aren't going to be questions in this book about the exact numbers of goals or saves, although someone out there is bound to know the answers. There may well be a few about me and my time with the show so I'll skip all the usual personal thoughts about being in the presenter's chair just in case it gives away any clues.

Why a book of questions about football?

Well, we in the *Match of the Day* office, both in front of and behind the camera, are the same as football fans in every part of the UK. We all enjoy testing each other with trivial and often utterly pointless questions about this great game of ours.

We hope that amongst the 3,000 questions – yes, 3,000! – there will be lots that you know, many that you half remember and a good few that you will have absolutely no chance of knowing unless your name is John Motson!

We have included sections about BBC Football and all five of the regular *Match of the Day* presenters, as well as the key commentators and pundits, plus many of the great players and managers, competitions, supporters, grounds, nicknames and trivia (a *lot* of trivia…). Regardless of who you support or which era you most closely identify with, we hope that there will be questions that all followers of football can find challenging and enjoyable.

Whether your memories begin with watching Greaves, Charlton and Moore in the black and white days of the 1960s or following Beckham, Henry and Messi in the 21st century there should be something for everyone, as the popular saying goes.

And if you like being tested on the decades before the BBC began regularly covering football, or even before the BBC actually existed, there are plenty of testers from the days when shorts were long, studs were dangerous and moustaches seemingly compulsory.

Plus there is a quiz on every one of the seasons that *Match of the Day* has been on air when _____ first presented it, and _____ played _____. (Apparently it was a very good game, but you'll have to fill in all the details yourself when you come across the answers in the relevant quizzes!)

We hope that you get as much out of playing these quizzes as our team did when we put them together and, at the very least, this should help pass the time on those long away trips on a Saturday afternoon before the programme!

Have fun and thanks for watching.

THE
QUESTIONS

1
Pre-Match Warm-up

1
Quick Fire

1   Who managed Manchester United between 1986 and 2013?

2   Bristol has two professional football teams. One is Bristol City, what is the other called?

3   What is the name of the BBC's regular Saturday night football highlights show?

4   In which year did England win the football World Cup?

5   Who were the first British team to win the European Cup?

6   In which season did the Premier League begin in England?

7   Which team play at White Hart Lane?

8   Which Manchester United player married Victoria Adams?

9   With which side is Roy Race most associated as player and manager?

10   What nationality is Pele?

11   Who became the owner of Chelsea in 2003?

12   In which country were the 2010 World Cup finals staged?

13   Which team was managed in the 1970s by Bill Shankly and Bob Paisley?

14   In 1986 who claimed that they had scored a goal against England aided by 'the Hand of God'?

15   Which football team does Noel Gallagher support?

2
Name the Country

Name the countries that these teams play in:

1 Ajax

2 Bayern Munich

3 Udinese

4 Braga

5 Dynamo Kiev

6 Ferencvaros

7 Olympiakos

8 Fenerbahce

9 Lens

10 Real Zaragoza

11 Standard Liege

12 Limerick

13 CSKA Sofia

14 Molde FK

15 Grasshoppers

3
Which City?

Which town or city is home to the following clubs?

1 Celtic and Rangers

2 Everton

3 Aston Villa

4 Galatasaray

5 Anderlecht

6 Espanyol

7 Benfica

8 Port Vale

9 Fiorentina

10 Feyenoord

11 Juventus

12 FC Schalke 04

13 Lazio

14 Sampdoria

15 Boca Juniors

4

Leading Goal-Scorers 2012–2013

Who were the leading Premier League goal-scorers for each of these clubs in the 2012–2013 season?

1   Manchester United

2   Manchester City

3   Chelsea

4   Arsenal

5   Tottenham Hotspur

6   Everton

7   Liverpool

8   West Bromwich Albion

9   Swansea City

10 West Ham United

11   Norwich City

12   Fulham

13   Stoke City

14   Southampton

15   Aston Villa

5
True or False

1   American singer Billy Joel was inspired to write his hit 'Uptown Girl' when he went to watch West Ham v Liverpool as a VIP guest with his girlfriend Christie Brinkley but was forced to change the name from 'Upton Girl' by his US record label.

2   One of Bobby Moore's middle names was 'Chelsea'.

3   'You'll Never Walk Alone', which is sung by Liverpool fans, was written by Gerry and the Pacemakers.

4   Desmond Lynam recorded and recited the Rudyard Kipling poem 'If' at the end of the 1990 World Cup.

5   Former Tottenham Hotspur winger Tony Galvin had a degree in Russian Studies from Hull University.

6   Real Madrid's legendary forward Alfredo di Stefano kept getting restless and played for three different countries, Argentina, Colombia and Spain.

7   In 1979, the Scottish Cup tie between Falkirk and Inverness Caledonian Thistle was postponed 29 times because of bad weather.

8   In 2008, BBC Commentator Jonathan Pearce broke the world record for the most number of balloons, 17, that could be blown up in a minute by mouth.

9   Former England defender and the epitome of the Bulldog Spirit Terry Butcher was actually born in Singapore.

10 Hardman footballer Vinnie Jones appeared alongside Jason Statham and Sting in the hit gangster film *Lock, Stock and Two Smoking Barrels*.

11 Liverpool manager Bill Shankly had a middle name that belied his working class roots. His full name was William Farquhar Shankly.

12 Aston Villa goalkeeper Nigel Spink qualified as a circus juggler after he retired as a player in 2001 and performs throughout Europe.

13 Coventry City was originally named Singer's FC as it was founded by a bicycle company of the same name who were based in the area.

14 Sylvester Stallone claimed to be a fan of Everton and once appeared on pitch waving a club scarf.

15 As well as owning several racehorses and being known for his love of wine, Sir Alex Ferguson has been painted by his idol David Hockney.

6
More True or False

1   As well as being one of the greatest English batsmen of all time, cricketer Denis Compton also won the League and the FA Cup with Arsenal.

2   Derbyshire club Glossop North End played one season in the First Division in 1899–1900.

3   Between 2003 and 2004, Arsenal were undefeated in a record 59 consecutive Premier League games.

4   Before turning to management, Jose Mourinho played for Inter Milan and Sampdoria but retired at 28 through injury.

5   John Motson once played Nanny Fanny Motty in a charity version of *The Sleeping Beauty* at the Abbey Theatre in St Albans in 2007.

6   Former Premiership heartthrob David Ginola stared as a handsome, romantic butcher in a film called *Rosbeef* in 2004.

7   In 1937, the Charlton Athletic goalkeeper Sam Bartram had assumed that all the match action was at the Chelsea end before being informed by a policeman that the match had been abandoned 15 minutes earlier because of the thick fog at Stamford Bridge.

8   Having retired as players, Bobby and Jack Charlton started a chain of greengrocers in the North East called 'Brothers in Farms'.

9   Didier Drogba scored in four different FA Cup finals for Chelsea.

10 Former Manchester City legend Francis Lee made millions from running a toilet roll business after retiring as a player and gained the nickname 'the Bog Roll King'.

11 Goalkeeper John Burridge played for 29 different clubs including Sheffield United, Blackpool and Southampton but he paid an expensive penalty when he was caught red-handed selling fake designer clothing from the back of a van at one of his grounds.

12 England and Barcelona manager Terry Venables co-created a hit 1970's ITV series about a fictional detective.

13 Brian Clough was twice approached to stand for Parliament as a member of the Liberal party.

14 Author and comedian Tony Hawks once tracked down each member of the Moldovan national team who had lost a World Cup qualifier to England and beat them at tennis, just to win a drunken bet.

15 Kick-off at the 1978 FA Cup final between Ipswich Town and Arsenal was delayed by 15 minutes after Bruce Forsyth pulled a muscle in his back whilst conducting the crowd from the top of a podium on the pitch in the then traditional pre-match sing-a-long. He had to be treated at the ground before being moved to a local hospital.

2
Welcome to the BBC

7

Gary Lineker

1   What is Gary's middle name?

2   In which season did Gary make his Division Two debut for his first club, Leicester City?

3   Gary made his England debut in 1984 against which side?

4   How many hat-tricks did Gary score for England?

5   Which manager signed Gary for Barcelona in 1986?

6   In 1996, Gary became the regular presenter of which BBC football show from inside a large virtual football?

7   Who is the only England player to have scored more than Gary's 48 goals for the national team?

8   What is the name of the Japanese side that Gary played for in the final two seasons of his career?

9   In which year did Gary take over from Desmond Lynam as the main presenter of *Match of the Day*?

10 Arthur Smith and Chris England wrote which Olivier Award-nominated play that included Gary's name in the title?

11 He holds the record for the most goals scored by an England player in World Cup finals. How many did he score?

12 In 1986, he was the leading scorer in Division One but had to settle for runners-up spots in both the FA Cup and Division One. Which team was he playing for?

13 The only major British competition that Gary won was the 1991 FA Cup. Which team was he playing for?

14 In Gary's final match as an England player, against Sweden in Euro '92 he was taken off by manager Graham Taylor and replaced by which Arsenal player?

15 Since 2002 Gary has presented every edition of which biennial BBC fundraiser?

8
Jimmy Hill

1   Jimmy was born in Balham, London, in which year?

2   Which year did Jimmy make his debut for Brentford?

3   Jimmy made more than 300 appearances for which club between 1952 and 1961?

4   When Jimmy was chairman of the PFA, he successfully campaigned for the maximum wage for footballers to be scrapped. What was the maximum that a player could earn each week before the rules were changed in January 1961?

5   When Jimmy became manager of Coventry City in 1961, his only part-time assistant was a young player who had broken his leg. He later managed Chesterfield, Newcastle United and Derby County. What is his name?

6   Jimmy acted as technical advisor on the BBC football-based drama series *United!* between 1965 and 1967. What was the name of the fictional football team that it featured?

7   Who was the regular presenter of the new weekly football shows

The Big Match and *On the Ball* that were launched by Jimmy when he was Head of Sport at London Weekend Television?

8   What name did Jimmy persuade Richard Davies to adopt as he thought it sounded 'warmer'?

9   At which ground did Jimmy act as an emergency replacement linesman in September 1972?

10 Who did Jimmy succeed as the presenter of *Match of the Day* when he moved to the BBC in 1973?

11 One of the most iconic sets of opening titles for *Match of the Day* featured a giant image of Jimmy's head being held up on 2,000 cards at which football ground?

12 Jimmy ran the Detroit Express franchise in the North American Soccer League in the late 1970s. Which striker, signed on loan from Birmingham City, scored 36 goals in 33 appearances for the team?

13 At the end of which season did Jimmy's spell as the regular presenter of *Match of the Day* come to an end?

14 What was the name of the weekend football show that Jimmy first presented on Sky Sports in 1999?

15 Which football club unveiled a statue of Jimmy outside its ground in 2011?

9

BBC TV Football Presenters

Identify the presenter:

1   Reporter and presenter who fronted *Football Focus* from 1999 to 2004 and presented many editions of *Match of the Day* during his 19 years with BBC Sport

2   Former Arsenal and Wales captain who presented *Match of the Day* several times in 1964 and 1965

3   The voice of *Look North*, who first worked for BBC Sport in 1983 and once presented a hastily arranged *Match of the Day* from Leeds to cover an FA Cup replay

4   Double-winning Arsenal goalkeeper who first presented *Football Focus* in 1974

5   Head of BBC Sport who also presented the original *Football Preview* on *Grandstand* before it became *Football Focus*

6   West Bromwich Albion fan who presented *MOTD2* when it began in 2004

7   Took over as presenter of *Football Focus* in 2009

8   Better known as a commentator, he first presented *Match of the Day* in December 1969 and occasionally fronted the show when David Coleman was away

9   The first woman presenter of *Football Focus* and *Match of the Day*

10 *Grandstand* presenter who also hosted *Football Focus* for two seasons between 1994 and 1996

11 Radio 5 Live's voice of sport since 2000, who presented an edition of *Match of the Day* in 2004 straight after six hours of a live radio show

12 Before becoming the main presenter of *Grandstand*, hosted several early editions of *Match of the Day* and was part of the BBC's presentation team for the 1966 World Cup coverage

13 Presenter of *Football Focus* from 2004 and *The Football League Show* from 2009

14 Presenter of *Sportsround* who became the youngest person to host *Football Focus* when he fronted the show for eight weeks in 2006

15 Former international gymnast who presented *Final Score* from 2009 to 2013

10
Football on BBC TV: The Early Years

1   The first ever live televising of footballers took place on Wednesday 15 September of which year? It only consisted of two minutes of mute pictures from Highbury at 3.45pm, and went out as part of a magazine show called *Picture Page*.

2   Which Arsenal manager, when asked about his squad, said, 'They are from Scotland, Yorkshire, Wales, all over the place ... just provided they are British subjects. We couldn't put a foreigner in the team'?

3   When the BBC resumed after the Second World War, what was the maximum distance that they could travel from their Alexandra Palace home in order to cover a live football match?

4   What was significant about the role of Edgar Kail in 1946?

5   Who in 1954 introduced a show in vision saying, 'The accent is on soccer and that's why we have asked Kenneth Wolstenholme to occupy the *Sportsview* chair to introduce *Saturday Sports Special* to you each week at around ten o'clock. So Kenneth, please take over and good luck for the new *Sportsview* unit Saturday programmes', before walking off the set?

6   The first edition of *Match of the Day* was broadcast on BBC Two on 22 August 1964. Who was the presenter?

7   BBC One's line-up that night included *The Telegoons*, *Juke Box Jury* hosted by David Jacobs, *Dr Finlay's Casebook* and *Perry Mason*. Who played the title character in *Doctor Who* that day?

8   How much did the BBC pay the Football League for the right to cover the highlights of one match a week for 36 weeks in that first season?

9   In the first few seasons, the highlights of only one match were permitted. Which game was featured in the first programme?

10 Which BBC Two controller had to agree to let the show switch to BBC One at the start of the 1966–1967 season?

11 In which year did the BBC's broadcast of Tottenham Hotspur against Manchester United in the Charity Shield become the first time in Britain that a football match had been shown in colour?

12 How much was a TV licence in 1969?

13 A new *Match of the Day* theme tune was introduced at the start of the 1970–1971 season, replacing Leslie Statham's 'The Drum Majorette'. Who wrote the new, and now iconic, music?

14 In August 1973, the *Radio Times* featured *Match of the Day* on their front cover with the headline 'Snatch of the Year'. What did it refer to?

15 In which season did *Football Focus* begin?

11
Football on the Box

Name these shows:

1   BBC Saturday night highlights show that began in 1964

2   Saturday lunchtime BBC football preview show first presented in 1974

3   1960s BBC midweek sports show that was named after its presenter and featured the Commentators Competition and the Kop Choirs Competition

4   ITV weekend football highlights show presented by Brian Moore from 1968

5   The BBC's first weekly sports show to feature football news and highlights, presented on Thursday nights from 1954 by Peter Dimmock

6   European Football show presented by James Richardson on Channel 4 from 1992 to 2002

7   Fan forum on BBC Choice presented by Matt Smith and Mark Bright

8   ITV Saturday lunchtime show running from 1985 to 1992 and presented by two former English and Scottish footballers

9   Sky TV's Saturday morning show, whose hosts have included Tim Lovejoy and Helen Chamberlain

10   BBC Scotland football show that began in 1975, with presenters including Dougie Donnelly and Dougie Vipond

11   Sunday night football show first presented on BBC Two by Adrian Chiles in 2004

12   BBC Two show presented by Frank Skinner and David Baddiel in the mid 1990s

13   BBC Children's programme fronted by Matt Smith, Lee Sharpe and Katy Hill in 2000

14   Highlights show presented by Manish Bhasin late evening on BBC One since 2009

15   The BBC's first weekend highlights show, presented by Kenneth Wolstenholme when it began in September 1955

12
BBC TV Voices of Football

1   A BBC football commentator for almost 40 years who also presented *Sportsnight* and once had to identify the Romanian team in the 1998 World Cup when they ran out with identical haircuts, cropped short and dyed blonde, against Tunisia

2   Australian-born reporter who read the football scores on *Grandstand* from the first show in 1958 until he died in 1995

3   After a career that included spells with Gillingham, Bournemouth and QPR, he was a regular BBC pundit after retiring in 2001 but moved to Canada in 2008 to take up religious studies

4   Born in 1930, this long-serving reporter and commentator for ITV and the BBC also spent several years involved in ballet and opera productions

5   Former Crystal Palace and Sheffield Wednesday striker who has been a regular pundit on *Football Focus* and Radio 5 Live

6   West Ham United and England midfielder who became a long-serving BBC football pundit and commentator on retiring in 1984

7   Versatile Yorkshireman who commentated on football for Radio 5

Live, *Match of the Day*, ITV, Setanta and ESPN

8   The reader of the Saturday football results on *Grandstand* and *Final Score* from 1995 to 2011, when he retired just before his 82nd birthday after a 60-year broadcasting career

9   QPR, Tottenham Hotspur and England manager who formed a memorably argumentative punditry partnership with Jimmy Hill on *Match of the Day* in the early 1990s

10 Tenaciously direct reporter and interviewer who has worked at many major football tournaments, been a regular contributor to *Football Focus* and hosts *Sportsweek* on Radio 5 Live

11 Former Eurosport and ITV commentator who joined the BBC in 2004 and succeeded John Motson in commentating on England's matches in the major tournaments

12 One of the BBC commentators at the start of the Premier League who moved to ITV in 1996 and established himself as their leading voice

13 Hull-born reporter, who is a regular on *Football Focus* and *Final Score* and has been involved in numerous major tournaments

14 Former Tottenham Hotspur and Manchester United striker who has been a regular pundit on *Match of the Day*, *Football Focus* and *Final Score* since the early 1990s

15 Arsenal and England fullback who became a regular pundit on BBC TV on his retirement in 2002 and transferred to ITV in 2012

13

John Motson and Barry Davies

1   Barry attended the same school as two other legendary commentators, ITV's Brian Moore and the BBC's Peter West. What was the school?

2   How many World Cup finals has John attended as a BBC commentator?

3   Barry made his World Cup commentary debut for ITV in which year?

4   In which year did John retire from commentating on live matches for BBC TV?

5   In which year did Barry commentate on the World Cup final?

6   In 1972, John's star rose when he commentated on an epic FA Cup third-round replay between Newcastle United and which other side?

7   How many FA Cup finals did Barry commentate on for BBC TV?

8   When John appeared on BBC Radio 4's *Great Lives*, series who did he nominate as his Great Life?

9   Barry has commentated on more Olympic Games than any other BBC broadcaster. How many had he covered up until 2012?

10 Which team does John support?

11 Which team did Barry only reveal that he supported after he had retired from *Match of the Day*?

12 When does John like to get to the ground when he is commentating?

13 Which branch of the medical profession did Barry study?

14 At which ground was John famously filmed in 1990 whilst wearing his sheepskin coat during a snowstorm?

15 Who had Barry just seen score a goal when he exclaimed, 'Look at his face, just look at his face'?

14
Kenneth Wolstenholme

1   In which year was he born?

2   Ken won several bravery awards during eight years spent in which service?

3   His first football commentary was a Third Division (North) game between York City and Stockport County. What was the name of York's then home ground?

4   Ken was the football commentator for which brand new midweek show that was launched on the BBC in 1954 and presented by Peter Dimmock?

5   Who was the commentator for ITV at the 1966 World Cup final?

6   How many FA Cup finals did Ken commentate on for the BBC?

7   Which football team did Ken support?

8   Ken's last commentary for the BBC was the European Cup final at Wembley in 1971. Ajax beat which Greek team 2-0?

9   Which international league did Ken commentate on for Channel 4

after he left the BBC?

10 How much did Ken earn for commentating on the 1966 World Cup final?

11 He regularly featured as the character of Frank Lee Brian in which Radio 4 comedy series written by Harry Thompson and Marcus Berkmann?

12 Who succeeded Ken as the BBC's FA Cup final commentator?

13 Which member of England's 1966 World Cup-winning team had been to the same school as Ken, Farnworth Grammar School?

14 Who was the host of the BBC TV quiz show *They Think It's All Over*, when it began in 1995?

15 Ken published his autobiography in 1999. What is the title of the book?

3
Fans Arrive

15
Former Ground Names 1

These are the former grounds of which English football teams?

1   Roker Park

2   Filbert Street

3   Plough Lane

4   Gay Meadow

5   Burnden Park

6   Maine Road

7   The Old Showground

8   Baseball Ground

9   Highfield Road Stadium

10 Layer Road

11 Elm Park

12 Ayresome Park

13 Fellows Park

14 Victoria Ground

15 The Dell

16

More Former Ground Names

1   Fleetwood Town have the same stadium name as Arsenal's old ground. What is it?

2   Millwall used to play at The Den. Where do they play now?

3   Where did Bolton Wanderers stage their home games before moving to the Reebok Stadium?

4   Leeds Road once belonged to which Football League club in Yorkshire?

5   The Canaries left The Nest in 1935. Who are they and where did they move to?

6   Who used to play at Loakes Park?

7   Which club played at Belle Vue until December 2006?

8   Where did Swansea City play before moving to the Liberty Stadium?

9   On 8 May 2010, Chesterfield hosted Bournemouth in the last match at which stadium?

10 Where did Brighton and Hove Albion play before moving to the American Express Community Stadium?

11 Notts County used which Test match cricket venue for football until 1910?

12 Which former Football League club used to play at Feethams?

13 Who formerly played at Boothferry Park?

14 What do Wigan's former home and *The Simpsons* have in common?

15 Stoke City moved to the Britannia Stadium in 1997. Where were they before this?

17
English League Stadiums with a Capacity below 30,000

Name the teams:

1   Brunton Park

2   The Hawthorns

3   New York Stadium

4   KC Stadium

5   Oakwell

6   Valley Parade (Coral Windows Stadium)

7   Britannia Stadium

8   Keepmoat Stadium

9   Prenton Park

10   (MEMS) Priestfield Stadium

11 Bescot Stadium (Banks's Stadium)

12 Whaddon Road (Abbey Business Stadium)

13 Turf Moor

14 Bloomfield Road

15 Kassam Stadium

18
Scottish Football Grounds

Who plays here?

1   Rugby Park

2   Easter Road

3   Tynecastle Stadium

4   Pittodrie Stadium

5   Ibrox Stadium

6   Hampden Park

7   Tannadice Park

8   Fir Park

9   Excelsior Stadium (New Broomfield)

10 Palmerston Park

11 Stair Park

12 East End Park

13 Dens Park

14 Station Park

15 Bayview Stadium

19

A European Tour

Which grounds do these European Clubs play at?

1 Barcelona

2 AC Milan and Inter Milan

3 Bayern Munich and 1860 Munich

4 FC Porto

5 Real Madrid

6 AS Roma and SS Lazio

7 Red Star Belgrade

8 Borussia Dortmund

9 Paris Saint-Germain

10 FC Basel

11 Spartak Moscow

12 PSV Eindhoven

13 Juventus

14 Shakhtar Donetsk

15 Atletico Madrid

4
Meet the Teams

20
Arsenal

1   Arsene Wenger became manager in October of which year?

2   Who scored the last-minute goal against Liverpool to clinch the Division One title in the final game of the 1988–1989 season?

3   Which Irish centre-back made 722 appearances between 1975 and 1993?

4   Which legendary manager won two League titles and the FA Cup between 1925 and 1934?

5   Who joined Arsenal from Bordeaux for a reported £13m in 2000?

6   Having been undefeated in the Premier League during the entire 2003–2004 season, what nickname did the team acquire?

7   Where is Arsenal's training ground?

8   George Graham won six major trophies during his time in charge. Which national team had he represented on 12 occasions as a player?

9 Theo Walcott and Alex Oxlade-Chamberlain joined Arsenal from which side?

10 Which former Manchester United stalwart acted as caretaker manager for a total of 25 games either side of the short reign of Bruce Rioch?

11 Who was voted Player of the Year in 2007, 2008 and 2010?

12 Who managed the 1970–1971 Double-winning side?

13 Which player captained Arsenal to FA Cup glory in the 1979 final when they beat Manchester United 3-2?

14 Which trophy did they win in 1994 having beaten Parma 1-0 in the final?

15 Patrick Viera won four FA Cups during his time with Arsenal. With which other British side did he also win the FA Cup?

21
Aston Villa

1 In which English city are the club based?

2 Who scored the only goal of the 1982 European Cup final when they beat Bayern Munich?

3 In which year did American businessman Randy Lerner become chairman of the club?

4 From which club did Juan Pablo Angel join Villa for £9.5m in 2001?

5 Who thrashed Villa 8-0 in December 2012 in the Premier League?

6 With 23 goals in all competitions, which German finished the 2012–2013 season as top scorer for the club?

7 Who did Villa beat 2-1 in the 1957 FA Cup final?

8 Which former player was their manager when they lost the 2000 FA Cup final 1-0 to Chelsea?

9 How many League titles did they win between 1893–1894 and 1980–1981?

10 Which animal appears on the club badge?

11 What surname was shared by the club's manager and the opening goal-scorer when they beat Manchester United 3-1 to win the 1994 League Cup final?

12 Who was Aston Villa's ever-present goalkeeper when they won the League Championship in 1980–1981?

13 Which is the only team to have spent more years in the top flight than Villa?

14 Who was appointed manager in June 2012?

15 What nationality was Charlie Aitken who holds the club's appearance record with a total of 657 between 1959 and 1976?

22
Birmingham City

1 Which former Newcastle United and Fulham player became manager in June 2012?

2 When they were founded in 1875 what was their name?

3 Which club did Bob Latchford join when he left Birmingham City in 1974?

4 What is the name of their ground?

5 In which year did they get beaten 3-1 by Manchester City in the FA Cup final?

6 Who was manager when they won the League Cup in 1963?

7 Who, with 14 goals, was leading scorer when they came second in the Championship and returned to the Premier League in 2008–2009?

8 Which competition did they win in 1991 and 1995?

9 Who did they sign from Valencia for £6m in 2010?

10 Who did they beat 2-1 to win the 2011 League Cup final?

11 Who scored 133 goals in 329 games for the club before moving to Nottingham Forest?

12 In 2008, they sold Olivier Kapo to which team for £3.5m?

13 Which former Barnet and Southend manager was in charge of the club between 1993 and 1996?

14 In which season were they relegated to Division Three for the only time in their history?

15 Which manager twice led them into the Premier League?

23
Blackburn Rovers

1   In which year was the club founded?

2   Who was appointed captain in March 2013 having joined in 2011 from Birmingham City?

3   Blackburn Rovers won the Premier League in 1994–1995. When had they last been English champions?

4   Who was their manager when they won the Premier League?

5   What is the name of their ground?

6   In 2001, they bought Andrew Cole for £8m from which club?

7   In which year did Mark Hughes, Paul Ince and Sam Allardyce all manage the club?

8   Which former Carlisle United striker scored the opening goal of the 2002 League Cup final when they beat Tottenham Hotspur 2-1?

9   Who succeeded Kenny Dalglish as manager in June 1995?

10 When was the only time that they won the FA Cup in the 20th century?

11 What trophy did they win in 1987, beating Charlton Athletic 1-0 in the final?

12 What is the name of the new owners who purchased the club in 2010?

13 Who was their leading goal-scorer when they won the Premier League?

14 Who beat in them in the semi-final of the 2006–2007 FA Cup?

15 Who scored 168 goals in 474 league appearances for the club between 1978 and 1992?

24
Celtic

1   What is the name of their ground?

2   Which former Ipswich Town manager was in charge for the nine months before Neil Lennon became manager?

3   By what name are they collectively known with Rangers?

4   When they won the 2012–2013 League title, which club was in second place, 16 points behind?

5   In which season did they win the League, Cup, League Cup and European Cup?

6   Which team did they beat 9-0 in the Scottish Premier League in November 2010?

7   What nationality was Jozef Venglos, who managed the team in the 1998–1999 season?

8   Who led Celtic to nine league titles, seven Scottish Cups, six Scottish League Cups and the European Cup as captain?

9   Which Swedish striker scored 242 goals for Celtic between 1997 and 2004?

10 Who was in goal when Celtic won the European Cup having previously won two FA Cups with Newcastle United?

11 Which English-born forward was their leading scorer in the 2012–2013 season with 29 goals in 50 games?

12 How many goals did Jimmy McGrory score against Dunfermline in their 1928 meeting in the Scottish Division One?

13 Which former Nottingham Forest and Notts County player managed them to the final of the 2003 UEFA Cup, where they lost 3-2 to Porto?

14 What is their official club nickname?

15 In which year did Jock Stein become manager?

25
Chelsea

1   In which year were they founded?

2   Who managed them to their first League title in 1954–1955?

3   Which player holds the record for most appearances, with 795 between 1961 and 1980?

4   How many league goals did Jimmy Greaves score in 1960–1961? It remains a record.

5   In which season did they become the first team to score 100 Premier League goals?

6   Which side beat them 8-1 in 1953?

7   Which goalkeeper kept 21 clean sheets in the 2004–2005 Premier League season?

8   What was the main feature to appear on Chelsea's crest until 1952?

9   Who was their manager when they won the Premier League in 2004–2005 and 2005–2006?

10 Who did they beat in the 2012 Champions League final?

11 How many goals did Kerry Dixon score for the club?

12 Who was their last English-born manager? He was in charge from 1988 to 1991.

13 Which English team did they beat in the semi-final of the 1971 European Cup Winners' Cup?

14 Tommy Docherty was manager between 1962 and 1967. What was the only major trophy that the club won during that time?

15 Who was voted Chelsea's Player of the Year in 2012 and 2013?

26
Everton

1   What was the name of the club when they were founded in 1878?

2   What is the name of their ground?

3   Who were Everton's opponents when they won the 1985 European Cup Winners' Cup final?

4   Who scored a club record 383 goals in 433 appearances?

5   In May 2005, they lost 7-0 to Arsenal. Who was the Everton manager at the time?

6   Which player made 750 first-team appearances between 1981 and 1998?

7   Which Premier League side bought Joleon Lescott and Jack Rodwell from Everton in 2009 and 2012?

8   In which championship-winning season did they win 29 league matches?

9   Who managed Everton to the First Division titles in 1984–1985 and 1986–1987?

10 Which team did they beat 8-0 in the second round of the League Cup in 1978?

11 Who spent his entire career at the club and made 534 appearances between 1958 and 1971 and also won 26 caps for England?

12 Who did they beat 1-0 in the 1995 FA Cup final?

13 In 2008, they paid Standard Liege £15m for which player?

14 How many goals did Graeme Sharp score in his 426 games for the club?

15 Which star of their 1960s side was nicknamed 'the Golden Vision'?

27
Huddersfield Town

1   In which county is the club based?

2   What was their final position in the 2012–2013 Championship table?

3   How many consecutive Division One titles did they win under Herbert Chapman in the 1920s?

4   What is the name of their ground?

5   With 574 appearances between 1913 and 1934, which player was a key member of Chapman's great side?

6   Which goalkeeper played in every league game when they won the Division Two title in 1969–1970?

7   In 1996, they paid £1.2m for Marcus Stewart to join them from which club?

8   Which former Barnsley and Coventry City manager took charge at the club in February 2013?

9   Who proved to be less than super as manager when Manchester City beat them 10-1 in 1987?

10 Which 1966 World Cup winner spent 12 years with the club?

11 In which season did they win the FA Cup?

12 Who managed them on three separate occasions – 1964–1968, 1975–1977 and 1977–1978?

13 Which locally born player scored 150 goals for the club during two spells between 1992 and 2009?

14 Between 1956–1957 and 2012–2013, how many seasons did they spend in the top division?

15 Who cost a reputed £8m when he was signed from Blackburn Rovers in August 2012?

28
Leeds United

1   In which year were they founded?

2   Which former Wimbledon player managed them between 2006 and 2008?

3   What was the points deduction imposed in 2007 for entering into administration that saw the club relegated to the third tier?

4   Who did they beat 1-0 to win the 1972 FA Cup final?

5   Under Don Revie, they won the League title twice. How many times did they finish in second place whilst he was in charge?

6   Luciano Becchio finished the 2012–2013 season as the club's leading goal-scorer, despite being transferred to which Premier League side on 31 January?

7   Which World Cup winner holds the record for most Leeds United appearances, 773?

8   In 2000–2001, Leeds United reached the semi-finals of the Champions League, where they were knocked out by which Spanish side?

9   Who bought the club and became chairman in 2011?

10 Right-back Gary Kelly spent his entire career with Leeds United and played 531 games between 1992 and 2007. Which national side capped him 51 times?

11 Following Brian Clough's infamous 44-day reign, who succeeded him as manager?

12 In which season did they win the last ever Division One title before the advent of the Premier League?

13 What is the name of their home ground?

14 Which player was bought from West Ham United for £18m and sold to Manchester United for more than £30m?

15 Who was appointed manager in April 2013?

29
Liverpool

1   Who was appointed manager in June 2012?

2   How many Division One titles did they win during the years when Bill Shankly and Bob Paisley managed the club?

3   What is the name of the ground that Liverpool play at?

4   In which year did they win the FA Cup for the first time?

5   How many times have they won the European Cup/Champions League?

6   Who made 857 appearances for Liverpool between 1960 and 1978?

7   Who was the manager when they completed the League and FA Cup Double for the first time in 1985–1986?

8   In which year did Jamie Carragher make his Liverpool debut?

9   Who made his Liverpool debut against West Bromwich Albion in 2012 at the age of 16 years and 6 days?

10 Which four-word motto appears on top of the Liverpool club badge?

11 Between 1996 and 2004, Michael Owen scored 158 goals for Liverpool. Which club did he leave them to join?

12 Which was the only trophy that Liverpool won under Roy Evans?

13 Who joined Liverpool in January 2011 from Ajax for a fee reported to be £23m?

14 Which full-back made a record 417 consecutive appearances between October 1976 and September 1983?

15 Who played for Liverpool between 1978 and 1984 before returning as manager from 1991 to 1994?

30
Manchester City

1   What was the pre-sponsorship name of their current ground?

2   When did they win the Division One title for the first time?

3   Who was their first-choice goalkeeper throughout the Premier League winning 2011–2012 season?

4   Who managed the team 269 times between 1974 and 1979 and has also acted as caretaker manager on four other occasions?

5   Which Argentinian joined them from Atletico Madrid in 2011 for a reported £38m?

6   Who did they beat 2-1 to win the 1976 League Cup final?

7   In which season were they relegated to Division Three for the only time in their history?

8   Their famous black and red away strip was deliberately copied by Malcolm Allison from which team?

9   Who was their most successful manager, winning the League, FA Cup, League Cup and European Cup Winners' Cup?

10 In which year did they lose an FA Cup final to Tottenham Hotspur under the management of John Bond?

11 Former owner Thaksin Shinawatra had been Prime Minister of which country?

12 Which shirt number was retired following the death of Marc-Vivien Foe in 2003?

13 Alan Oakes appeared for the team more than any other player, making his debut in 1959. In which year did he play for Manchester City for a 676th and final time?

14 Which club did they sell Mario Balotelli to in 2013?

15 Which side did Manchester City beat 3-2 to clinch the Premier League title in the final game of the 2011–2012 season?

31
Manchester United

1   Before Alex Ferguson arrived at the club, when had they last won the Division One title?

2   Which player retired for a second time at the end of the 2012–2013 season, having made 718 appearances for Manchester United?

3   What was the club's original name between 1878 and 1902?

4   Who managed the club immediately before Alex Ferguson took over in 1986?

5   In 2004, Wayne Rooney joined Manchester United from which club?

6   Who scored the winning goal when they beat Liverpool 2-1 in the 1977 FA Cup final?

7   Who was awarded the European Golden Shoe, UEFA Club Footballer of the Year and FIFA World Player of the Year in 2008?

8   Who scored a club record 249 goals in 758 appearances between 1956 and 1973?

9   The 1985 FA Cup final was memorable for Norman Whiteside's winning goal and Kevin Moran's sending off against Everton. Who was the United captain?

10 In which season did they win the Treble of the Champions League, Premier League and FA Cup?

11 Which striker moved from Nottingham Forest to Manchester United in 1980 for a £1.2m fee?

12 In which year was the Munich Air Crash, which claimed 23 lives, including eight players?

13 What is the name of the American family who own the club?

14 In 1993, Manchester United won the first ever Premier League title. Who finished in second place?

15 Peter Schmeichel spent almost all of the 1990s in the United goal. Which national team capped him 129 times?

32
Middlesbrough

1   Who became club chairman in 1994?

2   In which county is the club?

3   In 1998, Paul Merson was sold for an estimated £7m to which club?

4   Which trophy did they win in 1975–1976, beating Fulham 1-0 in the two-legged final?

5   Which future Republic of Ireland manager was in charge at the club between 1973 and 1977?

6   In which season did they win the League Cup?

7   Who made more than 400 appearances for the club between 1925 and 1939 and holds most of their goal-scoring records, including scoring 63 goals in the 1926–1927 season?

8   Who beat them 2-0 in the 1997 FA Cup final?

9   Who captained the club for six seasons from 1973 and helped lead them to the 1973–1974 Division Two title?

10   Who was their manager for 314 matches between 1994 and 2000?

11   In 2008, they spent £12.8m buying which player from SC Heerenveen?

12   Who spent almost a decade at the club as a player and became manager in 2010?

13   In 1958, they set a club record league score of 9-0 against which team?

14   Which club legend was blond, nicknamed the Golden Boy, 5'5" tall and made 26 appearances for England between 1946 and 1951?

15   What nationality was goalkeeper Mark Schwarzer who played 446 times for the club?

33
Newcastle United

1   What is the name of Newcastle's ground?

2   Which short-lived competition did they win in 1974 and 1975?

3   Which player was sold to Tottenham Hotspur for £2m in 1988?

4   Who was manager when they came second in the Premier League in 1995–1996 and 1996–1997?

5   Which bird has appeared on the club's crest and is also the club's main nickname?

6   Jackie Milburn, Bobby Mitchell and George Hannah all scored when Newcastle United won their most recent FA Cup in 1955. Which side did they beat 3-1?

7   Which goalkeeper made 462 appearances for the club between 1997 and 2009?

8   What nationality was Nikos Dabizas who played for the team between 1998 and 2004?

9   Which legendary player scored six goals in one match against Newport County in a Division Two match in 1946?

10 In which season did they win the last of their 4 Division One titles?

11 Who, with 13 goals, was the club's lead scorer in the Premier League in the 2012–2013 season?

12 In 1969, they won the Inter-Cities Fairs Cup final and beat which Hungarian side 6-2 on aggregate?

13 Which Argentinian became the club's first non-British manager when he took charge in March 1991?

14 Who is the club's all-time record scorer with 206 goals?

15 Which manager led them back into the Premier League in 2009–2010 as Championship champions?

34
Norwich City

1 In which year were they founded?

2 Which member of England's 1966 World Cup-winning team played for them from 1975 to 1980?

3 What is the name of their ground?

4 Who was their manager when they won the 1985 League Cup final against Sunderland?

5 Which actor and writer, who has played Jeeves and Oscar Wilde, is a fan of the team?

6 Who was their first-choice goalkeeper between 1963 and 1980?

7 Which striker was voted their player of the year in 2010, 2011 and 2012?

8 In which season did they come third in the Premier League?

9 What nationality was Johnny Gavin, who scored a record 132 times for the club in two spells between 1948 and 1958?

10 Who beat them 1-0 in the 1992 FA Cup semi-final?

11 Who made 662 appearances for the club and then managed them between 1962 and 1966?

12 From which side did Norwich City sign Sebastien Bassong from for £5.5m in 2012?

13 Which manager took them back into the Premier League as Division One champions in the 2003–2004 season?

14 Which county is Norwich in?

15 Who was appointed manager in June 2012?

35
Rangers

1 In which city are they based?

2 As of 2013, the club holds the world record for the most domestic trophies won by a single club. How many is that?

3 In which year did they win their only European Trophy, the UEFA Cup Winners' Cup?

4 Which English Centre forward played for the team between 1990 and 1995, making a brief return in 1997?

5 Which Spanish striker scored the only goal of the 2009 Scottish Cup final when they beat Falkirk 1-0?

6 Who was their manager between 1920 and 1954, winning 18 titles and 10 Scottish Cups?

7 Which player had Paul Le Guen stripped of the club captaincy three days before he then resigned as manager in January 2007?

8 How many consecutive titles did they win in a long run of success that began in 1988–1989?

9   Who twice scored six goals in a single game, against Ayr United and Dunfermline Athletic, in the 1930s?

10 Which non-playing goalkeeper in France's 1998 World Cup-winning squad made occasional appearances for Rangers between 1998 and 2001?

11 In 2000, they paid a reported £12m to buy Tore Andre Flo from which English team?

12 Following liquidation, in which division did Rangers play in the 2012–2013 season?

13 Two men have managed them twice. Jock Wallace was one; who was the other, who was in charge in 1991–1998 and 2007–2011?

14 What is the name of their home ground?

15 Who, with 355 goals, is the club's leading scorer?

36
Reading

1 Established in 1871, when did the club join the Football League?

2 Between 1947 and 1952 they were managed by which prolific former Southampton and Chelsea striker?

3 Which was their first ever season in the top division of English football?

4 Which club paid Reading £7m for Gylfi Sigurdsson in 2010?

5 What is the name of their stadium?

6 Which goalkeeper began his professional career at the club and played for them between 1992 and 1995?

7 Who was the Northern Ireland international who was player manager between 1994 and 1997?

8 Who scored a club record of 191 goals for the club in two separate spells?

9 In 1988, they beat Luton Town 4-1 in the final of which Trophy?

10 Who made 603 appearances for the club between 1978 and 1991?

11 In which season did they lose 3-0 to Cardiff City in an FA Cup semi-final?

12 Who managed them for just 23 games in 2009?

13 Which player made 156 consecutive first-team appearances and went 1,103 minutes without conceding a goal?

14 Against which team did they concede three goals within the first six minutes of an FA Cup fifth-round match in 2007?

15 Which manager took them into the Premier League in 2006 and saw them relegated again in 2008?

37
Southampton

1 Southampton is in which county?

2 Who was manager when they won the 1976 FA Cup?

3 They were relegated from the Premier League in 2005, ending how many consecutive seasons in the top league?

4 Who scored a record 227 goals in two spells between 1966 and 1982, invariably celebrating with a distinctive windmill arm action?

5 In which season did they finish runners-up in Division One?

6 Which former Scottish international was in charge when they reached the 2003 FA Cup final?

7 Who replaced Nigel Adkins as manager in January 2013?

8 What is the club's official nickname?

9 When they were first promoted to Division One in 1966 which future England striker was responsible for scoring 30 of their 85 league goals?

10 Who did they beat 4-1 in the 2010 Football League Trophy final?

11 How many England caps did Matthew Le Tissier win?

12 Who was the club chairman who appointed Harry Redknapp as manager in 2004, shortly after he had left as boss of Portsmouth?

13 What nationality was Egil Ostenstad, signed by Graeme Souness?

14 At the end of which season were they given a ten-point deduction for going into administration and dropped into the third tier?

15 In June 2012 Jay Rodriguez joined them for a club record £7m from which team?

38
Tottenham Hotspur

1   What was the name of the ground they played at before moving to White Hart Lane?

2   Which manager signed Osvaldo Ardiles and Ricky Villa in 1978?

3   What bird is featured on the club crest?

4   What nationality is Gareth Bale who scored 26 goals in the 2012–2013 season?

5   Which club paid a reported £33m to buy Luka Modric in 2012?

6   Which team did they beat 13-2 in a 1960 FA Cup match?

7   Who made 854 appearances for the club between 1969 and 1986?

8   Who finished top scorer five times between 1992–1993 and 2002–2003?

9   Which side had Tom Huddlestone played for before he joined Spurs in 2005?

10   Spurs beat Nottingham Forest 2-1 in the 1991 FA Cup final. Who was their goalkeeper?

11   In which season did they first win the Division One title?

12   When did the team and Chas and Dave release 'Hot Shot Tottenham' as their FA Cup final song?

13   Who succeeded Harry Redknapp as manager in 2012?

14   Which former QPR and England captain managed the club between 1994 and 1997?

15   How many times did they score three or more goals during the 49 matches of their Double-winning season of 1960–1961?

39
West Ham United

1   What is the correct name of the ground that they play at?

2   Who succeeded Billy Bonds as club captain in 1984?

3   In which year were they presented with the BBC Sports Personality of the Year Team award?

4   Who was the club's manager between 1950 and 1961?

5   What was the original name of the club?

6   Which player was a member of their 1975 and 1980 FA Cup-winning sides and later saw his son win the same trophy with Chelsea?

7   Who is the club's record goal-scorer, with 326 between 1920 and 1935?

8   Which goalkeeper moved from QPR to West Ham United in 1979 for a record fee of £565,000?

9   Who joined them as manager in 2011 and took them back into the Premier League via the play-offs?

10 In which season did they achieve their highest ever placing of third in the top division?

11 Who rejoined the club in 2013, a decade after he had moved to Chelsea?

12 In 2012, they paid almost £14m for Matt Jarvis when he joined them from which club?

13 Which General Manager left the club in 1977 to take charge of England?

14 Who was voted player of the year on five occasions between 1972 and 1984?

15 In 2007, which Australian became the first club captain from outside of Europe?

40

Wigan Athletic

1   Wigan's chairman when they won the 2013 FA Cup was Dave Whelan. In which year had he broken his leg whilst playing in the FA Cup final for Blackburn Rovers?

2   In which year were Wigan founded?

3   Which former Manchester United captain managed them briefly in 2001 before returning for a longer spell between 2007 and 2009?

4   In which season did they reach the League Cup final but lost to Manchester United?

5   Which side beat them 9-1 in the Premier League in 2009?

6   To which club did they pay a reported £6.5m for Mauro Boselli in 2010?

7   Which Scottish player was voted the club's Player of the Year for the 2012–2013 season?

8   Which competition did they win in 1984–1985 and 1998–1999?

9   From which team did Roberto Martinez join Wigan as manager in 2009?

10 Who made a club record 317 league appearances in two spells between 1981 and 1994?

11 Who moved to Manchester United from Wigan in 2009 for £16m?

12 Who was manager when they lost an FA Cup first-round game to Canvey Island in 2001?

13 Which season was their first in the Premier League?

14 Which striker became the first Wigan player to represent England whilst a full member of the squad?

15 What name did their ground change to in March 2009?

41
Wolverhampton Wanderers

1 Which manger led them to three titles and three second places in Division One?

2 Which European final did they reach in 1972?

3 Who was their captain when they beat Blackburn Rovers in the final of the 1960 FA Cup?

4 Who scored 306 goals in his 561 games for the club?

5 Where did Steven Fletcher move in 2012 for a fee reported to be £12m?

6 Which former Liverpool captain lifted the League Cup when they beat Nottingham Forest 1-0 in the 1980 final?

7 In which season did Mick McCarthy manage them into the Premier League as Championship champions?

8 What is the name of their ground?

9 Which team that included Rodney Marsh and Mike Summerbee did Wolves beat 2-1 in the 1974 League Cup final?

10 In which season were they awarded, and scored, the first ever penalty in the Football League?

11 Who was their captain for all three League titles wins in the 1950s?

12 What nationality was Stale Solbakken, who managed them for the first half of the 2012–2013 season?

13 Which manager won back-to-back promotions in 1988 and 1989 and took them from Division Four to Division Two?

14 Which businessman and fan owned the club between 1990 and 2007?

15 Which player was top scorer for Wolves in the league eight times in nine seasons from 1972–1973 but only played once for England?

5
The Manager's Team Talk

42
Sir Matt Busby

1   Where was he born in 1909?

2   Which side did he play for between 1928 and 1936?

3   In which season did he win the FA Cup as a player?

4   In March 1936, he was taken to Liverpool for £8,000 by which manager?

5   How many Scotland caps did he win?

6   In which year did he become manager of Manchester United?

7   How many times did he take Manchester United to the Division One title?

8   Who was his captain when Manchester United won the FA Cup final in 1948, beating Blackpool 4-2?

9   Which other side did he manage in 1948?

10   What nickname was given to his side in the early 1950s?

11 On 6 February 1958, he lost eight of his players when their plane crashed at Munich Airport following a European Cup tie against which team?

12 Who was his first-choice goalkeeper during his final championship winning season of 1966–1967?

13 In which year did he lead Manchester United to success in the European Cup, winning the final?

14 Who succeeded him as manager of Manchester United?

15 In 1971 he became the first person to be featured twice as a special guest on which TV programme?

43
Brian Clough

1 Where was he born, in 1935?

2 How many goals did he score in his 274 appearances for Middlesbrough and Sunderland?

3 How old was he when he retired from playing due to an injury?

4 Who did he appoint as his assistant manager when he took charge of Hartlepool United?

5 In which season did he manage Derby County to their first ever league title?

6 After leaving Derby County, which Division Three side did he join?

7 Which actor portrayed him in the film *The Damned United*?

8 How many days did he last as manager of Leeds United?

9 Who did he succeed as manager of Nottingham Forest?

10 His first trophy at Nottingham Forest was the 1978 League Cup. Who captained the side when they beat Liverpool 1-0 in a replay

of the final?

11 In 1978, Nottingham Forest won the First Division in their first season after promotion. Who was the last manager to have won the title with two different clubs?

12 Which club did Clough pay £1m when he made Trevor Francis the first million-pound player?

13 Nottingham Forest's first European Cup came in 1979 when they beat which Swedish side 1-0 in the final?

14 Who scored for Nottingham Forest when they retained the European Cup in 1980 with a 1-0 win against Hamburg?

15 He retired at the end of which season, just after Nottingham Forest were relegated?

44

Sir Alex Ferguson

1 Where was he born, in 1941?

2 Which was his first club as a player?

3 His first management job was with East Stirlingshire. Which year did he start?

4 Between 1978 and 1986, he managed Aberdeen to three Scottish titles and how many Scottish Cups?

5 What is the name of his footballer son, who had long spells with Wolverhampton Wanderers and Wrexham?

6 His first trophy with Manchester United was the 1990 FA Cup, which was won 1-0 in the replay against Crystal Palace following a 3-3 draw in the final. Who replaced goalkeeper Jim Leighton after he was dropped for the second game?

7 Which side did they beat 2-1 in the final of the 1991 European Cup Winners' Cup?

8 In which season did he win his first Premier League title?

9 Which 22-year-old midfielder did he buy from Nottingham Forest for a record British fee of £3.75m?

10 In 1999, Manchester United won the Premier League and FA Cup, but who scored in the final minute of play against Bayern Munich to add the Champions League trophy and give them the Treble?

11 What was the name of his assistant manager, who left Manchester United to take over as manager of Middlesbrough?

12 Manchester United won the Champions League for a second time in 2008 when they beat Chelsea on penalties in the final. In which city was the match played?

13 Who did he appoint as club captain after Bryan Robson?

14 In 2006–2007, they won the Premier League for the first time since 2002–2003. Who was their leading scorer in the League, with 17 goals?

15 When was he knighted?

45

Jose Mourinho

1 Which manager employed him as an interpreter at Sporting Lisbon?

2 In 2000, he began his managerial career at which club?

3 Whilst at Porto, he won two League titles, the UEFA Cup and the Champions League. Which French team did they beat 3-0 in the final to lift Europe's main trophy?

4 Which manager did he replace when he joined Chelsea in June 2004?

5 How old was he when he became manager of Chelsea?

6 He signed Didier Drogba for a reported £24m from which club?

7 In 2005, how much was he fined by the FA, after an appeal, for meeting with Ashley Cole while he was still under contract at Arsenal?

8 When Chelsea won the Premier League title in 2004–2005, who was the only player to start every game?

9   He won the FA Cup in 2007 when Chelsea beat which side 1-0, in the first final to be played at the new Wembley Stadium?

10   Who was his assistant manager from the time he first joined Chelsea in 2004 until his departure in 2007?

11   Which club did Chelsea pay £21m for Shaun Wright-Phillips?

12   Having joined Inter Milan in 2008, he won the Champions League for a second time two years later. Which Argentinian striker scored both goals when Milan beat Bayern Munich 2-0 in the final?

13   After two of his players were sent off in a 0-0 draw with Sampdoria, he was banned for three games for making what gesture towards a TV camera?

14   Between February 2002 and April 2011, he did not lose a single home league match with any of the teams that he managed. How many games was that in total?

15   In 2011, he won the Spanish League with a record 100 points. Which team was he managing?

46
Bill Nicholson

1 Where was he born, in 1919?

2 From 1938 to 1955, which was the only team that he played for?

3 In which season did he win the League title as a player?

4 He made his England debut against Portugal in 1951 and scored with his first touch after just 19 seconds. How many England caps did he win in total?

5 Which England manager did he assist at the 1958 World Cup finals?

6 In which year was he appointed manager of Tottenham Hotspur?

7 Who, with 33 goals in all competitions, was Tottenham Hotspur's leading goal-scorer in their 1960–1961 Double-winning season?

8 Who was the captain of Tottenham Hotspur when the won the FA Cup in 1961 and 1962?

9 In 1963, Tottenham Hotspur beat which Spanish side 5-1 in the final of the European Cup Winners' Cup?

10   Who scored both goals when Tottenham Hotspur beat Aston Villa 2-0 in the 1971 League Cup final?

11   Which British team were their opponents when Tottenham Hotspur won the first ever UEFA Cup final in 1972?

12   In which year did he resign as manager of Tottenham Hotspur?

3   Of the 79 players he selected whilst manager, who, with 480 appearances, did he select most frequently?

14   What was the name of the autobiography that he published in 1984?

15   Who succeeded him as Tottenham Hotspur manager?

47
Bob Paisley

1   Where did he first play amateur club football?

2   During the Second World War, what was his role in the 8th Army?

3   Which team did he spend his entire league career with from 1939 to 1954?

4   His first match in charge of Liverpool was against Luton Town in August of which year?

5   He won the League Cup three times, with the first coming in 1981 after a replay. Ray Stewart scored in the first match and Paul Goddard in the second, but they finished on the losing side with which club?

6   Liverpool won the UEFA Cup at the end of the 1975–1976 season. Who did they beat 4-3 on aggregate across the two legs of the final?

7   Who was the Liverpool captain when they won the European Cup in 1976–1977 and 1977–1978?

8   How many league titles did he win as manager?

9   In his nine seasons in charge, which was the only one that he failed to win any trophies?

10 He became the only manager to win the European Cup for a third time when Liverpool beat Real Madrid 1-0 in the 1981 final. Who was the defender who scored the goal?

11 In 1978, he signed Graeme Souness for £350,000 from which club?

12 Which player was used by Paisley so often as a late-scoring option that he became known as 'supersub'?

13 In 1981, he replaced long-serving goalkeeper Ray Clemence with Bruce Grobbelaar. Which club did he buy him from?

14 He won yet another League title and League Cup Double in 1982–1983, his final season in charge. Who, with 31 goals, was the club's leading scorer?

15 Who succeeded him as manager of Liverpool?

48

Sir Alf Ramsey

1 Which was the first club side that he played for, between 1943 and 1949?

2 How many times was he capped by England as a player?

3 Which side did he manage to the Division One title in 1961–1962?

4 What nickname was given to his England teams because of the particular and new way that he instructed them to play?

5 Despite goals from Bobby Smith and Bobby Tambling, his first match as England manager resulted in a 5-2 loss to which team in February 1963?

6 Who scored four goals when England beat Northern Ireland 8-3 in 1963 and repeated the feat when they defeated Norway 6-1 in 1966?

7 In May 1964, England recorded their biggest win under Ramsey when they put ten goals past which home team?

8   In the 1966 World Cup finals, England drew the opening game 0-0. Who were their opponents?

9   Who did he select for the knockout stages when Jimmy Greaves was injured in the group match against France in the 1966 World Cup finals?

10 At the age of 21, who was the youngest player that Ramsey selected for his World Cup winning team?

11 In the 1970 World Cup quarter-final, England lost 3-2 to West Germany, despite having been 2-0 up with 20 minutes to go. Who was England's goalkeeper?

12 Who was the chairman of the FA who sacked Ramsey in 1974?

13 He managed England 113 times between 1963 and 1974. How many were won?

14 Which side did he become caretaker manager of in the 1977–1978 season?

15 How old was he when his England reign ended?

49

Don Revie

1 Which was the first club that he signed for in 1944?

2 In which year did he win the FA Cup as a Manchester City player?

3 Who did he succeed as manager of Leeds United, initially becoming player-manager, in 1961?

4 How many times was he capped as a player by England?

5 Who was captain of Leeds United for a decade after being appointed by Revie in 1966?

6 He twice led Leeds United to the Division One title but how many times did they finish in second place?

7 He won only one of the four FA Cup finals that Leeds United reached during his time in charge. That came in 1972, when they beat Arsenal 1-0. Who was the goal-scorer?

8 In 1962, he gave a first-team debut to which player, who went on to score 238 goals in 703 appearances for the club?

9 Which team were on the receiving end of a 7-0 thrashing by Leeds

United in March 1972, when they also spent several minutes passing the ball to each other?

10 Many neutral supporters as well as Leeds United fans felt that biased refereeing was at least partly responsible for Leeds United losing the 1973 European Cup Winners' Cup final to which side?

11 Revie's first title with Leeds United came in 1968–1969. When was the second?

12 Which caretaker manager had been in charge of England for seven games between the sacking of Sir Alf Ramsey and the appointment of Revie?

13 In 1975, who scored all the goals when England beat Cyprus 5-0?

14 Who succeeded Revie as manager of Leeds United?

15 In 1977, Revie resigned as England manager and took charge of which international side?

50
Sir Bobby Robson

1   In which county was he born, in 1933?

2   He left school at 15 to work as an apprentice in which trade?

3   Which professional side did he sign for in 1950?

4   In March 1956, he was signed by manager Vic Buckingham for £25,000 and joined which team?

5   How many caps did he win for England as a player?

6   He scored in England's record 9-3 demolition of which team at Wembley in 1961?

7   Who captained Ipswich Town when they beat Arsenal 1-0 in the 1978 FA Cup final?

8   When Bobby was appointed England manager, he controversially dropped which iconic player from the squad for his first game against Denmark?

9   Who was England's goalkeeper when they lost the 1990 World Cup semi-final penalty shootout to West Germany?

10 Who did he manage to consecutive the Dutch league titles in 1990–1991 and 1991–1992?

11 Which Spanish team did he managed between May 1996 and June 1997?

12 When in Portugal he added a further two league titles and a cup winner's medal to his collection at which club side?

13 Sir Bobby was sacked by which Newcastle chairman, despite having led them to fifth spot the previous season?

14 In 2006, he was appointed International Football Consultant to which national side?

15 In which year was he awarded a knighthood?

51
Bill Shankly

1   He was born in September 1913 in Glenbuck. How many of his brothers were also professional footballers?

2   What was his first job when he left school?

3   In 1932–1933, he played for his first club. Who were they?

4   In 1933, he joined Preston North End and remained there until 1949. What was his weekly wage when he signed?

5   In 1938, he won the FA Cup against which side that he would later manage?

6   Which year did he join Division Two side Liverpool?

7   He converted a storage space into an area where he, Bob Paisley and others could discuss tactics. By what name did it become better known?

8   In which season did Liverpool win the first of their League titles under Shankly?

9   Which team did Liverpool beat 2-1 in the final to lift the 1964–1965 FA Cup?

10 With 30 goals, which player was the leading scorer for Liverpool when they won the League title in 1965–1966?

11 What was on the sign that he placed above the players' tunnel in full view of the opposition players?

12 In 1972–1973, he won his only European trophy, the UEFA Cup. Who did Liverpool beat 3-2 across the two legs of the final?

13 The 1972–1973 team that won the Division One title contained four English players who started all 42 games. Ian Callaghan, Emlyn Hughes and Larry Lloyd were three of them. Who was the fourth?

14 He retired as Liverpool manager in July of which year?

15 What is inscribed on the Shankly Gates at Anfield?

52

Jock Stein

1   Born in 1922, what was his main job while he also played football part-time with Albion Rovers?

2   What was his real first name?

3   In 1950–1951, he played as a full-time professional for which Welsh side?

4   Between 1951 and 1957, he played for Celtic. What caused him to retire?

5   Where did he begin his management career?

6   Between 1965 and 1978, how many times did he win the Scottish League title with Celtic?

7   In which year did he combine the managerial jobs of Celtic and Scotland?

8   When he won the Scottish Cup for the first time with Celtic, in 1965, beating Dunfermline Athletic 3-2 in the final, he played ten Scots and which Republic of Ireland inside-right?

9 In which year did he lead Celtic to their first ever domestic Treble?

10 Celtic beat Inter Milan 2-1 in the final of the 1967 European Cup when they became the first British side to win the competition. Who scored the winning goal?

11 In 1970, Celtic once again reached the final of the European Cup but this time lost 2-1 to which side?

12 How many days did he spend as manager of Leeds United?

13 He took over as full-time Scotland manager in 1978. For how many games was he in charge?

14 He led Scotland to the 1982 World Cup finals, but they were eliminated having only won once in the group staged. Which side did they beat 5-2?

15 He died at the age of 62 during an International match between Scotland and which other side?

53
Arsene Wenger

1   In which year was he born, in Strasbourg?

2   In 1988, he managed which side to the French championship?

3   Prior to joining Arsenal, he spent almost two years at Nagoya Grampus Eight. Which country do they play in?

4   Who did he succeed as manager of Arsenal?

5   In which season did he win his first League and Cup Double with Arsenal?

6   In 1999–2000, Arsenal lost the UEFA Cup final on penalties. Who were their victorious opponents?

7   Who scored the winning goal against Manchester United at Old Trafford to secure Arsenal the Premier League title in the penultimate game of the 2001–2002 season?

8   What was officially named 33179 Arsenewenger in his honour in 2007?

9   Which other Premier League manager once claimed that Wenger had an 'unhealthy obsession' with his club?

10 Arsenal won the 2003–2004 Premier League without losing a single game. How long was their unbeaten run, which finally came to an end in October 2004?

11 In 2005, Arsenal won the FA Cup for a fourth time under Wenger when they beat Manchester United on penalties. The only miss of the ten kicks came when Paul Scholes saw which keeper save the ball low to his right?

12 In 2007, William Gallas was sacked as captain. Who did Wenger hand the armband to?

13 What is his nickname?

14 He used his profits in the transfer market to build a new training ground for Arsenal. What county is it in?

15 In 2006, Arsenal reached the Champions League final but were beaten 2-1 by Barcelona. Only two of their 18-strong playing squad were English and one of them scored their only goal. Who was he?

6
First Half

54
Desmond Lynam

1   In which Irish town was Des born?

2   What was the first BBC radio show that Des regularly presented?

3   Who did Des succeed as the presenter of *Grandstand* in 1984?

4   When did he become the main presenter of *Match of the Day*?

5   Which football team does he support?

6   Who did Des succeed as the presenter of *Countdown*?

7   Which poem by Rudyard Kipling did Des record after the 1998 World Cup finals?

8   When Des joined BBC Radio he was mainly a commentator on which sport?

9   With which presenter did Des swap *Grandstand* and *Sportsnight* duties?

10 Which Welshman was his regular co-presenter on the BBC's Wimbledon highlights show for many years from 1983?

11 Des and Jenny Hull presented which BBC One show that explained the way that things worked?

12 In which profession did Des work as a salesman for much of the 1960s?

13 How many times did Des present *Sports Review of the Year*?

14 What was the name of the football programme on ITV that Des presented between 2001 and 2004?

15 What is the name of Des's 2005 autobiography?

55
World Cup 1930–1962

1   1930: Only 13 nations took part, but who were crowned the first World Champions?

2   1930: What record does the Peru v Romania group game hold to this day?

3   1934: Hosts Italy beat which nation after extra time in the final?

4   1934: What made 4.30pm on 27 May 1934 so unusual in World Cup history?

5   1938: What made this – in footballing terms – a notable tournament for Germany?

6   1938: Italy beat Hungary in the final in which city?

7   1950: England suffered a shock 1-0 defeat in Belo Horizonte to which nation?

8   1950: The hosts, Brazil, were surprisingly beaten by which team in the final?

9   1954: Which country hosted the tournament?

10 1954: Which nation finished as runners-up for the second time?

11 1958: Just Fontaine finished as leading scorer with a record tally. How many did he score?

12 1958: Which legend made his World Cup debut at the age of 17?

13 1962: What was the name given to the controversial encounter between Chile and Italy?

14 1962: Which future England manager was a member of their 1962 squad?

15 1962: Which Brazilian scored in their quarter-final, semi-final and final victories?

56
World Cup 1966

1   What was the name of the dog that found the Jules Rimet trophy under a bush when it was stolen prior to the finals?

2   Outside of London, six stadiums were used. Name them.

3   The shock of the tournament saw North Korea beat Italy 1-0. Who scored the goal?

4   The group match between Uruguay and France couldn't be played at Wembley as intended and was the one match played at White City Stadium. Why?

5   Name the Argentinian who was sent off against England at Wembley in the quarter-finals, refused to leave the pitch and was escorted away by several policeman?

6   What was the name of the tournament mascot, a lion?

7   Who scored three of England's four goals in the group stages?

8   North Korea led which nation 3-0 in the knockout stages before eventually succumbing 5-3?

9 The Soviet Union finished fourth. Who was their legendary goalkeeper?

10 1966 was his first appearance at a World Cup. He went on to win the tournament as both a player and a coach of Germany. Who is he?

11 Who finished the tournament as the leading goal-scorer in his country's first appearance at a World Cup finals?

12 Name the England starting 11 for the World Cup final?

13 What nationality was the linesman who said England's third goal was over the line?

14 Which club did Sir Alf Ramsey manage before taking over as England manager?

15 Who presented the trophy to England?

57
World Cup 1970

1   The ninth World Cup was the first staged in North America. Who were the hosts?

2   Why was England captain Bobby Moore arrested prior to the tournament in Colombia?

3   What was notable about Viktor Serebryanikov's first appearance in the 1970 World Cup?

4   Which player scored hat-tricks in two consecutive games against Bulgaria and Peru?

5   Who performed a wonder save to deny Pele in the group stages?

6   1970 proved a landmark in terms of broadcasting of the World Cup. Why?

7   On debut who scored the penalty that decided England's final group game against Czechoslovakia?

8   Which Brazilian player scored in all six of his team's matches?

9   What could referees use for the first time in 1970?

10 Who was Head Coach of Brazil?

11 It is the only venue to have hosted two World Cup finals. Name this Mexico City stadium.

12 Who was in goal for England in their quarter-final defeat to West Germany?

13 What did Franz Beckenbauer have to do in the Germans' 'Game of the Century' semi-final defeat by Italy?

14 Which Brazilian scored what is considered to be one of the greatest goals in World Cup history in the final?

15 What happened to the Jules Rimet trophy after the World Cup?

58
World Cup 1974

1   What did Italian Silvio Gazzaniga do in 1974 that can be seen at the World Cup to this day?

2   Which Caribbean nation qualified for the World Cup for their first and only time?

3   Only one British team made it to West Germany. Who?

4   How did Chile's Carlos Caszely make history in their opening group match against West Germany?

5   Who defeated Zaire 9-0, a record-equalling winning margin at the World Cup?

6   Pioneered by Ajax, what was the name of the style of play used by the Netherlands?

7   Jurgen Sparwasser scored a significant goal politically in the group stages. What was the match?

8   Against which nation did Johan Cruyff first demonstrate the 'Cryuff Turn' to the world?

9 Which Pole finished the tournament as the leading scorer with seven goals?

10 Where did defending World Champions Brazil finish the tournament?

11 Gunter Netzer made history when West Germany won the World Cup. How?

12 Which stadium hosted the final?

13 Who was the English referee who awarded two penalties in the final?

14 Gerd Muller scored the winner in the final, but name the two other goal-scorers.

15 Which German legend lifted the World Cup trophy?

59
World Cup 1978

1   Who hosted the World Cup for the first time, and why was there talk of moving the tournament in the preceding months?

2   Name the forward-thinking, chain-smoking Argentinian coach?

3   Which Scottish player was expelled from the tournament after being found to have taken a banned stimulant?

4   Name one of the two countries that qualified for the World Cup finals for the first time.

5   Who was the Welsh referee who disallowed a last-second Brazil 'winner' against Sweden?

6   Scotland famously defeated the Netherlands 3-2 in their final group game. Which midfielder scored two goals?

7   How was it that a local team from Mar del Plata, Club Atletico Kimberley, made headlines?

8   In a game known as the 'Miracle of Cordoba', which nation defeated West Germany 3-2 and ended their reign as World Champions?

9   Who scored a wonder strike for the Netherlands against Italy, ensuring their passage to the World Cup final for a second tournament in succession?

10 Who did Argentina controversially defeat 6-0 to edge out Brazil and qualify for the final?

11 What did FIFA introduce in 1978, though it was never used?

12 Who finished the tournament as the Golden Boot winner?

13 Which Dutchman scored in the final and also became the first substitute to be sent off at a World Cup after coming on against West Germany?

14 Name the Argentinian midfielder who played in the final and later signed for Tottenham?

15 Who was the right-winger who scored the decisive third goal for Argentina in extra time in the final?

60
World Cup 1982

1   Spain '82 marked the expansion of the World Cup to how many competing nations?

2   What event caused the British government to consider whether or not to withdraw England, Scotland and Northern Ireland from the tournament?

3   Which African newcomer shocked West Germany 2-1 in their first match?

4   What match was described as the 'Disgrace of Gijon' and what impact did it have on future tournaments?

5   Hungary beat which Central American nation 10-1 in the group stages?

6   Which Englishman scored after only 27 seconds against France?

7   Northern Irishman Norman Whiteside broke which World Cup record when appearing at the tournament?

8   Which Scotsman opened the scoring in their match against Brazil?

9   Thanks to Gerry Armstrong's goal, Northern Ireland famously defeated Spain in which city?

10 What was the score in England's two second-round games that ultimately saw them eliminated?

11 Who scored the hat-trick against Brazil that sent Italy through to the semi-finals?

12 Which German committed 'one of history's most shocking fouls' on Patrick Battiston of France in their semi-final and yet escaped sanction?

13 Which stadium hosted the 1982 final?

14 Name the midfielder famed for his wild goal celebration in the final as he sprinted towards the Italian bench screaming?

15 Which Italian became the oldest player to ever win the World Cup?

61
World Cup 1986

1   Which nation was originally due to host the tournament, but resigned in 1982 for largely economic reasons, allowing Mexico to take over?

2   Who coached Scotland at the 1986 World Cup?

3   Which goalkeeper played his last match for Northern Ireland on his 41st birthday in their last group game against Brazil?

4   What crowd phenomenon was first seen globally at this World Cup and remains prevalent across a variety of sports to this day?

5   Having qualified for the World Cup for the first time, who surpassed expectations and finished top of their group above West Germany?

6   Against whom did Ray Wilkins get sent off for England in the group stages?

7   Northern Ireland gained a solitary point against whom in a difficult Group D?

8   Who scored the hat-trick against Poland that sent England through to the last 16?

9   Who knocked Spain out of the World Cup 5-4 on penalties and went on to achieve their best ever placing of fourth?

10   Who was the goalkeeper involved in the infamous 'Hand of God' goal scored by Diego Maradona?

11   In the same match Maradona scored the 'Goal of the Century'. Which four English outfield players did he pass en route to the goal?

12   Which nation knocked out the holders, Italy, in the Round of 16?

13   Name the two head coaches of the 1986 finalists?

14   Which club was Diego Maradona playing for when winning the World Cup in 1986?

15   Who scored the winner for Argentina in the final?

62
World Cup 1990

1   Who managed England at the 1990 World Cup?

2   Who finished as the competition's top goal-scorer?

3   Which African team beat defending champions Argentina 1-0 in the opening match?

4   Name two of the three other teams in England's Group F?

5   Who scored the winning goal for West Germany in the final and when?

6   Which two England players missed their penalties in the shootout defeat to West Germany?

7   Who knocked out Spain before going out on penalties to Argentina in the quarter-finals?

8   Which Central American nation shocked Scotland and beat them 1-0 in the group stages?

9   Name the two cities away from the Italian mainland that hosted matches in 1990?

10 What was so unusual about the Republic of Ireland's progress to the quarter-finals?

11 Pedro Monzon made history at Italia '90 – how?

12 Who scored Scotland's two goals in their group win over Sweden?

13 What was notable about Claudio Caniggia's goal for Argentina in their semi-final v Italy?

14 Which England World Cup-winner managed the Republic of Ireland at Italia '90?

15 Who became the only man to both captain and manage a World Cup-winning team?

63

World Cup 1994

1 What happened for the first time when Brazil played Italy in the final?

2 What crowd record does World Cup '94 hold to this day?

3 Diego Maradona left the tournament early. Why?

4 Which Columbian defender was tragically murdered in Medellin ten days after he scored an own goal v USA?

5 Who surprisingly beat Germany in the quarter-finals and eventually finished fourth?

6 Name the captain of Brazil who picked up the trophy from American vice-president Al Gore?

7 How did Oleg Salenko make a name for himself at World Cup '94?

8 The outcome of Group E is unique in World Cup history. Why?

9 Who scored the Republic of Ireland's winner in their 1-0 victory over Italy?

10 Saaed Al-Owairian scored one of the goals of the tournament by running from his own half to score for whom in a 1-0 victory against Belgium?

11 Who became the oldest goal-scorer in World Cup finals history when he scored Cameroon's solitary goal in their group game v Russia?

12 What famous goal celebration did the Brazilian use in their 3-2 quarter-final win v the Netherlands and why?

13 Why was the USA-Switzerland group match played at the Pontiac Silverdome so unusual?

14 Which two Republic of Ireland personalities were fined following their 2-1 defeat to Mexico?

15 What were referees allowed to do for the first time at World Cup '94?

64
World Cup 1998

1 Scotland lost 2-1 to Brazil in the opening match of the tournament. Who scored their goal?

2 What was the most northerly host city of France '98 and the one closest to the UK?

3 Who finished as the tournament's top scorer with six goals?

4 Which two referees from the UK officiated at France '98?

5 In the group stages, France only conceded once. Which great Dane scored the goal?

6 What was the result of the highly sensitive Group F fixture between Iran and the USA?

7 England lost 2-1 and finished second in the group stages to whom?

8 Paul Ince and David Batty missed, but which three Englishman scored in the last 16 penalty shootout v Argentina?

9 Who was sent off in the 47th minute of the same match?

10   Laurent Blanc made history in France's last 16 victory v Paraguay. How?

11   What was the name of the new stadium built in Paris which hosted the final?

12   Which former Arsenal striker scored a memorable winner for the Netherlands in their quarter-final v Argentina?

13   Which Brazilian dominated the pre-match conversation at the final and why?

14   Which team finished the competition in a highest ever third place?

15   France beat Brazil 3-0 in the final. Who scored their goals?

65
World Cup 2002

1   The 17th World Cup was the first to be held in Asia. Who were the hosts?

2   France surprisingly lost 1-0 in the opening match of the tournament to which nation?

3   Which two teams finished the group stages with maximum points?

4   The Republic of Ireland lost their captain just before the World Cup. Who was it and why?

5   Egyptian referee Gamal Ghandour caused the Spanish government to get involved in the 2002 World Cup. Why?

6   He coached his fifth different nation at his fifth consecutive World Cup. Who was he?

7   Which nation surprisingly finished third in the tournament?

8   England avenged their 1998 defeat to Argentina by beating them in the group stages. Who scored?

9   Who scored from 42 yards to knock England out of the competition?

10 Robbie Keane scored two very late equalisers in games against which two nations?

11 Who scored the winning goal in one of the semi-finals and was then forced to miss the final due to suspension?

12 What record did Hakan Sukur break?

13 Which famous official was referee for the final?

14 Germany have been World Cup runners-up on the most occasions. How many times and when?

15 Who scored both goals in the final for Brazil?

66
World Cup 2006

1   Which two nations featured in the highest-scoring opening match in World Cup finals history?

2   Which team from the Caribbean qualified for the World Cup for the first time?

3   England won two and drew one of their group games. Who did they draw against?

4   All eight seeded teams progressed to the knockout stages. Who were they?

5   Which European nation surprisingly finished two points clear of France at the head of Group G?

6   Who was the only African nation to progress to the knockout stages?

7   Lionel Messi scored the sixth and final goal for Argentina in their group win against whom?

8   Which two nations took part in the so called 'Battle of Nuremberg', which featured a record-breaking 4 red and 16 yellow cards?

9   Which English referee booked Croatia's Josip Simunic three times in their game v Australia?

10 Which former East German city hosted matches at the Zentralstadion?

11 Only one Englishman scored in the quarter-final penalty shootout defeat to Portugal. Who?

12 Who won the Golden Boot?

13 Who was sent off in the final, and what had he done?

14 He scored the tournament-winning goal for France at Euro 2000, but missed the decisive penalty in the shootout v Italy in 2006. Who was he?

15 Who was Italy's captain who lifted the World Cup trophy?

67
World Cup 2010

1   What animal was the mascot Zakumi?

2   Johannesburg had two stadiums as venues. What were they?

3   Which team finished the tournament as the only undefeated nation?

4   South Africa had one victory in the tournament, but it was against which former World Champions?

5   A mistake by England keeper Robert Green led to who scoring for the USA in the group stages?

6   Who scored England's winner v Slovenia that took them through to the last 16?

7   Germany surprisingly lost 1-0 in Group D to which nation?

8   Which club side contributed the most players to the tournament?

9   Which Uruguayan denied Ghana a place in the semi-finals by deliberately handling the ball on the goal-line in the dying moments of extra time?

10 Who was the German goalkeeper for Frank Lampard's infamous 'goal' that wasn't given after clearly crossing the line?

11 Four players finished the tournament as joint highest goal-scorers with five goals. Name three of them.

12 What instrument used by spectators caused much debate throughout the tournament?

13 The Honduran squad made history in 2010. How?

14 Which Englishman refereed the 2010 World Cup final?

15 Who scored the winning goal for Spain in their final victory v Netherlands?

68
Which Nationality?

**These players have all played in the top flight in England,
but which country are they from?**

1   Ali Al Habsi

2   Shaun Goater

3   Paulo Wanchope

4   Ryan Nelsen

5   Steven Pienaar

6   Stephane Sessegnon

7   Javier Hernández

8   Kenwyne Jones

9   Emmanuel Adebayor

10 Vincent Kompany

11 Luis Saurez

12 Georgiou Kinkladze

13 Cristiano Ronaldo

14 Osvaldo Ardiles

15 George Weah

69

Spanish Players in Britain

1   Who won the Champions League with Real Madrid in 2000 and played for Bolton?

2   Who left Arsenal for Barcelona in the summer of 2011?

3   Pepe Reina joined Liverpool from which Spanish club in 2005?

4   Who owns shares in his hometown club, Oviedo, and is a big hit with Swansea fans?

5   David Silva wears what number shirt at Manchester City?

6   Whose 'lucky' shirt number is 10? He joined Chelsea from Valencia in 2011.

7   Who has played for Wigan, Swansea and Chester City and is now a manager?

8   Rafa Benitez has managed which two Premier League clubs?

9   Who was born in 1990 and made his competitive debut for Man Utd at Wembley in August 2011?

10 Who has won the Champions League and FA Cup with Liverpool and also the World Cup and Euros with Spain?

11 How much did Chelsea reportedly pay Liverpool for Fernando Torres?

12 Carlos Cuéllar left Rangers for which English club?

13 Which former Spurs player scored for Real Zaragoza from 40 yards in the last minute of the 1995 European Cup Winners' Cup final v Arsenal?

14 Which Spanish midfielder joined Arsenal from Everton in 2011?

15 Jose Enrique joined Liverpool from which club?

70
Italian Players in Britain

1   Nicknamed 'the White Feather', who scored a hat-trick on his PL debut v Liverpool in 1996?

2   What words did Mario Balotelli reveal on his T-shirt when he scored v Man Utd in 2011?

3   Which two top-flight London clubs did Carlo Cudicini play for?

4   Who played for 17 clubs in total, but made his name in England at Sheffield Wednesday?

5   Who was born in Switzerland and scored one of the fastest goals in Cup final history?

6   Paulo di Canio played for three clubs in England. Name them.

7   He cost over £4m, but made only four appearances for Man Utd. Name the goalkeeper.

8   Who was Brendan Rodger's first signing for Liverpool?

9   Which ex-Everton player was head-butted by Zinedine Zidane in the 2006 World Cup final?

10   Who played alongside Diego Maradona at Napoli and made 229 appearances for Chelsea?

11   Where was Fabio Capello coach before taking the job with England in 2008?

12   Which English club did Roberto Mancini briefly play for in 2001?

13   Which midfielder signed for Crystal Palace in 1997 from Juventus?

14   Dino Baggio made nine appearances in the Premier League for which club?

15   He played for and managed Chelsea and has won all three major European club competitions?

71
German Players in Britain (and vice versa!)

1 Who played for Chelsea for four seasons and was capped 98 times by Germany?

2 Who is nicknamed 'Der Hammer' and played for Aston Villa, West Ham and Everton?

3 How did Jurgen Klinsmann famously celebrate scoring for Tottenham?

4 Robert Huth has played for which three English clubs?

5 Uwe Rosler took over the managing of which Football League club in 2011?

6 Which German scored the last goal at the 'old' Wembley in October 2000?

7 Markus Babbel scored for Liverpool in the 2001 UEFA Cup final against whom?

8 Who played over 100 times for Tottenham and is their assistant manager?

9   Who was ever-present in goal for Arsenal's unbeaten 'Invincibles' team of 2003–2004?

10   His father is a former British soldier and an Everton fan, but he signed for Spurs in January 2013?

11   Kevin Keegan played for which German club?

12   Which England international, born in Canada, made his name at Bayern Munich?

13   Which German famously broke his neck in the 1956 FA Cup final and played on?

14   Who played for Liverpool, Middlesbrough and Tottenham and has a surname starting with Z?

15   Signed by Arsenal in 2012, which striker has played well over a hundred times for Germany?

72
French Players in Britain

1   Whilst with Liverpool, who earned the title of 'Lord of the Manor of Frodsham' and went on to play for Sunderland and QPR, amongst others?

2   Up to 2013, Nicolas Anelka had played for which six clubs in England?

3   Which two Frenchman performed a head-kissing ritual when playing for Man Utd in Champions League matches?

4   Which two World Cup-winning midfielders were instrumental figures in Arsenal's run of success in the late 1990s?

5   Who was the ex-Everton midfielder who broke Leeds' transfer record when he joined in 2000?

6   Which shirt number was Florent Malouda given on his arrival at Chelsea in 2007?

7   Louis Saha played in England for six Premier League clubs. Name them.

8   What was the reported transfer fee when Sami Nasri left Arsenal for Man City in 2011?

9   William Gallas has played for which three London teams?

10 Yohan Cabaye signed for Newcastle from which French club?

11 Which French World Cup-winner played for Chelsea for six seasons and won the FA Cup with them in 2000?

12 Sylvain Distin has played in England since 2001 for Newcastle Utd, Manchester City and which other two clubs?

13 Before moving to Manchester City, how many years did Gael Clichy spend with Arsenal?

14 Born in Senegal, which French international left-back has won multiple honours at Manchester United since his arrival in 2006?

15 Which former England manager signed David Ginola for Newcastle in 1995?

73
Scandinavian Players in Britain

1 Which Finnish central defender played for Liverpool for ten years from 1999?

2 Jussi Jaaskelainen has played for which two clubs in England?

3 Which Man Utd manager signed Jesper Olsen from Ajax?

4 He was Man of the Match in the first ever all Merseyside FA Cup final and managed Hull City and Swansea. Who is he?

5 Oyvind Leonhardsen had ten years in the Premier League with four clubs. Name them.

6 Who won the League Cup with Birmingham in 2011 and then went to Sunderland?

7 Brede Hangeland signed for which London club in 2008?

8 Which Danish father and son combination have both played in goal in the Premier League?

9 Name another Danish goalie, who has played for Sunderland, Aston Villa and Stoke in the top flight.

10 Who played for Sweden over 100 times and had a day named after him at Aston Villa?

11 In which city did Ole Gunnar Solskjaer win the Champions League for Man Utd in 1999?

12 Nicknamed the 'Flying Finn', who has played for over ten clubs in England and Scotland since 2001?

13 A Norwegian was the first person to win the Premier League with two different teams. Name the player and the clubs.

14 Which Danish midfielder played for Everton, Real Madrid and Celtic?

15 In a 2003 poll, he was voted Leeds' 'worst player in living memory' and yet scored the goal that knocked England out of Euro '92 and helped Sweden to third at World Cup '94. Who is he?

74
Eastern European Players in Britain

1   Who was Man City Player of the Year for two consecutive seasons in the 1990s and was famed for his dribbling ability?

2   Dimitar Berbatov has played for which three English clubs?

3   Tottenham paid Dinamo Zagreb £16.5m for which Croatian midfielder in 2008?

4   He controversially denied Laurent Blanc the opportunity to play in the World Cup final at France '98 and played for West Ham and Everton in England. Name the defender.

5   From which French club did Chelsea sign Petr Cech?

6   Nicknamed 'Stan', which Bulgarian played well over 500 games for Celtic and Aston Villa before retiring from football in May 2013?

7   Who was the winner of the Golden Boot at Euro 2004 and played for Liverpool, Aston Villa and Portsmouth?

8   Macedonian Georgi Hristov signed for which English club for a club record £1.5m in 1997?

9   Dan Petrescu played in the Premier League for four clubs; Sheffield Wednesday, Chelsea, Southampton and which other team?

10   Which winger has the distinction of having scored in the Glasgow, Merseyside and Manchester derbies and was signed by Sir Alex Ferguson for £650k in 1991?

11   Which Serb scored the winning goal for Chelsea in the 2013 Europa League final?

12   Which other Serb has been a mainstay of Manchester United's defence since 2006?

13   He is famous for his bizarre goal celebrations, including kicking the advertising hoardings when scoring for Newcastle. Name the Georgian.

14   Fellow Pole Pope John Paul II declared himself a fan of which goalkeeper, who dedicated his 2005 Champions League triumph to the late pontiff?

15   Andrij Shevchenko signed for Chelsea for £30.8m from which club?

75
South American Players in Britain

1   Sergio Aguerro won the Premier League for Manchester City in 2011–2012 by scoring in injury time in the last match against whom?

2   Temperamental World Cup-winner Alberto Tarantini ended his 23-game spell with Birmingham City in the 1970s by doing what?

3   Which club did Javier Mascherano play for before joining Liverpool?

4   Ex-Chelsea and Spurs star Gus Poyet won the 1995 Copa America with which country?

5   Which Brazilian played the full 120 minutes for Chelsea in the 2012 Champions League final and also converted his penalty kick in the shootout?

6   In what year did former Tottenham player, Ossie Ardiles, win the World Cup?

7   Which Colombian striker famously scored a hat-trick for Newcastle in a 3-2 Champions League victory over Barcelona?

8   Juan Sebastian Veron played for which two Premier League teams?

9   Which player featured on the 'Welcome to Manchester' billboards after moving from United to City in 2009?

10 Nolberto Solano played for various clubs in England across the divisions, but what country is he from?

11 Prior to joining Liverpool, Luis Suarez played for which European club?

12 Name the Ecuadorian winger who has played at both Wigan and Man Utd?

13 Name the Brazilian midfielder who was an integral part of Arsenal's 'Invincibles' team of 2003–2004?

14 Fabricio Coloccini joined Newcastle Utd from which Spanish side?

15 What are the first names of the Brazilian da Silva twins who have played in England since 2008?

76

The Far East, Australia and Britain

1   Married to an English soap star, which former Leeds and Liverpool star was voted Australia's greatest ever player in 2012?

2   Shinji Kagawa signed for Manchester Utd from which Bundesliga club in 2012?

3   Who was the first Asian player to win the Champions League when with Manchester Utd and won 100 caps for South Korea?

4   Name the goalkeeper who failed a drugs test in 2002 and played in England for Aston Villa, Man Utd and Chelsea?

5   Japanese star Junichi Inamoto was on the books of four British clubs. Name two of them.

6   Dubbed the 'most hated man in football', which controversial midfielder played for Crystal Palace, Wolves, Rangers and Millwall?

7   Who was the first Australian to score at a World Cup in 2006 and left Everton for the New York Red Bulls?

8   Which centre-back, who won the Scottish title five times with Rangers, also played for Newcastle Utd and Crystal Palace?

9   Name three of the four English clubs Australian Lucas Neill played for.

10 Which goalkeeper first played in England in 1997 and has over 100 caps for Australia?

11 From what country is Sun Jihai, who won the Football League First Division with Man City in 2001–2002?

12 Danny Tiatto was voted 'Player of the Season' during his spells with which two English clubs?

13 Which midfielder signed for Blackburn Rovers from Feyenoord and went on to make nearly 300 career appearances for the Ewood Park club?

14 South Korean Lee Dong-Gook had a disappointing spell in England and failed to score a single Premier League goal when playing for which North East club?

15 Which distinguished Australian forward, who had a successful career both north and south of the border with four clubs, also played for Croatia Zagreb?

77
American Players in Britain

1   Which American goalkeeper came to Man Utd in 2003 and subsequently joined Everton?

2   In January 2012, who became the first American to score a hat-trick in the English Premier League whilst at Fulham?

3   Claudio Reyna played for which three British clubs?

4   In October 2009, who saved four penalties for Aston Villa in one match (three in a penalty shootout)?

5   Who is the highest-scoring American player in World Cup history and had two loan spells at Everton?

6   With a record 310 consecutive appearances in the Premier League, this player has played for four clubs in England. Who is he?

7   Which forward, born in South Africa, most notably turned out for Luton Town, QPR and Coventry?

8   Which defender was nicknamed 'the Jackal' during his time at Fulham?

9   Which other Fulham import who became captain and had a local pub named after him?

10   Who was in the US squad for four World Cups and won the League Cup with Leicester City in 1997?

11   Famous for his dreadlocked hair, and with 164 caps for his country, who played one season at Coventry City?

12   Up to 2012–2013, Jonathan Spector had played in England for four clubs. Name them.

13   Who was the first American to play in the Premier League after he signed for Sheffield Wednesday in 1990?

14   Marcus Hahnemann won which honour with Reading in 2005–2006?

15   Who started in England with Southall in the ninth tier of the game, but made his name in his six years at Watford?

78
African Players in Britain

1   World Player of the Year in 1995, George Weah played for which two English clubs?

2   Didier Drogba is the all-time top goal-scorer for which country?

3   Which Nigerian played for Arsenal, West Brom and Portsmouth between 1999 and 2012?

4   Who was a cult hero at Leeds Utd and the scorer of some spectacular goals in the 1990s?

5   Name the two Touré brothers.

6   Zimbabwean Bruce Grobbelaar won a European Cup-winners medal with Liverpool in what year?

7   A member of the Arsenal 'Invincibles' of 2003–2004, who was the Cameroonian defender who made over 150 appearances for the club?

8   South African Mark Fish played over 100 times for which two English clubs?

9 Christopher Samba signed for QPR in 2013 from which club?

10 Fabrice Muamba moved to the UK aged 11, but he was born in which African state?

11 At the time of his signing for Chelsea in 2005, which Ghanaian international was the most expensive African footballer in history?

12 Who hails from Togo and has played for Arsenal, Tottenham, Man City and Real Madrid?

13 Who scored the first goal in the 2002 World Cup and was a regular for both Fulham and Portsmouth?

14 A favourite of Bolton fans who printed T-shirts in his honour with the inscription 'so good they named him twice' – name the midfielder?

15 Which South African is best known for his spells at Everton and has played for his country over 60 times?

79
Euros up to 1992

1   In what year was the UEFA European Championships (European Nations' Cup) first held?

2   The trophy is named after the first General Secretary of UEFA, who came up with the idea of a European Championship. What was his name?

3   Which two former nations met in the final of the first tournament in Paris?

4   Who was the host nation who won the trophy in 1964?

5   England played in their first Euros in 1968. Where did they finish?

6   West Germany beat the Soviet Union 3-0 in the 1972 final. Which German goal-scoring legend scored two of the goals?

7   Which Czech player famously chipped in the decisive penalty kick in the 1976 final shootout to defeat West Germany?

8   In 1980, England finished third in Group B and went out. Which team did they lose to?

9   Which West German scored both goals in the 1980 final to defeat Belgium 2-1, the winner a trademark bullet header?

10   Who finished the 1984 tournament as the leading goal-scorer?

11   Which stadium hosted the 1984 final?

12   The Republic of Ireland defeated England 1-0 in their opening group match of the 1988 finals. Who scored the goal?

13   Who scored a wonder goal in the 1988 final to win the tournament for the Netherlands?

14   Both England and Scotland were knocked out in the group stages in 1992. They won one match out of six between them. Which nation was defeated?

15   Which team replaced Yugoslavia late in the day and won the 1992 Euros?

80

Euro '96

1 Eight venues hosted Euro '96 in England. Name them?

2 What was the marketing slogan for the tournament?

3 What happened in Manchester one day before the group game between Germany and Russia?

4 What name was given to Paul Gascoigne's goal celebration following his spectacular goal against Scotland and why?

5 England defeated the Netherlands 4-1 to finish top of Group A. Who were the English goal-scorers?

6 Whose goal ultimately knocked Scotland out of the competition?

7 France finished top, but name the three other teams in Group B.

8 The two eventual finalists also met in the group stage. What was the score?

9 Only one team in Group D avoided a 3-0 defeat. Who was it?

10 England beat Spain 4-2 on penalties in the quarter-finals. Who was the England goalkeeper?

11 Who missed for England in the semi-final penalty shootout defeat to Germany?

12 The second semi-final also went to penalties. Which two teams were taking part?

13 Euro '96 was the first time a major football competition was decided by what method?

14 With five goals who ended the tournament as the leading scorer?

15 Who was the German captain who was presented with the trophy?

81
Euro 2000–2012

Euro 2000

1   Which two nations co-hosted Euro 2000?

2   Which country came back from 2-0 down in Group A to defeat England 3-2?

3   Which former Everton and Liverpool defender was adjudged to have handled the ball in extra time to present France with a controversial penalty winner in the semi-final?

4   Who scored the golden goal winner for France in the final?

Euro 2004

5   Which two teams did England defeat in Group B to qualify for the knockout stages?

6   Who came on as sub for the injured Wayne Rooney in the quarter-final and then missed the decisive penalty in the shootout v Portugal?

7   Which team surprised the hosts Portugal twice, beating them in both the opening match and the final?

8   And who scored the winner to give his nation a shock tournament victory?

Euro 2008

9   Both the co-hosts went out in the group stages. Name them?

10   Golden Boot winner David Villa scored a hat-trick against which team who Spain later met again in the semi-final?

11   Fernando Torres scored the only goal in the final. Who did Spain beat and where?

Euro 2012

12   What Group D fixture was suspended due to a torrential thunderstorm?

13   England was knocked out on penalties by Italy in what city?

14   Which Italian scored both goals in their semi-final victory over Germany?

15   By winning Euro 2012, Spain became the first nation to do what?

82
UEFA Champions League Finals

1   The first of the newly renamed UEFA Champions League finals took place in 1993. Which French team beat AC Milan 1-0?

2   Patrick Kluivert scored the only goal of the 1995 final, when AC Milan lost again. Who were the winning team?

3   Which future Chelsea manager captained Juventus in their 1996 win against Ajax in the final?

4   Whose substitution in the 81st minute of the 1999 final enabled Ole Gunnar Solskjaar to come on and score the winning goal for Manchester United against Bayern Munich?

5   Which eventual champions ended Manchester United's defence of their title when they knocked them out at the quarter-final stage?

6   In 2002, all three English teams – Arsenal, Liverpool and Manchester United – were beaten by which German side, who lost the final 2-0 to Real Madrid?

7   Jose Mourinho led Porto to the 2004 title. Which French team did they beat 3-0?

8   Who was the Liverpool manager who inspired his team to come back from a 3-0 half-time deficit against AC Milan to win on penalties?

9   Which English defender opened the scoring for Arsenal in the 2006 final, when they were defeated 2-1 by Barcelona in 2006?

10   Who scored both goals for AC Milan when they beat Liverpool 2-1 in the 2007 final?

11   In which city did Manchester United beat Chelsea on penalties to win the 2008 final?

12   Who was Manchester United's goalkeeper when they lost the 2009 final 2-0 against Barcelona?

13   How many Italians were in the starting line-up for Inter Milan in 2010, when they beat Bayern Munich 2-0 in the final?

14   On which ground did Manchester United lose the 2011 final 3-1 to Barcelona?

15   When Chelsea beat Bayern Munich on penalties in 2012 which of their starting XI had previously won the competition with Porto?

83
European Cup Finals

1 Which year was the first European Cup final?

2 Real Madrid won the trophy in the first five seasons. Which striker scored in all five finals?

3 In 1967, Celtic became the first British side to win the competition when they beat Inter Milan 2-1. How many of the team were born within a 30-mile radius of Glasgow?

4 When Manchester United beat Benfica 4-1 in the 1968 final, who was the only Scot in their team?

5 Which Dutch team won three in a row from 1971?

6 Bayern Munich won the competition three times from 1974 to 1976. Which English team did they beat 2-0 in the 1975 final?

7 In which season did Liverpool win their first European Cup?

8 Trevor Francis scored the only goal of the match when Nottingham Forest beat Malmo to win the trophy in 1979. Who was in goal for Forest?

9   Who captained Liverpool when they beat Real Madrid 1-0 in the 1981 final?

10 Who was the manager of Aston Villa when they won the 1982 final?

11 Which Italian team beat the defending champions, Liverpool, in the 1985 final with a goal from Michel Platini?

12 In 1987, a Portuguese side became champions for the first time since 1962, when which team beat Bayern Munich 2-1?

13 Ruud Gullit and Marco van Basten each scored twice for which side in the 4-0 win against Steaua Bucharest in 1989?

14 Which side became the first Yugoslavian team to win the final, against Marseille in 1991?

15 The last time that the competition was known as the European Cup was the 1992–1993 season. Which side became the first Spanish team to win since 1966?

84
European Cup Winners' Cup
1961–1999

1   Which Spanish team won it on four occasions?

2   Which British team lost the first final, in 1961, to Fiorentina?

3   The highest winning margin in a final came in 1963 when which English team beat Atletico Madrid 3-1 in the final?

4   What was the name of the West Ham United goalkeeper who won the ECWC with them in 1965 having also won cricket's County Championship with Worcestershire in the previous year?

5   With 14 goals for Chelsea and Southampton, who was the highest-scoring English footballer in the competition?

6   Which 18-year-old substitute won the Cup with Manchester City in 1970 and later won two European Cups with Nottingham Forest?

7   Which Spanish team did Chelsea beat in the 1971 final?

8   Which Scottish side beat Dynamo Moscow 3-2 to win the 1972 tournament?

9   Who managed Leeds United when they were beaten 1-0 by AC Milan in the 1973 final?

10 Pat Holland and Keith Robson scored for which English club who conceded four in the 1976 final against Anderlecht?

11 Who was the Everton manager in 1985 when they beat Rapid Vienna 3-1 in the final?

12 Alex Ferguson was in charge when Manchester United won the 1991 competition. With which club had previously been a winner in 1983?

13 In the 1994 final, Alan Smith scored for which English team when they beat Parma 1-0?

14 Which Italian substitute scored the only goal of the 1998 final, as Chelsea beat Stuttgart?

15 Roberto Mancini was a member of which Italian side who were the last ever winners of the competition in 1999. They beat Mallorca in the final.

85
UEFA Cup and Europa League Finals

1 Tottenham Hotspur won the first competition in 1972 when they beat Wolverhampton Wanderers 3-2 on aggregate. Which England international was the winning captain?

2 When Liverpool beat Borussia Monchengladbach in the 1973 final, they met three times. Why?

3 Who was the manager of Tottenham Hotspur when they lost the 1974 final to Feyenood?

4 In 1976, Liverpool won the trophy for the second time, having beater Club Brugge in the final. Which perm-haired English striker scored in both legs for Liverpool?

5 In 1981, Ipswich Town beat AZ '67 5-4 on aggregate in the final. What nationality were the losing club?

6 Which British team, which included Tony Parks, Danny Thomas and Paul Miller, beat Anderlect on penalties?

7 Which Spanish team became the first club to win back-to-back trophies in 1984–1985 and 1985–1986?

8   Which country provided the winners of the competition six times between 1988–1989 and 1994–1995?

9   Jurgen Klinsmann, Oliver Kahn and Lothar Matthaus were members of which team that beat Bordeaux in the 1996 final?

10   In 1997–1998, the final became one match for the first time. Which Italian side beat Lazio 3-0 to collect the trophy for the third time?

11   In 2000, Arsenal lost the final to Galatasaray on penalties. Who was the Arsenal goalkeeper?

12   Who did Liverpool beat 5-4 via a Golden Goal in the 2001 final?

13   Which Middlesbrough goalkeeper played in the 2006 final, where they were beaten 4-0 by Sevilla, in a facemask to protect a broken cheekbone?

14   In 2010, Roy Hodgson managed which team to the final, where they lost 2-1 to Atletico Madrid?

15   In which city did Chelsea win the 2013 Europa League final when they beat Benfica 2-1?

86
Women's Football

1   Which country hosted the Women's European Championships in 2013?

2   Who are the most successful women's club in England?

3   About whom did her national coach, Hope Powell, say she was 'one of those players that come along once or twice in a lifetime'?

4   Name the Brazilian forward who won FIFA World Player of the Year on five consecutive occasions from 2006?

5   The inaugural FIFA Women's World Cup was held in 1991. Of the six tournaments to date, which two nations have won it twice?

6   Which female player declined an offer from Perugia to join their Serie A men's team, fearing it would be used as a publicity stunt?

7   Which team beat Lyon in the UEFA Champions League final in 2013 to end the French side's 118-game unbeaten run?

8   Scotland have yet to qualify for the final stages of a major tournament and were unlucky to lose in extra time of a play-off for Euro 2013 to which nation?

9   What is 'The FA WSL'?

10   Which two American forwards have scored over 300 international goals between them over their careers?

11   In 1921, who said, 'The game of football is quite unsuitable for females and ought not to be encouraged.'

12   Arsenal has only lost the Women's FA Cup final once. Who beat them in extra time in 2010?

13   England lost in the final of the 2009 Euros to which nation?

14   The world record attendance for a women's match is officially reported as 90,185. Which two teams took part and what was the occasion?

15   In 2007, Arsenal became the first British side to win which honour?

87
Other Tournaments

1   The 2013 FIFA Confederations Cup final took place in which stadium?

2   Who takes part in the annual FA Community Shield?

3   Scarborough, Woking and Telford United are the most successful clubs with three wins each in what competition?

4   In what year did Man Utd miss the FA Cup to play in the Club World Cup in Brazil?

5   Which team are the current holders (2011) and most successful team in Copa America history?

6   In 1999, which team won the last ever UEFA Cup Winners' Cup final held at Villa Park?

7   Which team defeated Chelsea 1-0 to win the 2012 FIFA Club World Cup?

8   Sunday Mba won what trophy for Nigeria in 2013?

9   The New Saints were the 2012–2013 Champions of which league?

10   In 2013, Spennymoor Town beat Tunbridge Wells in the final of which competition?

11   Which Scottish team has won the Scottish Cup the most times?

12   Roberto Carlos scored a famous curling free kick in which 1997 pre-World Cup tournament?

13   Which South Pacific Island won their first OFC (Oceania) Nations Cup in 2012 and so qualified for the FIFA Confederations Cup?

14   In 2012, Chelsea lost the UEFA Super Cup final 4-1 to which team?

15   Now known as the Johnstone's Paint Trophy, what was the Football League Trophy called when it began in 1983–1984?

88
England Managers

1   Walter Winterbottom was the first and longest-serving manager and led the team in 139 matches between 1946 and 1962. Which club had he previously played for?

2   In which season did Alf Ramsey manage Ipswich Town to the First Division Championship?

3   Which caretaker manager won three, drew three and lost one of his seven games in charge of England following the sacking of Sir Alf Ramsey?

4   How many times did Don Revie manage England?

5   In November 1978, Ron Greenwood became the first England manager to select a black player for the team. What was the name of the man who made his international debut in England's 1-0 win in Czechoslovakia?

6   In the finals of Euro '88, Bobby Robson's team finished bottom of their qualifying group and lost all three matches. Which future England manager was in the England squad?

7   Who was chairman of Watford when Graham Taylor was first appointed as their manager in 1977?

8   What was the name of the fictional private detective that Terry Venables co-created in a series of novels with Gordon Williams?

9   Who did Glenn Hoddle appoint as assistant manager when he took on the England job?

10 Kevin Keegan is the only England manager to have been named European Footballer of the Year. He won the award twice, in 1978 and 1979. Which team was he playing for at the time?

11 Who did Peter Taylor appoint as England captain, for the first time, in his one match as caretaker manager when the team lost 1-0 to Italy?

12 Which Italian team had Sven-Goran Eriksson managed to success in Serie A, Coppa Italia and the UEFA Cup Winners' Cup before becoming England manager?

13 Who did Steve McClaren select as England's goalkeeper when they lost 3-2 at home to Croatia in 2007 and failed to qualify for Euro 2008?

14 Who was England's captain when Fabio Capello scored the only goal of the game for Italy against England at Wembley in November 1973?

15 Before taking the helm with England Roy Hodgson had managed three other national teams. The first two were Switzerland and United Arab Emirates. Which was the third?

89

England Captains

1   In 1872, who became the first ever England captain?

2   Which two legends share the record for the most England games captained?

3   Who captained England between 1980 and 1991?

4   Which England captain was nicknamed 'Crazy Horse'?

5   Gary Lineker captained his country 18 times. How many goals did he score for England?

6   He scored England's first ever goal in a European Championship game, was a non-playing member of the 1966 World Cup squad and captained his country three times. Who is he?

7   Who led England in their infamous match v Germany in Berlin in 1938, and what was the team told to do by British diplomats before kick-off?

8   Which former England captain has managed in Azerbaijan?

9   He captained England 22 times, and there is a statue of him outside Craven Cottage. Who is he?

10 Which goalkeeper has captained England on the most occasions?

11 Why was John Terry's captaining and goal in a 1-1 draw against Brazil in 2007 notable?

12 Which England captain has worked for BBC Radio for over 30 years?

13 Kevin Keegan was captain of England on 31 occasions. At which club did he start his career?

14 Which ex-captain became the first England player to be sent off in a World Cup finals game?

15 Which former England captain is a Doctor of Civil Law at Newcastle University?

90

English Legends

Identify the following

1   Scored 30 goals in 76 appearances for England between 1946 and 1958, spent his entire career with Preston North End. He was knighted in 1998.

2   Manchester City goalkeeper who won 14 wartime caps for England and 19 full ones. He later became a journalist and died in the Munich air disaster.

3   Pre-First World War star of Tottenham Hotspur and Chelsea. He scored 29 goals in his 23 appearances for England.

4   Scored seven goals for Arsenal against Aston Villa in 1935 and won five pre-war international caps. He later managed Chelsea to the 1955 League title.

5   Busby Babe who won two league titles and made his England debut at the age of 18. He died at Munich when he was 21.

6   Blackpool stalwart who scored 23 goals in 25 England appearances and a hat-trick in the 1953 FA Cup final.

7   Striker who scored 22 goals in his 23 international games and shocked the football world when he left Division One Chelsea to join Division Three Notts County in 1947 for a then record fee of £20,000.

8   The first player to be paid £100 a week and who spent 18 years at Fulham. He captained England in 22 of his 56 appearances.

9   Captained Sunderland to title and FA Cup success in 1936 and 1937, later played for Derby County and Hull City and managed Leeds United and Middlesbrough.

10 Left-back who captained Arsenal during the 1930s and won five league titles and two FA Cups. He also led England 21 times.

11 The first footballer in the world to win 100 caps, he led England in 90 games and spent his entire career at Wolverhampton Wanderers.

12 Inside-forward who played 341 league games for Middlesbrough between 1936 and 1954 and scored 11 goals for England in his 26 appearances.

13 'The Wizard of the dribble', who is the only player to have been knighted while he was still playing. Retired at the age of 50 whilst in his second spell with Stoke City.

14 Arsenal's all-time top goal-scorer until overtaken by Ian Wright, he scored 12 times for England in 21 pre-war appearances.

15 Derby County and Middlesbrough forward who scored 28 goals for England in his 23 appearances between 1895 and 1907.

91
Scotland National Managers

1   The first full-time manager of Scotland was appointed in 1954. What was his name?

2   Craig Brown was in charge of Scotland for more matches than any other manager. How many did he lead them in?

3   Tommy Docherty managed Scotland on 12 occasions, but which was the only Scottish club side that he played for, making nine appearances for them between 1947 and 1949?

4   Which confident manager insisted that Scotland would return from the 1978 World Cup finals in Argentina with 'at least a medal'?

5   Alex Ferguson played alongside which other future Scotland manager when Falkirk won the Scottish Division Two title in 1969–1970?

6   Who managed the Scotland squad at the 1958 World Cup finals in Sweden after Matt Busby was injured in the Munich Air Crash?

7   Who was the manager of Scotland in the 1974 World Cup finals when they were the only team in the tournament to remain undefeated?

8   How many consecutive League titles did Jock Stein win while he was in charge of Celtic?

9   Gordon Strachan was appointed manager of Scotland in January 2013. In which year did he win the first of his 50 international caps as a player?

10   Craig Levein watched his Scotland team lose a Friendly 5-1 to which other international side in May 2012?

11   Having failed to qualify for Euro 2008, Alex McLeish resigned and became manager of which Premier League club?

12   George Burley made 500 appearances for which English team?

13   Who was the only former Scotland manager to have won the World Cup as a player?

14   Walter Smith managed Scotland 16 times between 2004 and 2007. His middle name is the same as the surname of which other Scottish manager?

15   Which manager celebrated his first match in charge with a shock 3-2 win over the new World Champions, England, at Wembley in 1967?

92

Scotland Captains (by initials)

1 Captained them 48 times in his 53 appearances (GY)

2 Red-haired captain of Leeds who led Scotland 39 times (BB)

3 Won the FA Cup and League Cup double with Liverpool in 2000–2001 (GM)

4 Won five Scottish Premier League titles with Rangers and captained his country 28 times (BF)

5 After winning 54 caps for Scotland, he later managed Galatasaray, Benfica and Torino (GS)

6 Won many trophies with Celtic in 1976–1990 and was briefly caretaker manager at Aston Villa (RA)

7 Scored eight goals in 43 appearances for Scotland, including a famous one against Holland in the 1978 World Cup finals (AG)

8 Made a late Scotland debut aged 27 but captained the side in 22 of his 51 matches (CH)

9   During a spell with Borussia Dortmund, became the first British player to win the new Champions League (PL)

10 Made 755 official appearances for Rangers and then managed them from 1978 to 1983 (JG)

11 Legendary Celtic fullback who played 657 times for his club and won 62 caps for his country (DM)

12 Claimed to 'have more clubs than Arnold Palmer' and managed Scotland on 12 occasions (TD)

13 His 77 appearances make him Scotland's third most capped player. He won the Scottish Premier League three times with Aberdeen (AM)

14 He only captained his country in six of his 102 games (KD)

15 Former Arsenal captain who led Scotland out on one occasion, against Northern Ireland, in 1970 (MFM)

93
Great Scots

1   Won the league title with Tottenham Hotspur as a player and Derby County as manager and made 22 national appearances between 1957 and 1965

2   One of the 'Lisbon Lions' who won the 1967 European Cup, this 5'2" outside-right played 515 times for Celtic and scored 129 goals. He was capped 23 times for Scotland.

3   Scored 30 goals in 55 appearances for Scotland and won two league titles and the European Cup with Manchester United

4   A winger with Rangers and Motherwell who played 22 times for Scotland between 1979 and 1990 and scored a crucial penalty against Wales in the 1986 World Cup qualifying campaign

5   Nottingham Forest and Derby County left-winger who won two European Cups with Forest and was capped 28 times by Scotland

6   Rangers player and manager who spent more than a decade as a team captain on *A Question of Sport* between spells at the club

7   Opinionated midfielder who played 50 times for Scotland and had long spells with Aberdeen, Manchester United and Leeds United

before managing Celtic and Scotland

8 Won the League and FA Cup under Bill Shankly at Liverpool and later formed a long-running TV partnership with Jimmy Greaves

9 Liverpool captain who won three European Cups and eight league titles before becoming a *Match of the Day* pundit in 1992

10 Preston North End and Arsenal inside-forward before the Second World War, who provided many assists for the great strikers of the time. He was limited to eight international caps because Preston refused to release him to play for Scotland.

11 A right-back whose career with Rangers and Hearts lasted more than two decades. He won 38 Scottish caps and played in the 1974 and 1978 World Cup finals.

12 With 23 goals from 20 internationals and 406 goals in 554 league games for teams including Newcastle United and Chelsea between 1925 and 1934, this diminutive centre-forward was one of the greatest frontmen of the age.

13 A defender who spent his entire career at Celtic, captaining them to nine championships, and played 29 times for Scotland before managing Celtic, Manchester City and Aston Villa

14 A goalkeeper who represented Scotland 43 times between 1985 and 1998 and made more than 200 appearances for Oldham Athletic and Rangers

15 Left footed midfielder with Rangers, Sunderland and Nottingham Forest in the 1960s who played 34 times for his country

94
Northern Ireland Managers

1   Who played 56 games for Northern Ireland and then managed them 138 times?

2   Which manager of Northern Ireland has a BSc degree in Management Science from Loughborough University?

3   The first manager of Northern Ireland shares a name with the former lead singer of The Libertines. Who was he?

4   Before becoming manager of Northern Ireland, Nigel Worthington had led which team into the Premier League in 2003–2004?

5   Lawrie McMenemy was appointed manager of Northern Ireland in 1998, but when had he won the FA Cup as manager of Southampton?

6   Which manager was the first person to refuse to take part in *This Is Your Life* when confronted by Eamonn Andrews and his red book in 1961?

7   How old was Terry Neill when he became manager of Arsenal in 1976?

8   In Sammy McIlroy's first match in charge, he gave a debut cap to which player who would become the all-time leading goal-scorer for Northern Ireland?

9   Who was the manager of Northern Ireland when George Best made his first appearance in 1964?

10   Only one manager led Northern Ireland whilst still playing for the team. Who was he?

11   Lawrie Sanchez's mother was born in Northern Ireland but in which country was his father born?

12   Billy Bingham was a member of which First Division Championship winning team in 1962–1963?

13   Two future managers of Northern Ireland were part of Bertie Peacock's team which suffered the nation's biggest ever defeat, to England, in November 1963. What was the score?

14   Which manager was previously in charge of Tranmere Rovers, Wigan Athletic and Leicester City?

15   Michael O'Neill was appointed manager of Northern Ireland in December 2012. In which year had he won the last of his 31 playing caps for the National side?

95
Northern Ireland Legends

1   Left-back with Arsenal and later for Brighton and Hove Albion who won 51 caps for Northern Ireland

2   Tottenham Hotspur, Watford and Real Mallorca striker who scored the winner for Northern Ireland against Spain at the 1982 World Cup finals

3   Twice winner of the European Cup with Nottingham Forest who won two League Cups with them and also as manager of Leicester City

4   Capped 91 times by his country, he spent a decade with Luton Town, won the European Cup Winners' Cup with Manchester United and ended his career at Chelsea.

5   Scored 12 goals in 59 international games whilst playing for West Ham United, Southampton, Crystal Palace and QPR

6   Bearded Aston Villa captain who made 210 league appearances for them between 1972 and 1977 and a further 228 with Southampton

7   Having won 59 caps for Northern Ireland, he managed Hull City, Arsenal and Tottenham Hotspur.

8   German-born goalkeeper who won 88 caps between 1999 and 2011

9   Born in 1979, this striker had long spells with Preston North End and Leeds United and scored 36 goals in his first 94 appearances for his country.

10   A member of the famous Manchester United youth side of the early 1990s, he spent much of his career with Newcastle United, Blackburn Rovers and Sheffield United.

11   Scored five goals in 52 games for his country during long spells with Oxford United, Southampton and Ipswich Town. He managed the latter between 2006 and 2009.

12   Tottenham Hotspur and Arsenal goalkeeper who represented his country 119 times

13   A versatile midfielder who played in the 1982 and 1986 World Cup finals, and won the FA Cup with Manchester United in 1977

14   Born in Canada, this defender made almost 200 league appearances for Manchester United and had two spells with Toronto Blizzard. He was capped 73 times between 1976 and 1986.

15   Central defender who won the FA Cup during a decade with Ipswich Town and played 53 times for Northern Ireland

96
Wales National Managers

1   The first official manager of Wales was appointed in 1954 and, a decade later, he also became the first official pundit on *Match of the Day*. Who was he?

2   In August 1993, Wales reached their highest ever FIFA ranking under the management of Terry Yorath. What was the position?

3   As a player, Mike England won the FA Cup, two League Cups and the UEFA Cup with which English club?

4   Jimmy Murphy is the only manager to take Wales to the finals of a major championship. Which year did they manage to reach the World Cup finals?

5   Gary Speed was capped 85 times by Wales. How many goals did he score for the national side?

6   Which Welsh manager had previously been in charge of Bristol Rovers, Coventry City, Wimbledon and WBA?

7   BBC Sport presenter Gabby Logan is the daughter of which Welsh manager?

8   John Toshack took which club side from Division Four to Division One in just four seasons?

9   In October 2002, Mark Hughes's Welsh side produced a shock 2-1 win against Italy to go top in their Euro 2004 qualifying group. Who scored the winning goal?

10 Which Greek side did Chris Coleman manage prior to his appointment with Wales?

11 When Egypt won the African Cup of Nations in 1986, they were led by which former Welsh manager?

12 The longest-serving manager in Welsh history was Dave Bowen (1964–1974). He also had four separate spells between 1947 and 1972 with which particular football league club, twice as a player and twice as manager?

13 Who is the only Welsh manager to have also scored a hat-trick for Wales?

14 Which former Cardiff and Swansea boss who later managed Wales on one occasion in 1964 had led a squadron of 40 Lancaster Bombers on D-Day?

15 Who was manager during Wales's record run of six consecutive wins and two draws between June 1980 and May 1981?

97

Welsh Wizards

1　Prolific Liverpool goal-scorer who won two European Cups and spent a season with Juventus

2　Capped 54 times for Wales, this winger had three spells with Burnley and also played for Derby County, QPR and Sunderland

3　Manchester United winger who made his international debut in 1991 and is the most decorated footballer in English football history

4　Capped 73 times by his country between 1979 and 1992, his clubs included Crystal Palace, Arsenal, Luton Town and Chelsea

5　A two-decade league career saw him win the FA Cup with Liverpool and the League Cup with Aston Villa and score 22 goals in 75 games for his country

6　Prolific striker who won the League Cup with Manchester United, Chelsea and Blackburn Rovers. He played 72 times for Wales and managed them in 41 games.

7　A goal machine who scored 38 times in 40 Division One games for Leeds United in 1956–1957 before moving to Juventus and winning three Serie A titles

8   A defender and midfielder who had long spells with Swansea City, Oxford United, Sunderland and Fulham. He won the first of his 65 caps in 1989 under Terry Yorath.

9   A left-back who played 72 times for Wales, had three long spells at Wrexham and twice won the European Cup with Liverpool

10 249 goals in 691 league games for Swansea Town, Newcastle United and Cardiff City between 1947 and 1968 and a further 23 in 68 internationals led to him being nicknamed the Golden Boy of Welsh football.

11 Wales and Everton captain who led his club to 1980s success in the League, FA Cup and European Cup Winners' Cup

12 Zambian-born striker who is the only man to have scored hat-tricks in the Premier League, all three divisions of the Football League and in an international. He won his first cap in 2002.

13 In goal for Wales on 52 occasions between 1975 and 1982, he also played for Everton and Wrexham.

14 Versatile Manchester United and Middlesbrough player who won the 1990 FA Cup and 1991 European Cup Winners' Cup and 39 Welsh caps

15 Captain of Wales between 2007 and 2011 whose many clubs include Newcastle United, Blackburn Rovers, Liverpool and Manchester City

98
Republic of Ireland Players

1   Born in 1980, this striker played for teams as varied as Leeds United, Inter Milan, Celtic and LA Galaxy as well as scoring 59 goals in his first 127 internationals.

2   West Bromwich Albion's first £1m player who played 66 consecutive matches for the Republic of Ireland and won 110 caps in total

3   Aston Villa and Liverpool defender who won 102 caps and managed the national side on 17 occasions

4   Scored 21 goals in his 92 appearances and played for Arsenal, Manchester City and Sunderland

5   Won the first of his 88 caps whilst at Gillingham and later spent several years playing in France

6   Centre-back in Euro '88 and the 1990 and 1994 World Cup finals who twice won the League Cup with Aston Villa

7   Won five Premier League titles with Manchester United and gave away a penalty against Croatia on his international debut in 2001

8   Goalkeeper who won 80 caps between 1981 and 1996 and spent his entire career with Celtic

9   Hard-working Glasgow-born midfielder who won trophies with Oxford United, Liverpool and Aston Villa

10 Four times Manchester City's player of the year who moved to Aston Villa in 2009. He scored, conceded a penalty and was sent off as his national team lost 5-2 to Cyprus during the Euro 2008 qualifying campaign.

11 The first man to be sent off in an FA Cup final who also twice won the All-Ireland Gaelic Football championship

12 Won the FA Cup with Arsenal and Manchester United as well as the equivalent competitions in Belgium and Holland and scored 20 times for his country

13 Former Manchester United captain who walked out of the Republic of Ireland squad during the 2002 World Cup finals

14 Kent-born midfielder who played 70 times for his country before becoming a pundit for ITV

15 A career spent largely with QPR and Neuchatel Xamax included 56 caps and two spells as caretaker manager of the national side

7
Half-Time Entertainment

99
Football and the UK Singles Chart

1   Which band reached number 15 with Scotland's official 1998 World Cup theme tune, 'Don't Come Home Too Soon'?

2   Glenn Hoddle and Chris Waddle reached number 12 in 1987 with which song?

3   In 1966, who sang 'World Cup Willie'?

4   Chris Norman and Pete Spencer wrote Kevin Keegan's 1979 hit single 'Head Over Heels In Love', which reached number 31 in the UK and number 10 in Germany. Which band were they members of?

5   Songwriters Phil Coulter and Bill Martin wrote four UK number 1s, including 'Puppet On A String' for Sandy Shaw, 'Congratulations' for Cliff Richard and 'Forever And Ever' by Slik. What is the name of their football-linked track that also topped the chart?

6   Which comedian co-wrote 'World in Motion', New Order's chart-topping single for England's 1990 World Cup campaign?

7   'Ossie's Dream' was a number 5 hit for Chas and Dave and the Tottenham Hotspur FA Cup Final Squad in which year?

8   Which team reached number 14 in 1985 with 'Here We Go'?

9   Bobby Moore, Bobby Charlton, Gary Lineker and Nobby Styles are all mentioned in which football song?

10 Which chart position did Manchester United striker Andy Cole reach in 1999 when he released his version of the Gap Band's track 'Outstanding'?

11 Which football commentator spoke a verse in Liverpool's 1986 FA Cup final song, 'Anfield Rap'?

12 In 1997, Chris Rea re-recorded his classic track 'Let's Dance' with comedian Bob Mortimer but it peaked at number 44. Which team was it dedicated to?

13 Only one club side has so far topped the UK charts with an FA Cup final song. What was the team?

14 Which Football League newcomers managed to reach the top 40 with a track that was only initially released in their home town to celebrate the fact that they had been drawn against Liverpool in the third round of the 2003–2004 FA Cup?

15 In 1972, Marvin Hinton, Tommy Baldwin, John Dempsey and Steve Kember all sang on a track which reached number 5 in the UK singles chart. What was the song?

100
Football on Film

1   Who played Don Revie in the film *The Damned United*?

2   Which football-themed film saw Pele, Bobby Moore and John Wark star alongside Michael Caine and Sylvester Stallone?

3   In the 1997 film version of Nick Hornby's bestselling book *Fever Pitch*, Colin Firth played the lead character of football fanatic Paul Ashworth. Which team did he follow?

4   Gurinder Chadha co-produced, co-wrote and directed which film about women footballers?

5   Billy Meredith was one of the first footballing superstars and played for both Manchester City and Manchester United. In 1926, he played himself in which famous silent film about football?

6   Who wrote the 1979 film *Yesterday's Hero* which stared Ian McShane as an alcoholic ex-footballer?

7   Sean Bean, Emily Lloyd and Pete Postlethwaite stared in which 1996 film about the exploits of a factory worker playing for Sheffield United?

8   Who directed *The Golden Vision*, the 1968 BBC docu-drama about Everton's Alex Young, and then 41 years later also directed *Looking for Eric*, staring Eric Cantona?

9   Arthur Askey played a football-obsessed train driver in which 1955 feature film?

10 Which British actor played the cheating games teacher in a football match in *Kes*?

11 *See You At Wembley, Frankie Walsh* was a comedy based around the wedding of a fan of which British football team?

12 The classic 1939 film *The Arsenal Stadium Mystery* featured which Arsenal manager?

13 Which singer and actress played *Gregory's Girl* in Bill Forsyth's 1981 romantic comedy?

14 In 2001, Ricky Tomlinson played which fictional England manager in a film of the same name?

15 Julie Welch wrote which 1983 TV film about her time as a young supporter of Tottenham Hotspur?

101
Great Football Books

Who wrote the following?

1   *The Glory Game* (1972)

2   *Fever Pitch* (1992)

3   *Only a Game* (1987)

4   *The Damned United* (2007)

5   *The Football Man* (1968)

6   *Football Against the Enemy* (1994)

7   *Brilliant Orange: The Neurotic Genius of Dutch Football* (2000)

8   *Walking on Water* (2002)

9   *The Soccer Tribe* (1981)

10 *Steak... Diana Ross: Diary of a Football Nobody* (2003)

11 *A Life Too Short* (2011)

12 *Kicking and Screaming* (1995)

13 *Addicted* (1998)

14 *All Played Out* (1991)

15 *Goalkeepers Are Different* (1972)

102

1970s Entertainers

1 Despite scoring 97 league goals in 315 starts for QPR, this cult player only won five caps for England. One of his former managers expressed the wish that he could 'pass a betting shop like he passes the ball'.

2 The most sartorially flamboyant player of his generation was associated with 24 clubs in a 26-year career. His most famous goal came against Ipswich Town and included a header and three chips before turning and volleying into the net.

3 Named after the battleship that his father served on, he made his name by demonstrating his often dazzling skills with Fulham, QPR, Manchester City and, on nine occasions, with England.

4 A true entertainer who played 313 league games for Sheffield United before long spells with Leeds United and QPR. His curling shot during United's November 1978 4-0 home win against Southampton FC won ITV's *The Big Match* Goal Of The Season that year.

5 One of the greatest Leicester City players of all time, skilful on the ball and a smile on his face, he also won the European Cup Winners' Cup with Chelsea and was famous for wearing white

tights in cold weather.

6   Enormously talented but with a reputation for individualism rather than team play, his longest spells in a much-travelled career were with Nottingham Forest, Leeds United, Blackburn Rovers and Everton. His party trick was to leap over a mini.

7   With a career that included long spells with Arsenal, Juventus, Sampdoria, Inter Milan and West Ham United plus 72 caps for the Republic of Ireland, this skilled and elegant player can lay claim to being one of the greatest Irish footballers in history.

8   Born and brought up near the King's Road, this talented midfield playmaker was renowned for his flair and skill during his peak years with Chelsea and Stoke City.

9   Having made his debut for Birmingham City aged just 16, this agile, fast and skilful striker became the world's first Million Pound Man.

10 Ever-smiling Republic of Ireland international with a famously balding head, he was a favourite with Leyton Orient, QPR and Arsenal.

11 Opinionated, entertaining and controversial Northern Ireland striker who gained a cult following during his eight seasons at Wolverhampton Wanderers and was a member of ITV's famous 1970 World Cup studio panel.

12 Played for Manchester City, Derby County and England during the 1970s. He established a new penalty record in the 1971–1972 season when he scored 15.

13 'The King of Stamford Bridge' who won the FA Cup with Chelsea in 1970 and Southampton in 1976, he was renowned for a playboy lifestyle.

14 Supremely skilled attacking midfielder who made 647 appearances for West Ham United before becoming John Motson's regular co-commentator on live matches on BBC TV

15 Long-haired Arsenal and Derby County forward who famously scored a long-range winning goal for the Gunners in the 1970 FA Cup final at the age of 20 and celebrated by laying on his back

103

Celebrity Supporters 1

Which clubs do the following celebrities support?

1   Actor and singer Michael Crawford

2   Former athlete and London 2012 supremo Lord Coe

3   Radio presenter Lauren Laverne

4   Actor, and former captain of the Starship *Enterprise*, Patrick Stewart

5   Comedian Frank Skinner

6   Actress Catherine Zeta-Jones

7   Comedian and actor Les Dennis

8   Simply Red frontman Mick Hucknell

9   AC/DC singer Brian Johnston

10 Singer Dido

11   Actor Hugh Grant

12   Superstar DJ Fatboy Slim

13   Singer Rod Stewart

14   Actor and comedian Russell Brand

15   Singer Alison Moyet

104

Celebrity Supporters 2

Which clubs do the following celebrities support?

1 Singer Lily Allen

2 Singer Robbie Williams

3 Actor Jude Law

4 Actor Sean Bean

5 Model and presenter Melinda Messenger

6 Oasis songwriter, and High Flying Bird, Noel Gallagher

7 Master chef Delia Smith

8 Double Olympic Gold Medallist Mo Farah

9 Actor and comedian Bob Mortimer

10 Actor and comedian Bill Bailey

11 Broadcaster and journalist Sir Michael Parkinson

12 Comedian Mark Watson

13 Comedian Jasper Carrott

14 Politician, and former Foreign and Home Secretary, Jack Straw

15 Actress and comedian Jo Brand

105

Match of the Day – True or False

1   *Match of the Day* is now broadcast each week from a studio in Salford.

2   In 1974, the BBC's farming department produced a weekend of programmes about chickens that was called *Hatch of the Day*.

3   Robbie Williams appeared as a studio guest during the 1998 World Cup finals.

4   Desmond Lynam coined the nickname 'Our Man Albert' to refer to the BBC's football statistician, Albert Sewell.

5   Alan Sugar turned down the opportunity to become the regular presenter of *Match of the Day* when Desmond Lynam left the BBC to join ITV.

6   When *Match of the Day* began in 1964, the total audience was estimated to be 20,000 viewers.

7   *Match of the Day 3* was launched online at the start of the 2011–2012 season.

8   Presenter Ray Stubbs was a professional player with Sheffield Wednesday.

9   CBC sports show *Hockey Night in Canada* also uses the *Match of the Day* theme tune.

10 In 1990, Jimmy Hill escaped serious injury when a large studio light exploded and showered the *Match of the Day* set with hot shards of glass just seconds after he got up.

11 Former *Match of the Day 2* presenter Colin Murray was also a Radio 1 DJ.

12 In 1999, *Match of the Day* was broadcast from inside a giant plastic revolving football. The experiment was abandoned the following year.

13 In recent seasons, the actual Premier League Trophy features on the set each weekend and arrives with its own security team.

14 In 2007, a technical error meant that the soundtrack to the feature film *Rocky* was accidently broadcast for almost three minutes over Arsenal against Manchester United instead of John Motson's commentary.

15 Former *Match of the Day* presenter David Coleman was also a British and European 1500m champion.

106
Quotes of the 1970s

Who said...

1 'We lost the World Cup, but it was still the finest England Team I've played in.'

2 'What is it, being a footballer? If you take away *Match of the Day* and the press and the fans and the hangers-on, it's all very empty and lonely.'

3 'Pele couldn't get into my squad the way my lads are playing these days.'

4 'No team has worked harder than the winner of that match – or indeed the losers.'

5 'Pity I didn't get me eyebrows on telly sooner; really you can cop a lot of easy loot in this panel game lark, can't you?'

6 'Some people think football is a matter of life and death. I don't like that attitude. I can assure them it is much more serious than that.'

7 'When anyone starts calling me a Messiah all I have to do is go and see my parents.'

8   'I'd like to see a return of the wingers, the days of Matthews and Finney, Hancocks and Mullen, Huntley and Palmer, Fortnum and Mason.'

9   'I did the ordinary things that ordinary managers do, like reshaping the youth scheme. But on the whole I am far above ordinary.'

10 'For those of you with black and white sets, Liverpool are in the all-red strip.'

11 'I was potentially quite bright at school but when they'd be telling me about the reproduction of the spirogyra all I was thinking was how to get a left-back to overlap.'

12 'On our team coach, the radio dial always points to Radio 4, not Radio 1's pop. Show me a talented player who is thick and I will show you a player who has problems.'

13 'The ideal soccer board of directors should be made up of three men. Two dead and the other dying.'

14 'Duncan McKenzie is like a beautiful motor car. Six owners and been in the garage most of the time.'

15 'Sir Harold Thompson, chairman of the FA, treated me like an employee. These Arab Sheikhs treat me like one of them.'

107
British Goalkeepers

1   FA Cup winner who became the first goalkeeper to save a penalty in the final

2   Won 91 caps for Scotland between 1982 and 1998 and collected four Scottish Cup-winning medals with Aberdeen and the FA Cup with Manchester United

3   The main Arsenal goalkeeper throughout the 1950s who was also capped 41 times for Wales and played in the team that reached the quarter-finals of the 1958 World Cup

4   World Cup-winner who began his career at Chesterfield and later played for Leicester City and Stoke City

5   With 125 caps, this goalkeeper is also England's most capped player

6   A former hod-carrier and dustman who won the League, FA Cup and European Cup Winners' Cup and played a record 92 times for Wales

7   Born in Shrewsbury in 1987, he made his full England debut as a substitute against Trinidad and Tobago in 2008

8   Former Tottenham Hotspur and Arsenal favourite who won a record 119th cap for Northern Ireland on his 41st birthday, against Brazil in the 1986 World Cup finals

9   A Liverpool legend whose haul of major trophies included three European Cup and five League titles

10   Almost as famous for his ponytail and moustache, this former Leeds United and QPR goalkeeper was the first choice for England for almost eight years.

11   Following a move from non-league Chelmsford City, this player's second appearance for Aston Villa was as a substitute in their 1-0 win against Bayern Munich in the 1982 European Cup final.

12   Having begun his career at Watford, he later won the League Cup with Liverpool and the FA Cup with Portsmouth.

13   Sheffield United's star goalkeeper at the turn of the 20th century, who was reputed to weigh as much as 24 stone during his playing days

14   Headed a goal that gained extra time for Leeds United against Swindon Town in the 2003–2004 League Cup and then saved a penalty in the subsequent shootout before moving to Tottenham Hotspur in the summer.

15   Longstanding Sheffield Wednesday goalkeeper who represented England 33 times and was involved in a unique transfer swap with his goalkeeping brother Peter that took him to QPR and Peter to Sheffield Wednesday

108

British Transfer Records

1   The first £1,000 player moved from Sunderland to Middlesbrough in 1905. What was his name?

2   Which team broke the transfer record twice in a row when they paid £5,500 for Warney Cresswell in 1922 and £6,500 for Bob Kelly in 1925?

3   Tommy Lawton had scored 30 goals in 42 League games for Chelsea when he became the first player to be sold for £20,000 in 1947. Who bought him?

4   How much did Torino pay Manchester City for Denis Law when he moved to Italy in June 1961?

5   Which player broke the £200,000 barrier by moving across London from West Ham United to Tottenham Hotspur in 1970?

6   Who paid Liverpool £500,000 for Kevin Keegan in June 1977?

7   Which manager made Trevor Francis the first Million Pound player in 1979 when he was sold to Nottingham Forest by Birmingham City?

8   The football world was astonished when Manchester City manager Malcolm Allison paid £1,437,500 to Wolverhampton Wanderers for midfielder Steve Daley. What was his value 20 months later when he was sold to Seattle Sounders?

9   In October 1981, Manchester United took the record up to £1,500,000 when Bryan Robson moved to Old Trafford from West Bromwich Albion. During his 13 years at the club, as their longest-serving captain, he made which shirt number his own?

10 What world record transfer fee did the English press report Real Madrid paid Tottenham for the services of Gareth Bale in 2013?

11 Arsenal paid £7,500,000 to Inter Milan for which player in June 1995?

12 Who was bought for £8,500,000 by Liverpool and then sold for £7,000,000 to Aston Villa?

13 Rio Ferdinand moved from West Ham United to Leeds United for £18,000,000 and then to Manchester United for an estimated £29,000,000. But which lower league team did he play 11 games for whilst on loan during the 1996–1997 season?

14 Who was the manager of Chelsea when Andriy Shevchenko joined the club from AC Milan for £30,800,000?

15 How old was Cristiano Ronaldo when he became the most expensive player in history, moving from Manchester United to Real Madrid for £80,000,000?

109
Club Nicknames 1
(England)

1 Who are 'The Shrimpers'?

2 What is Morecambe's nickname?

3 Why are Bournemouth called 'The Cherries'?

4 Which non-league club are called 'The Lambs' and why?

5 What is Hartlepool's nickname?

6 Who are 'The Owls'?

7 Whose club chairman came up with the nickname 'The Shakers'?

8 Who are 'The Addicks'?

9 What is Blackpool's nickname?

10 Which Yorkshire club's nickname is a breed of dog?

11 If the Lions in London were at home to the Tigers, who would be playing?

12 What is Bradford City's nickname?

13 Who took their nickname from Benfica of Portugal?

14 What nickname do Brentford and Barnet have in common?

15 Who are 'The Cobblers' and why?

110
Club Nicknames 2 (Scotland, Wales and Northern Ireland)

1   Who are 'The Bhoys'?

2   What is Patrick Thistle's nickname?

3   Which team are known as 'The Wee Gers'?

4   What is Rangers' nickname?

5   Which Welsh team are 'The Wingmakers'?

6   Coleraine derives its nickname from a nearby river. What is the river?

7   Who are 'The Seasiders' of Northern Ireland?

8   Which intelligent-sounding Scottish team are nicknamed 'The Accies'?

9   What is Aberdeen's nickname?

10 Which team are 'The Buddies' of Paisley?

11 Cardiff City changed their home kit to red in 2012, but kept their nickname. What is it?

12 If 'The Glens' were to play 'The Hatchetmen', who would be playing?

13 Who are 'The Jam Tarts' or 'Jambos' of Edinburgh?

14 Which precious stone does Airdrie Utd have as its nickname?

15 Newport County shares its nickname with the title of a 1970s American detective series. What is it?

111
Club Nicknames 3 (Overseas)

1 Which French side are 'Les Verts' ('The Greens')?

2 PSV Eindhoven have 'poor people' as their nickname. What is it?

3 Who are 'The Meringues' ('Los Merengues') in La Liga?

4 What animal do Galatasaray have as their nickname?

5 Kaiserslautern and Hapoel Tel Aviv share a nickname with one of the Premier League's leading teams. What is it?

6 Who are 'The Red and Blacks' ('Rossoneri')?

7 Which Italian club are known as 'The Donkeys' ('I Ciucci')?

8 And who are 'The Flying Donkeys'?

9 Nantes and Norwich both have a type of bird as their nickname. What is it?

10 Who is known as 'The Old Lady' of Turin?

11 Which Brazilian club are known as 'Great Team' ('Timáo')?

12 Pele's former club, Santos, are known as 'The Dolphins'. True or false?

13 Who are 'Les Rouge-et-Bleu' ('The Red and Blue') of France?

14 Which German side are known as 'Star of the South' ('Stern des Súdens')?

15 What's the nickname of Shaktar Donetsk, taken from the people who work in the main local industry?

112
Footballing Brians

1   Presenter of *The Big Match* on ITV

2   Manager of Derby County and Nottingham Forest

3   Coventry City's 1987 FA Cup-winning captain

4   Managed Leicester City, Aston Villa and Hull City

5   Scored for Manchester United in their 1968 European Cup final win

6   Manager of Reading and Leeds United

7   Won the FA Cup as a player with Ipswich Town and Arsenal

8   Won three FA Cups and two league titles as captain of Manchester United

9   Twice winner of the League Cup with Nottingham Forest and managed Sheffield Wednesday

10   Played for Port Vale and Luton Town and managed Manchester City, Oxford United and Huddersfield Town

11 Barnsley player of the year for 2006–2007

12 Played for Leeds United and Burnley and won 66 caps for Wales

13 Danish international who played for Rangers, Ajax and Bayern Munich

14 Won the 1974 FA Cup and two league titles with Liverpool

15 Manchester United and Leeds United player who often appeared alongside his brother

113
Mascots

Which teams do these Mascots represent?

1   Angus the Bull

2   Fred the Red

3   Cyril the Swan

4   Billy the Badger

5   Gunnersauras Rex

6   Hoopie the Huddle Hound

7   Bubbles the Bear

8   Scrumpy the Robin

9   H'Angus the Monkey

10   Broxi Bear

11   Lucas the Kop Cat

12 Sammy the Shrimp

13 Zampa the Lion

14 Swifty

15 Pilgrim Pete

8
Second Half: Match of the Day Memories

114

David Coleman

1   When was he born?

2   Which newspaper did he work on at the start of his career?

3   Which BBC Sport show did he present from 1958?

4   In 1972, he conducted the first Royal interview on *Sports Review of the Year*. Who did he talk to?

5   How many FA Cup finals did he commentate on for BBC TV?

6   Which eponymous sports show did he present between 1968 and 1972?

7   In which year did he first commentate for BBC TV at the Olympic Games?

8   Other than football, what is the main sport that he commentated on?

9   In 1964, he conducted a famous interview on *Grandstand* with which band who had just arrived at London Airport?

10 He was the regular presenter of *Match of the Day* from 1969 until which year?

11 What name did the magazine *Private Eye* coin for their section about sporting commentary blunders?

12 Which quiz show did he present between 1979 and 1997?

13 He retired after commentating on which Olympic Games?

14 On 23 occasions he presented the BBC's TV coverage of which horse race?

15 How many autobiographies has he written?

115
1964–1965

1   One famous name was missing when the first season of *Match of the Day* began. A member of the Tottenham Hotspur's double-winning side was tragically killed by lightning in July while sheltering under a tree on a golf course at Enfield. Who was he?

2   Which 19-year-old scored a hat-trick in front of the cameras for Blackpool as they drew 3-3 with Fulham at Craven Cottage?

3   Stan Cullis was sacked by which club after 16 years in charge and having led them to three Division One titles and an FA Cup?

4   Tommy Docherty's young Chelsea side were winners of the League Cup, beating which other team 3-2 on aggregate in the two-legged final.

5   Which former Northern Ireland captain was used as an occasional pitch side pundit in the first series of *Match of the Day*?

6   This was the final season for the legendary winger Stanley Matthews, who retired shortly after being awarded a knighthood. How old was he when he played his final game for Stoke in February 1965?

7   Which bottom-placed team conceded 96 goals in Division One and were beaten 6-1 by Chelsea, 5-3 by Everton and drew 5-5 with Blackburn Rovers?

8   Why was *Match of the Day* cancelled on 30 January 1965?

9   West Ham United became only the second British team to win a European trophy when a 2-0 victory at Wembley gave them the European Cup Winners' Cup. Who did they beat in the final?

10 Liverpool beat Leeds United 2-1 in the FA Cup final to lift the trophy for the first time. What was the name of the Liverpool manager?

11 After a career spent at West Bromwich Albion, Fulham, Leicester City and Shrewsbury Town, Arthur Rowley retired with what is still an all-time English league record of how many goals from his 619 games?

12 Manchester United won the First Division Title on goal difference having finished level on 61 points with which other team?

13 Which team were promoted as Division Two champions?

14 The joint top Division One goal-scorers, with 29 each, were Jimmy Greaves at Tottenham Hotspur and which Blackburn Rovers striker?

15 In April Jack Charlton won his first International cap when England drew 2-2 with Scotland. His brother Bobby was in the same team, but how many caps had he already won before this game?

116
1965–1966

1   At White Hart Lane in October, Jimmy Greaves scored one of his greatest solo goals for Tottenham Hotspur as he accelerated past four players to score their third in a 5-1 win against which team?

2   Tottenham were also involved in another remarkable high-scoring home game in March when they went 5-1 up against Aston Villa before the visitors pulled it back to 5-5. Which father of a future England international scored four times for Villa?

3   Which team won the Division One title for the second time in three seasons?

4   What breed of dog was Pickles, who found the World Cup trophy in a bush in March 1966?

5   Who finished bottom of Division One, led by manager Jack Marshall, after a wretched run that had seen them take just two points from a possible 26?

6   Which Manchester United player was voted British and European Player of the Year?

7   Which newly promoted side returned immediately to Division Two

as a result of their dreadful away form. They conceded 60 goals away from home as Blackburn, Leeds United, Manchester United and Stoke City all scored six against them.

8   Who managed Manchester City to the promotion and the Division Two championship in his first season in charge at Maine Road?

9   Which striker finished as the leading goal-scorer in top flight with 38 League and Cup goals to his name?

10 Southampton had a 9-3 win in Division Two. Who were their opponents?

11 In the FA Cup final, Sheffield Wednesday looked to have the match sewn up when they took a two-goal lead against Everton with just over half an hour remaining. In a tremendous comeback, Mike Trebilcock scored twice in five minutes, but who hit the winner ten minutes before the final whistle to clinch a 3-2 win for the Merseyside team?

12 The League Cup final saw which side beat West Ham United 5-3 on aggregate?

13 How did Charlton Athletic's player Keith Peacock make history in a Division Two match against Bolton Wanderers on Saturday 21 August?

14 Celtic won the first of how many consecutive Scottish League Division One titles under manager Jock Stein?

15 What is the name of the future World Cup winner who made his England debut in a May friendly against Yugoslavia?

117
1966–1967

1   Three weeks after Bobby Moore had lifted the Jules Rimet trophy, the *Match of the Day* cameras were at his home ground to see the three West Ham heroes Moore, Geoff Hurst and Martin Peters take a collective bow ahead of their opening game. The day ended less cheerfully for the home crowd as they were beaten 2-1 by which local rival?

2   When West Bromwich Albion lost 4-3 at home to Manchester United, all seven goals came in the second half. Which Scottish player scored a hat-trick for the visitors?

3   Alan Ball was sold by Blackpool for a new British transfer record of £110,000. It was the game's first six-figure fee. Who did he join?

4   Welshman Ron Davies scored 37 goals in 41 Division One games. Who did he play for?

5   Who was the manager of Division Three side Queens Park Rangers when they beat holders West Bromwich Albion to win the League Cup?

6   Celtic became the first British side to win the European Cup when they beat Inter Milan 2-1. In which city was the final held?

7 Who scored five goals for Chelsea in their 6-2 win over Aston Villa?

8 Who was the trophy-lifting captain of Tottenham Hotspur when they beat Chelsea 2-1 in the FA Cup final?

9 Bobby Robson began his managerial career when he left Fulham to join which side as their player-manager?

10 Manchester United regained the Division One title but which team came second, four points behind?

11 Who beat the World Cup holders, England, 3-2 at Wembley in April?

12 Brian Clough was managing which side to eighth place in Division Four this season prior to his move to Derby County?

13 Which team, managed by a future *Match of the Day* presenter, were promoted to the top flight of English football for the first time in their history?

14 Manchester United goalkeeper Harry Gregg left the club in December 1967. Which team did he join?

15 Which future Arsenal captain was born in October 1966?

118
1967–1968

1 On 30 September 1967, who presented *Match of the Day* for the first time?

2 In the Charity Shield, Tottenham Hotspur's 22-year-old goalkeeper Pat Jennings scored when he kicked the ball up field. It was missed by every player and bounced over the head of his opposite number. Who was the Manchester United goalkeeper that day?

3 Which Division One side recorded the biggest win of the year when they beat Burnley 8-1?

4 Who succeded Tommy Docherty at Stamford Bridge following his resignation as manager of Chelsea?

5 Fulham came bottom of Division One. Which other side, managed by John Harris, were relegated alongside them?

6 Which Manchester City player joined the club in October 1967 following a club record £60,000 move from Bolton Wanderers?

7 Which side won the League Cup and the Inter-Cities Fairs Cup?

8   Manchester United became the first English side to win the European Cup when they beat which side 4-1 at Wembley?

9   Martin Chivers set a new British transfer record when he moved from Southampton to Tottenham Hotspur. How much was the fee?

10   Which side beat Everton 1-0 in the 1968 FA Cup final?

11   Manchester City won the Division One title for the first time since 1937. What was the name of their flamboyant coach who worked alongside manager Joe Mercer?

12   Only 56,365 spectators, the smallest crowd since 1921, attended the Scottish Cup final at Hampden Park to see Heart of Midlothian beaten 3-1 by which team?

13   Who was voted European Player of the Year?

14   Which team won promotion as Division Two champions?

15   Which famous television celebrity team contained a pair of Ogdens, a Fairclough and a Turpin?

119

1968–1969

1   *Match of the Day*'s first show of the season featured two members of the same family on opposing sides. Leicester included the most expensive player in the history of the Football League, Allan, who had moved from Fulham in the summer for £150,000. His brother Frank was leading the QPR attack. What is their surname?

2   Jimmy Greaves once again finished as the League's leading goal-scorer. His 36 League and Cup goals included four in their 5-1 win against which team?

3   Manchester City failed to defend their title. What was their final league position at the end of the season?

4   Which Division Three side replicated Queens Park Rangers' feat of the previous season by winning the League Cup and being promoted to Division Two?

5   Manchester City beat Leicester City 1-0 in the FA Cup final. Who scored the only goal of the game?

6   In their World Cup qualifying group Scotland won 8-0 and 5-0 against which country?

7   More than 10,000 people entered a BBC competition to find a new football commentator. The winner was Idwal Robling, a Welsh sales manager for a packaging company. Which Liverpool footballer was placed second?

8   Which side were promoted to Division One as champions?

9   Don Revie finally saw his Leeds United team become Division One champions. Who was the captain of the side?

10 George Cohen and Johnny Haynes were members of which relegated team?

11 What was the name of the new ITV Saturday lunchtime football preview show that began this season?

12 Which British team won the only European trophy of their history when they beat Ujpest of Hungary 6-2 across the two legs of the Inter-Cities Fairs Cup.

13 Who succeeded Sir Matt Busby as manager of Manchester United when he retired at the end of the season?

14 At the start of the FA Cup final, the referee George McCabe used the first ever coin of a new denomination for the toss, some six months before they went into circulation. What was the value of the coin?

15 Which team won the European Cup for the second time in seven years?

120

1969–1970

1   This season saw several changes for *Match of the Day*. The show moved from being pre-recorded pitch-side to a studio at Television Centre, and the highlights of two games could be seen in each programme. Who took over from Kenneth Wolstenholme as the main presenter of the show?

2   Which Everton defender scored one of the greatest ever own-goals when he headed into his own net during the Merseyside derby?

3   Who scored twice on his league debut for West Ham United when they beat Manchester City 5-1 at Maine Road?

4   Which British club beat Leeds United in the semi-finals of the European Cup but lost the Final 2-1 to Feyenoord after extra time?

5   One of the biggest shocks came in the FA Cup when Liverpool were knocked out by Watford in the sixth round. Whose flying header produced the only goal of the game?

6   Everton were crowned Division One champions for the second time in eight seasons. Who was their manager?

7   Brian Clough and Peter Taylor took Derby County to which position at the end of their first season in Division One?

8   Which side completed a Cup double, beating West Bromwich Albion 2-1 in the League Cup final and becoming only the third British side to win the European Cup Winners' Cup? They beat Gornik Zabrze 2-1 in the final played in Vienna.

9   When Tommy Docherty was employed by his new club in the hope that he would take them out of Division Two, they hadn't expected that they would end the season in Division Three. Who were his employers?

10   In an outstanding European season for English clubs, Arsenal beat which club 4-3 across the two legs of the Fairs Cup final?

11   Who became the first Chelsea captain to lift the FA Cup after their 2-1 victory over Leeds United in the replay of the final?

12   George Best and Tom Finney took part in the first edition of *A Question of Sport* when it was broadcast in January 1970. Who presented the show?

13   Which club saw their name change from Town to City during the season?

14   Bradford Park Avenue came bottom of Division Four and were voted out of the league. Which non-league club replaced them?

15   Who captained England and scored the third goal of their 3-1 win against Northern Ireland in the match where he won his 100th cap?

1   Arsenal completed the Division One and FA Cup Double. Who was their manager?

2   The *Match of the Day* audience was treated to a goal that was so unusual that it became known as a 'donkey kick'. Coventry had been awarded a free kick on the edge of Everton's box when which player stood over the ball, trapped it between both feet and leapt into the air flicking the ball backwards for Ernie Hunt to volley into the top-right-hand corner of the goal?

3   Ted McDougall scored 42 league goals for which Division Four side in the season before they changed their name?

4   Chelsea won the European Cup Winners' Cup final after a replay. Who were their opponents?

5   Who scored both goals for Tottenham Hotspur when they beat Aston Villa in the League Cup final?

6   In the fifth round of the FA Cup, Leeds United were beaten 3-2 by which Division Four side?

7   Which side finished bottom of Division One and had to wait 39 years to return to the top division?

8   Which Leeds player won the first ever Goal of the Month competition on *Match of the Day* for his goal against Manchester United in their opening match of the season?

9   Who was named Footballer of the Year?

10 Who scored Arsenal's first goal when they beat Liverpool 2-1 in the FA Cup final?

11 Liverpool signed 20-year-old Kevin Keegan from which club?

12 Wilf McGuinness was replaced in December by Sir Matt Busby. Who succeeded him as the new manager of Manchester United at the end of the season?

13 Which team finished runners-up in Division One for the fourth time in seven seasons but won the European Fairs Cup for the second time in four years, beating Juventus on away goals?

14 Who was the West Bromwich Albion player who ended the season as the leading goal-scorer in Division One? His tally of 28 included a hat-trick against Manchester United.

15 Who were promoted as Division Two champions?

122
1971–1972

1 Which fleece-loving commentator made his *Match of the Day* debut this season?

2 Chelsea opened their defence of the European Cup Winners' Cup with an extraordinary encounter against Hautcharage. They won the away leg 8-0, which included a hat-trick by Peter Osgood. Two weeks later, at Stamford Bridge, Osgood added another five as Chelsea won 13-0. Which country are Hautcharage from?

3 Who scored a hat-trick for Leeds United in their 7-0 demolition of Southampton?

4 The Division One race was one of the closest for many seasons, and at the start of the final week four clubs still had a chance. Who ended up clinching the championship by one point?

5 Gordon Banks, Mike Pejic and Jimmy Greenhoff were all part of which team which won their first ever trophy by beating Chelsea 2-1 in the League Cup final?

6 Norwich City were promoted as Division Two champions. Who was the manager who guided them to the top tier for the first time in their history?

7   The biggest shock of the season came when Southern League Hereford United took on Newcastle United in an FA Cup third-round replay. Malcolm Macdonald put the visitors ahead before Ronnie Radford unleashed a 40-yard shot that gave him sporting immortality, but who scored the winner?

8   This season saw the introduction of a short-lived competition that saw the highest-scoring side from each of the four divisions take part in a knockout tournament. What was it called?

9   A Dixie Deans hat-trick helped Celtic become the first team since 1887–1888 to score six goals in a Scottish Cup final, against who?

10   In the first all-British European final, Tottenham Hotspur beat Wolverhampton Wanderers 3-2 over two legs to lift which trophy?

11   Which player was sent off against Chelsea and dropped by his club in January for not turning up for training and was ordered by his manager to live in 'digs' and concentrate on getting fit?

12   In the FA Cup final, Allan Clarke's diving header took the trophy back to Leeds for the first time. Who did they beat?

13   Who scored twice for Rangers as they beat Dynamo Moscow 3-2 to win the Cup Winners' Cup?

14   Manchester City finished the season in fourth place in Division One. Which of their players scored 33 league goals, a total that remained unsurpassed in the top Division for 22 years.

15   Where was Brian Clough when he heard that he was the manager of the League Champions?

123
1972–1973

1   Who scored all of Tottenham Hotspurs' goals in their 4-1 win against Manchester United at Old Trafford?

2   Which future captain of England led Liverpool to the League Championship and UEFA Cup double?

3   Who became the fourth manager in 18 months to move into the manager's office at Manchester United?

4   Gordon Jago managed which team into the First Division?

5   Tottenham Hotspur won the League Cup for the second time in three years when whose goal was enough to see them defeat Norwich City in a dull final at Wembley?

6   The FA Cup final between Sunderland and Leeds United was decided by two key moments. Ian Porterfield put Sunderland ahead, but what was the name of their goalkeeper who, in the 70th minute, pulled off a sensational double save to deflect shots from Trevor Cherry and Peter Lorimer, the second onto the underside of the bar?

7   What did Bobby and Jack Charlton both do on 28 April?

8   Which team did Liverpool beat 3-2 on aggregate to win their first ever European trophy in the UEFA Cup final?

9   Who resigned as manager of Manchester City just eight months after taking over from Joe Mercer?

10 Against which side did Bobby Moore win his record 106th cap?

11 Which side were promoted to Division Three in their first year in the Football League?

12 Ron Greenwood steered West Ham United to equal their best ever position in the league. Where did they finish?

13 Johnny Rep scored the only goal of the European Cup final against Juventus to give which team their third consecutive win in the competition?

14 Which side dropped out of Division One for the first time since 1949, when they were relegated along with Crystal Palace?

15 Which former Newcastle United striker topped the Division One chart with 28 goals for West Ham United?

124

1973–1974

1   The season began with another presenter change on *Match of the Day*. The new man was the first to combine presentation with analysis. Who was he?

2   Who was Leeds United's first-choice goalkeeper when they won their second League title in six seasons and also kept for Scotland in the 1974 World Cup finals?

3   In a time of hooliganism, three-days weeks and dull football, many clubs saw their attendances drop sharply. Which Division One side lost 25 per cent of its paying customers this season?

4   The break-up of which team saw Peter Osgood and Alan Hudson depart for Southampton and Stoke City during this season?

5   How many games had Leeds United been unbeaten before losing 3-2 to Stoke City?

6   Cardiff City won which trophy for the ninth time in 11 seasons?

7   England failed to qualify for the 1974 World Cup finals. Needing a win, they could only draw 1-1 with Poland at Wembley thanks to the goalkeeping skills of which player?

8   Who scored the goal in the Manchester derby that sent Manchester United into Division Two?

9   Sir Alf Ramsey was sacked by the FA after how many matches in charge of England?

10   Which Southampton striker could not help his team avoid relegation despite finishing the season with 21 goals, more than any other player in Division One?

11   Derby County finished in third place despite having lost their managing partnership of Brian Clough and Peter Taylor. They resigned after a fallout with the chairman in October. What was his name?

12   Three up/three down promotion was introduced for the first time. Which side joined Middlesbrough and Luton Town in being promoted from Division Two?

13   Manchester United's failure to score was one of the main reasons for their relegation. Sammy McIlroy was their top scorer with how many league goals?

14   Which team beat Manchester City 2-1 to lift the League Cup?

15   Two goals by Kevin Keegan helped Liverpool to a 3-0 win over Newcastle United in the FA Cup Final. Prior to the match, Bruce Forsyth had led the crowd in pre-match singing but which international athlete won a special 3,000m race around the Wembley pitch?

125
1974–1975

1   The season began with Bill Shankly, having announced his retirement, leading Liverpool out for the last time, and Brian Clough, the newly appointed manager of Leeds United, walking alongside him. Who was appointed the new Liverpool boss?

2   How many days did Brian Clough spend as manager of Leeds United after Don Revie left to take the England job?

3   Which manager steered Derby County to their second Division One title in four years?

4   What was the score when Ipswich beat Newcastle United at Portman Road?

5   Which side beat Norwich City 1-0 in the League Cup final and capped a great season by being promoted to Division One for the first time since 1967?

6   Which 21-year-old West Ham striker scored both FA Cup final goals, ending Bobby Moore's trophy hopes with his new club, Fulham?

7   Recently retired Arsenal goalkeeper Bob Wilson became the presenter of which new weekly football spot in *Grandstand*?

8 Which team finally broke Celtic's decade-long dominance of the Scottish Championship?

9 Jimmy Armfield, the new manager at Leeds United, took them to the European Cup final, where they lost 2-0 to which German team?

10 Jack Charlton had steered Middlesbrough out of Division Two in his first season in charge, with a record lead of 15 points over second-placed Luton Town. Where did they finish in their debut term in the top flight?

11 Manchester United finally ran out of patience with George Best and transferred him to which club?

12 The goal of the season came in February when Blackpool took on Sunderland at Bloomfield Road in a Division Two match. Which player chested down a clearance just past the halfway line, took on the Sunderland defence and then curled a long-range shot past the diving Jim Montgomery?

13 How many goals did Malcolm Macdonald score for England against Cyprus in a European Championship qualifier at Wembley?

14 Following their relegation from Division Three, which team became the first former English champions to find themselves playing in the bottom division?

15 Who had retired as manager of Tottenham Hotspur four games into the season after almost 16 years in charge and having won the League Championship, three FA Cups, two League Cups, the European Cup Winners' Cup and the UEFA Cup?

126
1975–1976

1   The opening day of the season saw Gerry Francis score a fantastic goal that took the ball from one penalty area to the other in four moves. It was adjudged the Goal of the Season as his side beat Liverpool 2-0. Who was he playing for?

2   Manchester City beat Newcastle United 2-1 in the final of the League Cup with goals by Peter Barnes and Dennis Tueart. What was the name of their captain?

3   Yet another slump in support for football saw the game record its lowest set of attendances since the war. With just under 25 million paying spectators, the game had lost how many million since 1968?

4   Which future manager of Macedonia scored a hat-trick as West Ham United were demolished 4-0 by Liverpool at Upton Park?

5   Kenny Burns and Peter Withe each played more than 35 times for which Division One team this season?

6   Bob Paisley saw his Liverpool side win the Division One title. How many points separated them from QPR in second place.

7   Rangers completed the League and Cup Treble in Scotland. Who was their manager?

8   In the FA Cup final, Southampton beat Manchester United 1-0. Who scored the winning goal?

9   Bertie Mee retired as manager of Arsenal. Who controversially crossed North London to succeed him?

10 Franz Beckenbauer was named European Footballer of the Year for the second time in three seasons. Which club did he play for?

11 Liverpool also won the UEFA Cup with a 4-3 aggregate win over FC Bruges. Their squad consisted of 13 Englishmen, two Welshmen and a single representative from the Republic of Ireland. What was his name?

12 Scotland revamped their league structure. How many teams played in their new Premier Division?

13 Future England manager Graham Taylor won promotion out of Division Four with Lincoln City. How old was he?

14 Which side, managed by Bob Stokoe, were promoted when they finish top of Division Two ?

15 Where did Chelsea finish at the end of the season?

127

1976–1977

1   Which side set a then record for the most goals by one team on *Match of the Day* when they demolished York City 7-2 in their Division Three encounter? Peter Ward and Ian Mellor led the way with two goals each. The following month saw Ward score four and Mellor three as they put seven past Walsall.

2   In May 1977, Ally McLeod was appointed manager of the Scotland football team. Which team had he just led to a 2-1 success against Celtic in the final of the Scottish League Cup?

3   Referees were able to develop their own theatrical styles this season with the introduction of red and yellow cards. Which Blackburn Rovers player was the first in the Football League to be shown a red one?

4   At Highbury, Arsenal won 5-3 against Newcastle thanks to a hat-trick against his old club from Malcolm Macdonald. Who was the Newcastle manager when he was transferred?

5   Which group reached number 14 in the singles chart in March with their *Spot The Pigeon* EP that contained a track called 'Match Of The Day'?

6   For the second consecutive season, Liverpool won the League Championship by just one point. Which team were runners-up?

7   What was the name of the referee who was officiating in his final game when he had to ask the groundsman to repaint the penalty spot before Gerry Daly was able to score Derby County's fourth against Manchester City, and thereby avoid relegation?

8   It took three attempts before Aston Villa were able to beat Everton in the League Cup final. At which ground was their decisive 3-2 meeting?

9   Who denied Liverpool the Treble when they beat them 2-1 in the FA Cup final?

10 In June Kevin Keegan joined SV Hamburg for a new British transfer record fee. How much did they pay?

11 Who was the manager when Tottenham Hotspur were relegated to Division Two?

12 Which 21-year-old striker was voted Player of the Year and Young Player of the Year having won a League Cup winners medal and, with 25 goals, finished joint top scorer in Division One.

13 Brian Clough guided Nottingham Forest into Division One when they came third in Division Two, Eddie McCreadie was in charge of second-placed Chelsea, but who managed Wolverhampton Wanderers as they went up as Champions?

14 Liverpool won the European Cup for the first time in their history when they beat Borussia Monchengladbach in Rome. What was

the score?

15 Terry Venables managed which Division Three team into third place and a promotion?

128
1977–1978

1 Gordon McQueen set a new transfer record between two British clubs when he moved from which team to Manchester United for £495,000?

2 Which side won the Division One title at their first attempt?

3 The biggest win of the season, and a new *Match of the Day* record, came when Tottenham Hotspur beat Bristol Rovers 9-0 in their Division Two encounter. Colin Lee scored four on his debut, but who else competed a hat-trick?

4 When Stoke City were beaten 3-2 at home in February their opponents became the first non-league side to reach the fifth round of the FA Cup for 29 years. Who were they?

5 Which side's leaky defence saw them lose 5-1 at Coventry City, 6-0 at Everton and 6-2 to Manchester City?

6 Who scored the only goal of the game when Nottingham Forest beat Liverpool to win the League Cup final replay?

7 Which side secured their first FA Cup success when a Roger Osborne goal was enough to beat Arsenal in the final?

8 Who succeeded Don Revie as manager of the England team?

9 Liverpool reached their second successive European Cup final and became the first British club to retain the trophy when they beat FC Bruges 1-0. Where was the game played?

10 Brian Clough emulated the feat of which other manager in leading two different teams to the League title?

11 Alan Slough ended up on the wrong end of a 4-3 scoreline for Peterbrough United against Chester despite scoring three goals. What was unusual about his hat-trick?

12 Which future Premier League side were voted into the Football League at the end of the season at the expense of Southport?

13 With 30 goals to his name, which Everton striker was the leading scorer in Division One, helping his side to third place?

14 In August 1977, *Match of the Day* celebrated which milestone?

15 West Ham United were relegated after how many consecutive years in Division One?

129

1978–1979

1 Argentinean World Cup-winners Ricky Villa and Osvaldo Ardiles signed for Tottenham Hotspur. Which club did Ardiles previously play for?

2 The bottom-placed side in Division One won only five games and conceded 92 goals. Who were they?

3 Viv Anderson became the first black player to represent England when he started against which country, at Wembley, on 29 November?

4 Who cost £500,000 when he moved to West Bromwich Albion from Middlesbrough in January?

5 How many players did Bob Paisley use in the league as Liverpool regained the Division One title by scoring 85 goals, conceding just 16 and losing only four games?

6 In a pulsating FA Cup final, Arsenal beat Manchester United 3-2. Which Arsenal player had also been a winner with Ipswich Town in the previous season?

7 Who was the 17-year-old who scored a hat-trick on his debut for

QPR when they beat Coventry City 5-1 in Division Two?

8   Trevor Francis became the first million-pound footballer when he was signed by Brian Clough at Nottingham Forest. He also had regular columns in which children's sporting comic?

9   When Jock Stein took over the Scotland side, who replaced him as manager of Celtic?

10 Who led out Nottingham Forest at Wembley before they became the first team to defend the title when they beat Southampton 3-2?

11 Which former Wolverhampton Wanderers striker scored a hat-trick for Arsenal when they beat Tottenham Hotspur 5-0 at White Hart Lane?

12 Which British player was voted European Player of the Year for the second consecutive season, the only time this has ever happened?

13 Alan Mullery managed which team into Division One for the first time in their history?

14 When Liverpool beat Nottingham Forest 2-0 in December, they ended an unbeaten League run of how many games?

15 For which team did Ian Rush make his first ever league appearance, aged 17?

130

1979–1980

1   As transfer fees began to spiral, which team paid Wolverhampton Wanderers £1.4m for Steve Daley and a further £1.25m to Norwich City for Kevin Reeves?

2   Trevor Booking's glancing header gave West Ham victory in the FA Cup final against Arsenal. Who was their captain, who collected the trophy for a second time?

3   Who scored the BBC's Goal of the Season when he flipped up the ball, turned and sent an exquisite left-footed volley into the top-left corner past a diving Ray Clemence as Norwich City and Liverpool drew 3-3?

4   Which team won promotion for the first time in 41 years when Len Ashurst managed them to third place in Division Four?

5   In October, Billy O'Rourke, a 19-year-old goalkeeper made his club debut at Loftus Road and conceded seven. Who was he playing for?

6   One of BBC Radio Sport's presenters made his first appearances on *Match of the Day* this season, presenting the football news. What was his name?

7   Nottingham Forest finished fifth in the League but retained the European Cup by beating which German team 1-0?

8   The legendary Everton striker Dixie Dean passed away after suffering a heart attack whilst watching the Merseyside derby. How many league goals did he score in his record-breaking 1927–1928 season?

9   One trophy that Forest failed to retain was the League Cup. They did manage to reach their third successive final but lost 1-0 to Wolverhampton Wanderers. A mistake by which goalkeeper gave Andy Gray the chance to score?

10 Having won two League Championships in the 1970s, which team found themselves starting the new decade in Division Two?

11 Manchester United finished the season in second place, two points behind Liverpool. Who was their manager?

12 Alan Hardaker retired from which position in football after a 22-year reign?

13 After 14 years of dominance by Rangers and Celtic, which side finally broke Glasgow's hold on the top tier of Scottish football?

14 Which future England manager scored on his debut for the national team when they beat Bulgaria 2-0?

15 With 21 goals in 37 league games, which former Everton striker was the leading scorer for Liverpool in their Championship-winning season?

131

1980–1981

1 After 16 seasons on a Saturday night, *Match of the Day* moved to which new time slot?

2 Terry Venables, Ernie Whalley, Malcolm Allison and Dario Gradi all managed which team during this season?

3 Garth Crooks and Steve Archibald scored 47 goals in a prolific season for which side?

4 How many players did Aston Villa use this season as they won the Division One title for the first time?

5 Which British team beat AZ 67 Alkmaar 5-4 on aggregate to lift the UEFA Cup?

6 Liverpool won the European Cup for the third time when they beat Real Madrid 1-0 in Paris. They also collected the League Cup after a replay against which London side?

7 Who was the 1966 World Cup hero who was sacked as manager of Chelsea and replaced by John Neal?

8 Kevin Keegan Alan Ball, Dave Watson, Mick Channon, Charlie

George and Chris Nicholl all played for which team this season, finishing sixth in Division One?

9   Which Manchester City player had opened the scoring in the FA Cup final against Tottenham Hotspur with a diving header but was later in despair after being credited with an own goal when the ball was deflected by his shoulder past Joe Corrigan to bring the scores level?

10 Who became the first Dutchman to be named Footballer of the Year?

11 Which teenager was transferred twice for more than a million pounds during the season?

12 Which manager moved from West Bromwich Albion to Manchester United at the end of the season?

13 Which side were promoted to Division One just four seasons after being in Division Four?

14 Who managed Aston Villa to League success this season?

15 In winning the Division Four title, which Essex side topped a league for the first time in their history?

132
1981–1982

1   Having recently signed from Everton, Bob Latchford scored three for which team as they beat Leeds United 5-1 on the opening weekend of the season?

2   When three points were introduced for a win in this season, it was the culmination of a long campaign by which administrator who had advocated it in his 1961 book *Striking for Soccer*?

3   In October, Bryan Robson moved to Manchester United for a new British record fee of more than £1.5m. Which team sold him?

4   Liverpool were Division One champions for the fifth time in seven years thanks to an outstanding period of success after Christmas. How many of their final 25 games did they lose?

5   Which team finished in second place, four points behind Liverpool and five points ahead of Manchester United?

6   With 26 goals for Southampton, which player finished the season as the leading scorer in Division One?

7   Liverpool won a second trophy by successfully defending the League Cup when they beat Tottenham Hotspur 3-1. The

competition was sponsored for the first time this season. What was it known as?

8   The European Cup stayed in England for a sixth consecutive season when Aston Villa beat Bayern Munich 1-0 in the final. Which previous winner, with Nottingham Forest, scored the only goal?

9   Which Division One side installed an artificial pitch?

10 Who did Tottenham Hotspur beat in the final of the FA Cup after a replay?

11 Goal of the Season was scored by which West Bromwich Albion striker against Norwich in the FA Cup in February 1982?

12 The legendary former Liverpool manager Bill Shankly died in September aged 67. A Scottish International, he had been an FA Cup winner with which team in 1938?

13 John Barnes and Luther Blissett scored for which team as their win against Leicester City secured promotion from Division Two?

14 Liverpool players Sammy Lee and Graham Souness featured in which BBC drama series?

15 Who succeeded Ron Greenwood as manager of the England team?

133
1982–1983

1   Kevin Keegan moved down a division from Southampton to which side? On his first appearance in front of the *Match of the Day* cameras, he scored four as the team went to Rotherham United and won 5-1.

2   Who scored four of Liverpool's five in their 5-0 win against Everton at Goodison Park? It was the first Merseyside derby hat-trick since 1935.

3   Liverpool won their third consecutive League Cup when they beat Manchester United 2-1 after extra time in the final. Who was told by the team to go and collect the trophy, which he did with a scarf draped around his neck?

4   At the final whistle of Luton Town's 1-0 win against Manchester City, their manager David Pleat ran leaping, crouching and clapping across the pitch pausing briefly only to button his jacket. Whose late goal had ensured Luton's Division One survival in the final minutes of the season?

5   Robert Maxwell was chairman of Oxford and also bought a controlling interest in Reading. He announced that he was going to merge the teams. Before the plans collapsed what was the

proposed name of the new team?

6   In the League, Liverpool stormed away from the pack and won the title with five games to go. They finished 11 points clear of which second-placed team?

7   The only British success in Europe this season came when which side beat Real Madrid 2-1 in extra time to win the European Cup Winners' Cup?

8   Who was caretaker manager of Manchester City as they joined Brighton and Hove Albion and Swansea in being relegated from Division One?

9   Manchester United beat Brighton and Hove Albion 4-0 in the replay of the FA Cup final, but which Brighton player missed an easy chance to score in the final minute of the first match?

10   Which Scottish side won the championship for the first time in their history?

11   Name the future *Match of the Day* presenter who was the leading scorer in Division Two with 26 goals for Leicester City.

12   Following Bob Paisley's retirement at the end of the season, who took over as the next manager of Liverpool?

13   When England beat Luxembourg 9-0 at Wembley in December, Luther Blissett scored a hat-trick and became the nation's first black goal-scorer. Which Stoke City player became the second, in the same match and on his debut?

14 Which Irish international became the first player to score in two FA Cup finals for different clubs?

15 Dave Bassett led which team to the Division Four title?

134

1983–1984

1 Which team became the first British club to float on the Stock Exchange when they were valued at just over £9m? The shares were four times oversubscribed, wiped out the club's debt and delighted their new chairman, Irving Scholar.

2 Liverpool rounded off an incredible season by winning their fourth European Cup. Roma were beaten on penalties after goalkeeper Bruce Grobbelaar fooled around with wobbly legs on the goal line to try and put them off. It worked, but who was the left-back who hit the winning penalty of the shootout?

3 What was the name of the 21-year-old Scottish player who moved from Celtic to Arsenal for £800,000 and was believed to be the highest-paid player in the country?

4 One of the surprises of the season came when manager Bobby Gould brought in the English Dance Theatre to help the players of which side with mobility and balance?

5 What is the name of the former FC Koln player who scored five in one match when Arsenal beat Aston Villa 6-2?

6 Liverpool won the League Cup for the fourth consecutive season, beating which team 1-0 in a replay at Maine Road?

7 Kevin Keegan scored in his final league match ahead of retirement as Newcastle United beat Brighton and Hove Albion 3-1. How old was he?

8 In the UEFA Cup final, Tottenham Hotspur beat Anderlecht on penalties when which substitute goalkeeper became an instant hero by saving the crucial penalty?

9 FA Cup holders Manchester United made a shock exit when they were knocked out by lowly Bournemouth. The Division Three team beat them 2-0 in one of the biggest ever FA Cup upsets. Who was their manager?

10 Everton won the trophy for the first time since 1966 when they beat Watford 2-0 in the FA Cup final. Which musician was chairman of the losing team?

11 Who guided Aberdeen to the Scottish Double?

12 When he scored at Ipswich Town in front of the *Match of the Day* cameras in November, who became the first man to score 100 league goals for a Scottish and English club?

13 The first ever live league match on the BBC saw Manchester United beat Tottenham Hotspur 4-2. How many years had it taken the FA to agree to the BBC's request to show live football?

14 Which team, bought by Ken Bates for £1, were promoted as Division One champions?

15 Lawrie McMenemy guided Southampton to their best ever position. Where did they finish?

135
1984–1985

1   As the season began, a number of the best-known British players moved abroad. Graeme Souness left Liverpool for Sampdoria and Liam Brady joined Juventus. Which club did Ray Wilkins move to?

2   On 16 March, Tottenham Hotspur beat Liverpool at Anfield for the first time since which year?

3   On the way to being crowned Division One champions, which team beat Manchester United 5-0, Newcastle United 4-0 and defeated Watford 5-4 at Vicarage Road?

4   What nationality were Jan Molby, who joined Liverpool, and Jesper Olsen, who moved to Manchester United?

5   The highest-scoring match came in September when which side visited QPR? At half-time the visitors led 4-0 thanks to a hat-trick from Chris Waddle, but an incredible comeback by the home team saw the match finish at 5-5.

6   Everton beat Rapid Vienna 3-1 in the European Cup Winners' Cup final in Rotterdam to clinch their first ever European trophy. Who was Everton's captain?

7   The fans of which side saw their team manage only three wins and concede 91 goals to finish bottom of Division One?

8   Following the shock resignation of Keith Burkinshaw, Tottenham Hotspur were steered into third place in Division One by which former Chelmsford City, Wimbledon and Stevenage Athletic player?

9   Oxford United joined the Cities of Birmingham and Manchester in the Division Two promotion spots. Who was their key striker with 30 league goals?

10   Manchester United beat Everton 1-0 at Wembley, despite which of their team becoming the first player ever to be shown the red card in an FA Cup final?

11   On 8 December, in the first round of the Scottish Cup, Stirling Albion set a new record for the biggest first-class score of the century in Britain when they beat Selkirk. What was the score?

12   Chris Woods, Steve Bruce and Mick Channon were part of which team who won the League Cup thanks to their opponents, Sunderland, scoring an own goal and missing a penalty?

13   Gary Lineker's 24 league goals for Leicester City saw him finish joint top scorer with which Chelsea favourite?

14   Millwall won promotion to Division Two and were managed by which former Arsenal and Chelsea midfielder?

15   Manchester United allow an 18-year-old to go to Crewe Alexandra on a free transfer. His future transfer fees will be worth in excess of £20m. Who is he?

136

1985–1986

1   Whose amazing start saw them win their first ten matches to secure a nine-point lead over Liverpool by the end of September?

2   Crystal Palace signed which 21-year-old future TV and radio presenter from non-league side Greenwich Borough?

3   When West Ham United won 8-1 against injury-hit Newcastle United, one of their players scored a hat-trick against three different goalkeepers. Who put the ball past Martin Thomas, Chris Hedworth and Peter Beardsley?

4   Goals by Trevor Hebberd, Ray Houghton and Jeremy Charles ensured that which team beat QPR 3-0 in the final of the League Cup to lift their first major trophy?

5   Whose volleyed goal in the Chelsea box saw Liverpool win 1-0 to clinch their 16 League Championship? It was his first year as player-manager and their eighth title in 11 seasons.

6   Wimbledon were promoted at the end of the season to complete their astonishing journey from non League to Division One in how many years?

7   When Liverpool beat Everton 3-1 in the FA Cup final, they became only the third team to complete the Double in the 20th century. Ian Rush scored twice, but which South African born player also made it onto the score sheet for Liverpool that day?

8   Scotland's manager, Jock Stein, collapsed and died at the age of 62 from a heart attack towards the end of their World Cup qualifier against which side at Ninian Park on 10 September?

9   Which side were relegated out of Division Three having finished sixth in the top flight just four seasons before?

10   Who was sent off in his first match as player-manager of Rangers?

11   How many goals did the prolific partnership of Frank McAvennie and Tony Cottee score between them that season as West Ham finished third?

12   Who was named player of the season having scored 38 goals for Everton as they finished second in the League and FA Cup?

13   Which recent FA and UEFA Cup-winners were relegated from Division One along with Birmingham City and West Bromwich Albion?

14   When George Graham was appointed manager of Arsenal, who did he replaced?

15   Mark Hughes left Manchester United to join which Spanish team?

1986–1987

1   Alex Ferguson took over as the new boss of Manchester United after who had been sacked?

2   Which striker's 49 goals for Tottenham Hotspur this season was seven more than Jimmy Greaves's longstanding club record?

3   One of the big talking points of the season came in the FA Cup quarter-final, when Watford beat Arsenal 3-1 at Highbury. The referee missed the linesman's flag for an apparent foul in the Watford box, but the Arsenal players had already stopped as Luther Blissett ran the full length of their half to score at the second attempt past which goalkeeper?

4   When Liverpool lost 2-1 to Arsenal in the League Cup final, it ended an amazing seven-year record of never losing a game when Ian Rush scored. How many matches did this sequence last for?

5   Which team had to drop out of the League Cup when they refused to lift their ban on visiting fans?

6   At the end of the season, Howard Kendall resigned as Everton manager and was replaced by his assistant Colin Harvey. Which Spanish team did Kendall move to?

7   Whose deflection looped over the head of Ray Clemence to give Coventry City their first major trophy when they beat Tottenham Hotspur 3-2 in the FA Cup final?

8   Play-offs were used for the first time to determine the final promotion and relegation places in order to reduce the size of Division One. Which team, who finished fourth from bottom, beat Leeds 2-1 to retain their place in the top flight?

9   Newcastle United finished just two places above the new Division One play-off zone, but which future manager of theirs was named European Footballer of the Year?

10 Lawrie McMenemy was sacked from which Division Two side in March, shortly before they were relegated?

11 St Mirren won the Scottish Cup for the first time since when?

12 Doug Ellis was the chairman of which team, who came bottom of Division One just five years after being crowned champions of Europe?

13 Which Guernsey-born 17-year-old made his debut for Southampton this season?

14 Everton won their second title in three seasons. How many points did they finish ahead of second-placed Liverpool?

15 Glenn Hoddle left Tottenham Hotspur at the end of the season. Which French League Club did he join?

138

1987–1988

1 Peter Beardsley and John Barnes joined which team for the start of the season?

2 Which side finished in bottom place having lost 7-4 and 5-2 to Luton Town?

3 In the Football League's Centenary season, which Division Three side produced the highest League score since 1964 when they beat Chesterfield 10-0?

4 Who produced one of the best individual performances of the season when he completed a hat-trick inside four minutes at the end of Nottingham Forest's 4-0 win against Queens Park Rangers?

5 Which side finished in second place, nine points behind the Division One Champions Liverpool?

6 Who scored 52 goals in all competitions for Wolverhampton Wanderers?

7 Bobby Campbell was caretaker manager at which Division One team who were relegated as part of the play-offs?

8   Luton Town won their first major trophy when they beat Arsenal 3-2 in the Littlewood's Cup final. Which Brian scored the first and third goals for the winners?

9   Which Liverpool player saw his penalty kick saved by Dave Beasant as Wimbledon won the FA Cup final 1-0?

10 Chris Kamara was fined for causing grievous bodily harm to Jim Melrose of Shrewsbury. It was the first time that a player in England had been convicted in a civil court for an on-field incident. Who did Karama play for at the time?

11 Celtic won the Double in Scotland under new manager Billy McNeill. Which newly signed former West Ham United player scored twice in their 2-1 Cup final win against Dundee United?

12 This was the last season that which man presented *Match of the Day*?

13 Paul Stewart, Tony Adcock and David White all scored hat-tricks as Manchester City beat Huddersfield Town 10-1 in Division Two. Which former Tottenham Hotspur and Brighton and Hove Albion midfielder scored the first of the 10?

14 Just two years after financial problems almost put them out of business, Bruce Rioch steered which side into Division One?

15 Following David Pleat's resignation who became the new manager at Tottenham Hotspur?

139
1988–1989

1   After 15 years being fronted by Jimmy Hill, who was the new *Match of the Day* presenter now that ITV had won the exclusive rights to show League football?

2   Before the season began, Paul Gascoigne moved from Newcastle United to which London side for £2m?

3   Everton paid West Ham United £2.2m to buy which striker who opened his new career with a hat-trick in Everton's 4-0 win against Newcastle?

4   Which Liverpool player was jailed for three months for reckless driving?

5   Nigel Clough scored twice in the Littlewoods Cup final when Nottingham Forest beat the holders, Luton Town, 3-1 to win their first major trophy for how many seasons?

6   When Arsenal met Liverpool, who scored with the final kick in the final minute of the last game of the season to snatch the Championship away from a traumatised Anfield?

7   In Scotland, Alex Smith and Jocky Scott jointly managed which

side to second place in the Premier Division behind Rangers?

8   In the third round of the FA Cup, Tony Rains and Matt Hanlan were the stars of the day as Barrie Williams managed which side to an astonishing 2-1 victory over Coventry City and into FA Cup folklore?

9   On 22 October, three brothers, Danny, Ray and Rod, all appeared for Southampton against Sheffield Wednesday. It was the first time in 68 years that three brothers had played together in the same First Division team. What was their surname?

10 At the end of the season, John Lyall was sacked after 15 years in charge of which relegated Division One team?

11 Liverpool beat Everton 3-2 in an FA Cup final that was overshadowed by the Hillsborough disaster. Who was the Liverpool captain who lifted the trophy?

12 Chelsea and Manchester City won promotion from Division Two alongside which team managed by Steve Coppell?

13 Graeme Souness controversially signed which player from Nantes who was claimed to be the first Catholic to play for Rangers?

14 Which former Arsenal player managed them to their first Championship since 1971?

15 Howard Wilkinson resigned from Sheffield Wednesday in October after six years at the helm and took charge at which Division Two side?

140
1989–1990

1   FIFA announced that players who were level were no longer offside and that caused a great deal of debate throughout the season. It was the first time that the offside law had been changed since which year?

2   Crystal Palace were beaten 9-0 by Liverpool in September. It was the biggest Division One victory since Fulham had beaten Ipswich Town in December 1963. Who was the Palace goalkeeper?

3   Who had joined Tottenham Hotspur from Barcelona and opened his account at White Hart Lane with a hat-trick as Spurs beat Queens Park Rangers 3-2?

4   Osvaldo Ardiles led which team into the First Division for the first time in their history but was stunned when the club found themselves relegated to the Third instead? It was punishment for irregular payments made to their players by the previous regime. On appeal they remained in Division Two.

5   Having won yet another Division One title, Kenny Dalglish came on for his final Liverpool appearance in their last home game of the season against which team managed by Arthur Cox?

6   A would-be chairman juggled a ball on the pitch at Old Trafford and announced that he was going to buy Manchester United, but after a vitriolic press campaign against him he withdrew a couple of months later. Who was he?

7   Stoke City sacked Mick Mills as manager and replaced him with which World Cup-winner?

8   This season, Brian Clough celebrated his 1,000th match as a manager and Nottingham Forest beat which Joe Royle-led side 1-0 to retain the League Cup?

9   Bobby Robson announced that he was resigning after the World Cup to return to club management with which Dutch side?

10   Four England World Cup players, Terry Butcher, Trevor Steven, Chris Woods and Gary Stevens, were playing for which Scottish team?

11   Sheffield Wednesday were relegated to Division Two as neighbouring United went the other way. Who was Wednesday's manager?

12   Alex Ferguson won his first trophy with Manchester United when they beat Crystal Palace 1-0 in their FA Cup final replay. Who scored the only goal of the game?

13   Graham Taylor managed which team to second place in Division One?

14   Which former Oldham Athletic and Portsmouth centre-forward finished as the league's top scorer, with 32 goals, but wasn't able

to secure promotion for Newcastle United out of Division Two?

15   John Aldridge left Liverpool for which team in Europe?

141

1990–1991

1   On the opening weekend, who was fined a week's wages when he walked out of the dressing room at half-time to go and sit in his goalmouth after Everton went 2-0 down against newly promoted Leeds United?

2   Which new radio station was launched in August and greatly expanded the coverage of football on the airwaves?

3   In early September, Liverpool beat Manchester United and Everton on their way to recording how many consecutive victories which equalled Everton's 96-year-old record?

4   Who had succeeded Bobby Robson as the new England manager?

5   The biggest win was achieved by Crystal Palace when they put eight past Southend United in the League Cup, with hat-tricks for both Ian Wright and Mark Bright. Where did they finish in Division One?

6   Tottenham Hotspur beat Nottingham Forest 2-1 in the FA Cup final, but Paul Gascoigne, in an infamous moment of recklessness, put himself out of football for a year when he tackled which Forest

player, with his feet way above the grass, early in the final?

7   Arsenal finished seven points ahead of Liverpool having lost just one League match and only three of the 50 games that they played in all competitions. How many goals did David Seaman concede in the entire campaign?

8   Who scored the only goal of the League Cup final as Sheffield Wednesday surprisingly beat Manchester United?

9   In the first season that British clubs were readmitted to European competition following their ban after the Heysel tragedy, Manchester United reached the final of the Cup Winner's Cup and beat Barcelona 2-1. Who was the losing manager?

10   Arsenal's captain, Tony Adams, was jailed on 19 December for a drink-driving offence and spent two months inside which prison, whose previous footballing connection had been in 1979 when it was used to stage the football match in the film version of the BBC sitcom *Porridge*?

11   After six years that had seen him win three championships and two FA Cups, Kenny Dalglish resigned as Liverpool manager on 22 February when they were on top of the table and had just drawn 4-4 with which team in the FA Cup?

12   Stan Mortensen died in May 1991 at the age of 69. He had scored a hat-trick for Blackpool in which FA Cup final?

13   Which Millwall player was the league's leading goal-scorer this season with 38 goals?

14 Who replaced Colin Harvey as manager of Everton?

15 On 2 March, which player made his professional debut for Manchester United as they lost 2-0 at home to Everton?

142

1991–1992

1   After several years of speculation, it was announced in February that a new, breakaway League was going to be formed. What was it called?

2   Which Division Four newcomers lost 4-7 at home to Crewe Alexandra but only conceded 16 more goals at home and recovered to finish seventh in the League?

3   Who took over from Osvaldo Ardiles as manager of Newcastle United?

4   Which side had to leave the League when they were unable to guarantee their fixtures and became the first League club to fold since Accrington in 1962?

5   Which Division One side beat Sheffield United 5-2, Sheffield Wednesday 7-1 and Southampton 5-1 but could only finish fourth?

6   After 26 years away from the top flight, Blackburn Rovers returned to Division One by beating Leicester City 1-0 in the play-off final. Who was their manager?

7   Which team collected their first trophy of any kind since 1972

when they beat Dunfermline Athletic 2-0 in the final of the Scottish League Cup?

8   Who moved to Middlesbrough after nine years in charge of Charlton Athletic?

9   Eric Cantona helped Howard Wilkinson take Leeds United to the last ever Division One title. Which club had he left to move to Yorkshire?

10 Manchester United won the League Cup for the first time when which Scottish striker's 14th-minute goal was the only score in the final against Nottingham Forest?

11 Three teams missed out on the Premier League when they were relegated. West Ham United and Notts County filled the bottom two places; which team went down with them?

12 Which England player moved from Nottingham Forest to Sampdoria for £1.5m?

13 Michael Thomas and Ian Rush scored the goals that gave Liverpool a 2-0 victory and the FA Cup for the third time in seven seasons. Who were their Division Two opponents in the final?

14 Gary Lineker left Tottenham Hotspur to join Grampus8 in which country?

15 Sheffield Wednesday finished third in Division One, their best position since 1961. Who was their player manager?

143
1992–1993

1   When Desmond Lynam introduced the first *Match of the Day* of the new Premier League season, which former Liverpool player made his debut as a pundit, alongside Trevor Brooking?

2   Premier League referees were no longer the men in black. What colour were their new shirts?

3   The season started with a goal rush at the Charity Shield when which player scored a hat-trick as Leeds United beat Liverpool 4-3?

4   How many substitutes were each team allowed in the Premier League?

5   Which Liverpool striker hit the crossbar when standing in front of a completely open Aston Villa goal and under no pressure?

6   Brian Deane entered the history books as the scorer of the first goal in the Premier League when he put which team 1-0 up against Manchester United after just five minutes?

7   Blackburn Rovers beat Norwich City 7-1 with Alan Shearer scoring twice. He had recently joined Rovers for a record fee of some £3.3m from which side?

8 Manchester United were the first winners of the Premier League and it was their first title since 1968. Who was Alex Ferguson's assistant manager?

9 When Arsenal beat Sheffield Wednesday 2-1 to win the League Cup, ten of the team were English. Which Republic of Ireland player completed the line-up?

10 Who retired from management having seen his Nottingham Forest team relegated from the Premier League in the final game of the season?

11 Arsenal and Sheffield Wednesday met again in the FA Cup final. Who scored in the final minute of extra time in the replay to give George Graham's team their second trophy of the season?

12 Bobby Moore died in February 1993 aged just 51. He had been suffering from cancer. As well as leading England to their 1966 World Cup success, he had captained his country in how many of his 108 appearances?

13 What is the name of the Tottenham Hotspur chairman who sacked Terry Venables and replaced him as manager with Osvaldo Ardiles?

14 Walter Smith won the Treble with which side in Scotland?

15 When Ian Rush notched up his 287th goal for Liverpool as part of their 2-2 draw at Manchester United, whose club record did he break?

144
1993–1994

1 Which side finished bottom of the Premier League having won only five games but conceded 100 goals?

2 Who took over at Anfield when Graeme Souness resigned as Liverpool manager?

3 The most unusual pre-match warm-up came at Villa Park, where Ron Atkinson had arranged for which chart-topping tenor to sing a few bars of Puccini in the changing room? It seemed to work as they beat QPR 4-1.

4 Manchester United retained the title and finished eight points ahead of Blackburn Rovers and 15 in front of third-placed Newcastle United, who reached that position thanks to 34 league goals from which striker?

5 Who were the first sponsors of the new Football League?

6 Aston Villa beat Manchester United 3-1 in the League Cup final. Which Welsh striker scored twice for Villa?

7 Alan Smith scored the game's only goal in the 19th minute as Arsenal beat which team in Copenhagen to lift the European Cup Winners' Cup?

8   Everton were almost relegated on the last day of the season but recovered from 2-0 down to win 3-2 against Wimbledon. Who had left Norwich and taken over as manager in January?

9   Manchester United completed the Double by beating which side 4-0 in the FA Cup final?

10 Graham Taylor resigned as England manager after failing to reach the World Cup finals. Needing to win by seven goals, they conceded a goal after eight seconds and won 7-1 against which side?

11 Who became the UK's most expensive goalkeeper when he moved to Blackburn Rovers from Southampton for £2.4 million?

12 Alan Smith managed which side into the Premier League as Division One champions?

13 Everton suffered one of their heaviest ever home defeats when, despite having gone one up against Norwich, they lost 5-1. Which Nigerian international scored four?

14 Former player Francis Lee took over as chairman of which team from Peter Swales after buying his 29.9 per cent of shares?

15 In the final of the Scottish FA Cup, which side won the trophy for the first time in their history with a 1-0 win against Rangers?

145
1994–1995

1   When Tottenham Hotspur won 4-3 at Sheffield Wednesday on the opening day of the season, one of their goals was scored by a German who had joined them for £2m from Monaco in the summer. Who was he?

2   Blackburn Rovers won the Premier League, their first title since 1914. Who was their chairman, who had provided millions of pounds for the club to spend on new players?

3   Newcastle United sold Andy Cole to Manchester United for £7m, and he then scored five times as they beat which side 9-0 in the Premier League?

4   Which 19-year-old scored three goals in four minutes for Liverpool against Arsenal?

5   When Eric Cantona was sent off against Crystal Palace, he leapt feet-first into the crowd and attacked an abusive spectator. What was the length of the ban that he received?

6   Dutch striker Bryan Roy's 13 league goals helped take which newly promoted team to third place in the Premier League?

7   When Arsenal met Real Zaragoza in the final of the European Cup Winners' Cup, they were beaten in the last minute of extra time when which player lobbed David Seaman from some 50 yards to make it 2-1?

8   Steve McManaman scored twice in the League Cup final as Liverpool secured the first trophy of the season by winning 2-1 against which team that featured Alan Stubbs, Jason McAteer and Keith Branagan?

9   Which Arsenal player confessed to drug, drink and gambling addictions and spent six weeks in a rehabilitation clinic?

10   Who was the winning manager when a Paul Rideout goal was enough to give Everton victory against Manchester United in the FA Cup final?

11   Middlesbrough won the Division One title in their first season under which manager?

12   Which side paid £2m to Manchester United to buy Dion Dublin?

13   Who, with 34 goals, was the Premier League's leading goal-scorer?

14   Leeds United paid a club record £3.4m to Eintracht Frankfurt for which striker?

15   37-year-old Glenn Hoddle was the manager of which team when he announced his retirement from playing?

146

1995–1996

1   Who said of Manchester United, before they went on to win the Double, 'You can't win anything with kids ... He's got to buy players, it's as simple as that'?

2   Who left Leicester City when they were pushing for promotion to the Premier League and joined Division One strugglers Wolverhampton Wanderers?

3   New signings Les Ferdinand and David Ginola helped which side to nine wins in their first ten league games?

4   Manchester United were ridiculed when they changed out of their grey shirts at which team when they were 3-0 down at half time? The new blue and white strip made no difference and they eventually lost 3-1.

5   Which team lost 7-0 and 5-1 to Blackburn Rovers?

6   Aston Villa won the League Cup for the second time in three years when they beat Leeds United 3-0 in the final. Who was their manager?

7   Which former Swindon Town and Brentford player took Bradford

City into Division One via the play-offs in his first season as manager?

8   Eric Cantona's goal gave Manchester United a 1-0 win against Liverpool in the FA Cup final but the game was also remembered for the cream suits worn by the losers. Who designed them?

9   In the last game of the season, Manchester City were drawing 2-2 with Liverpool when their manager Alan Ball was told that other results meant that a draw was enough. It was the wrong information and bewildered fans watched as who time-wasted with the ball in the corner when they needed a win? They went down for third time in 13 seasons.

10 One of the BBC's best-loved voices was silenced in August when Len Martin died aged 76. He had been reading the football and racing results on *Grandstand* since it began in which season?

11 Alan Shearer reached which new landmark when Blackburn beat Tottenham?

12 Which England player was voted Scottish Player of the Year after his 19 goals helped Rangers to the Double?

13 The football transfer market was transformed when an EU ruling stated that once a player's contract had expired he could move freely to any club within the EU. Which Belgian player brought the test case?

14 Which Brazilian international moved to Middlesbrough for a fee of £4.75m?

15 John Aldridge became player manager of which Division One side?

147
1996–1997

1   Who succeeded Bob Wilson as only the third full-time presenter of *Football Focus*?

2   Arsene Wenger was appointed manager of Arsenal after Bruce Rioch had lasted how long in charge of the team?

3   What fee did Newcastle United pay Blackburn Rovers for Alan Shearer?

4   When Wimbledon lost 3-0 to the eventual champions, Manchester United, a 21-year-old called David Beckham scored from the halfway line in the 90th minute after spotting who was off his goal line?

5   On 20 December, which team took the unprecedented step of cancelling their game against Blackburn as 23 of their players were injured or ill? That decision cost them a three-point fine and meant that they were relegated at the end of the season.

6   Danny Wilson managed which team into the top division for the first time in their 110-year history?

7   Which Division Two team reached the semi-finals of the FA Cup?

8   Who replaced Kevin Keegan as manager of Newcastle United after he unexpectedly quit?

9   Chelsea beat Middlesbrough 2-0 in the FA Cup final. Who scored the fastest Cup final goal at Wembley after just 42 seconds?

10   George Graham replaced Howard Wilkinson as manager of which team?

11   Which club beat Falkirk 1-0 in the Scottish Cup final to win the trophy for the first time since 1929?

12   Stan Ternent managed which team to their second successive promotion as they reached Division One?

13   Manchester United lost their 40-year unbeaten home record in Europe to which Turkish side?

14   Steve Claridge's goal in extra time of the League Cup final replay ensured that which team beat Middlesbrough?

15   Who was the chairman of Portsmouth who also agreed to manage Australia?

148
1997–1998

1   Manchester United opened their title defence with a 2-0 win against Tottenham Hotspur. The Spurs fans gained a small dose of satisfaction when which former striker missed a penalty against his old team, having moved in the summer?

2   On 13 September, whose hat-trick against Bolton Wanderers at Highbury took him to 180 goals and past Cliff Bastin's 58-year-old Arsenal record of 178?

3   In the early weeks of the season, which side conceded five goals to Arsenal, six to Chelsea and seven to Manchester United?

4   Which manager paid Celtic £5.7m to take Paulo Di Canio to Sheffield Wednesday?

5   On 3 May, Arsenal's tenth consecutive win set a new League record and ensured that Arsene Wenger had become the first foreign manager to win the title. They clinched it by beating which team 4-0 to secure the championship for the 11th time?

6   Who replaced Gerry Francis as manager of Tottenham Hotspur?

7   Which side had double success in the League Cup final against

Middlesbrough and the European Cup Winners Cup final against Stuttgart?

8   Who became the youngest England international of the century when he played against Chile at Wembley in February?

9   Arsenal completed the Double when goals by Marc Overmars and Nicolas Anelka saw off which team in the final?

10   Southampton ended a run of three defeats when they beat Leicester 2-1. Matt Le Tissier opened the scoring and then Francis Benali headed his first goal in how many games?

11   Who won promotion into Division Two at the end of their first season in the Football League and were managed by Sammy McIlroy?

12   Who was appointed Chief Operating Officer at Fulham?

13   Which side, managed by, Joe Royle, were relegated to the third flight of English football for the first time in their history?

14   Derby County had moved to a new £23m stadium, which was opened by the Queen. 25,000 turned up to see the first match against Wimbledon, but 11 minutes into the second half the lights failed and the match was abandoned. What is the name of the ground?

15   Which relegated team demonstrated the gulf between the Premier League and Division One as they scored 41 goals this season compared to 100 when they were promoted in the previous year?

149
1998–1999

1   Which promoted team got off to a strong start when Chris Mendonca's hat-trick helped them beat Southampton 5-0 on the second weekend of the season?

2   Which former Arsenal player took over at Leeds United when George Graham left to replace Christian Gross at Tottenham Hotspur?

3   Whose imitation 'snorting' of the white line after scoring a penalty in Liverpool's 3-2 win over Everton led to widespread condemnation, large club and FA fines and a four-match ban?

4   Nottingham Forest lost 8-1 to Manchester United. Who scored four of the goals for the winning team?

5   Manchester United beat Bayern Munich 2-1 to win the European Cup. In which city was the final played?

6   The one trophy that eluded Manchester United this season was the League Cup. Who beat Leicester City 1-0 to win it for the first time since 1973?

7   Carlisle United's goalkeeper made the headlines when he rushed upfield in extra time of their last game of the season, against

Plymouth Argyle, and headed in the goal that secured their league status. Who was he?

8 Manchester United lifted their fourth FA Cup of the decade when they beat Newcastle United 2-0 and completed the Double for the third time. Which manager led out Newcastle at the start of the match?

9 England manager Glenn Hoddle was sacked and replaced by Kevin Keegan. Who had been in charge in between them for a brief caretaker spell?

10 Paulo di Canio received an 11-match ban after he pushed the referee when playing for Sheffield Wednesday against whom?

11 John Hartson's new teammates at which club set fire to his expensive suit when he joined them from West Ham United for £7m?

12 Blackburn went bottom when they lost 2-0 at home to Southampton, and 45 minutes later Roy Hodgson was sacked as manager. Who took over as caretaker for the fourth time in 12 seasons?

13 Which former manager of Holland won the Scottish Treble in his first season in charge of Rangers?

14 Who collected the Premiership trophy for the first time as Manchester United captain?

15 Stuart McCall, Lee Mills and Peter Beagrie were all part of which side which won promotion to the top league for the first time in 77 years?

150
1999–2000

1. Who became the fifth full-time presenter of *Match of the Day* after Desmond Lynam moved to ITV?

2. There was wide condemnation of Manchester United when, despite being the holders, they withdrew from the FA Cup in order to take part in which event in Brazil?

3. Bobby Robson returned to England to manage Newcastle United. Which side had he been managing in Europe?

4. Which young side led the Championship for much of the early part of the season having won 14 of their first 19 matches?

5. Which Norwegian striker scored a hat-trick when Tottenham Hotspur beat Southampton 7-2?

6. Arsenal sold Nicolas Anelka for £23m, a record fee involving a British club. Who did he sign for?

7. Manchester United won the Premier League for the sixth time in eight seasons. How many points were they ahead of second-placed Arsenal?

8   Leicester City sold Emile Heskey to Liverpool for £11m and beat Tranmere Rovers 2-1 in the final of the League Cup. By what name was it now known?

9   Having been managed by Egil Olsen for most of the season, who lost 2-0 against Southampton on the final day of the campaign and were relegated after 14 years in the top flight?

10 Which 19-year-old became British football's most expensive teenager when he moved from Wolverhampton Wanderers to Coventry City for £6m?

11 Rangers collected their 11th title in 12 years in Scotland, finishing 21 points ahead of which second-placed team?

12 Which 37-year-old manager led Preston North End to the Division Two title?

13 On 26 December, which side began their match at Southampton without a single British player in their starting 11? It was the first time it had ever happened.

14 Chelsea beat Aston Villa 2-0 in the last FA Cup final to be played at the old Wembley Stadium. In which year had the final been held there for the first time?

15 Who scored 30 Premier League goals for Sunderland as they finished seventh?

151
2000–2001

1   Chelsea beat Manchester United 2-0 to win the Charity Shield but a month later their manager, Gianluca Vialli, was sacked. Who replaced him?

2   Goalkeeper Kevin Pressman was sent off after just 13 seconds of a Division One match against Wolverhampton Wanderers for a deliberate handball outside the box. It was the quickest dismissal in League history, although replays suggested that he had been very unlucky as the ball appeared to have hit his chest not his hands. Which team was he playing for?

3   Which Australian scored all four goals when Leeds United beat Liverpool 4-3?

4   Liverpool beat Birmingham City 5-4 on penalties to win the League Cup final, but which side had they beaten 8-0 when they visited them in the fourth round?

5   Kevin Keegan walked out on England after they lost 1-0 to which side in a World Cup qualifier at Wembley despite the fact that there was another vital match against Finland just four days later?

6   Liverpool beat Alaves 5-4 to win the UEFA Cup and their first

European Trophy for 17 years. It was won by a Golden Goal after the game finished 4-4 at the end of extra time. Who headed an own goal to end the final and start Liverpool's celebrations?

7   Liverpool beat Arsenal 2-1 in the FA Cup final. Who was the manager who led them to three trophies this season?

8   Walter Smith signed Paul Gascoigne on a free transfer from Middlesbrough to play at which club?

9   Ipswich Town came fifth in the Premier League. Which striker scored 19 league goals for them?

10   How old was Rio Ferdinand when he became the most expensive English footballer and moved from West Ham United to Leeds United for £18m?

11   Despite having Carlton Palmer, Craig Bellamy and John Hartson in their squad which team was relegated at the end of the Premier League season along with Manchester City and Bradford City?

12   In front of a post-war record crowd of 67,637 at Old Trafford, Manchester United secured their seventh title in nine seasons when they beat Coventry 4-2. They also finally signed which player from PSV Eindhoven for a new club record £19m?

13   Brian Talbot managed which side into the Football League as Conference champions just nine years after the club had been formed?

14   Which 35-year-old was voted Player of the Year by his peers and the football writers?

15   Who managed Fulham to the Division One title?

152
2001–2002

1   Manchester United recovered from 3-0 down at Tottenham Hotspur to win 5-3. Who was the relieved winning goalkeeper?

2   Which West Ham United 23-year-old midfielder went from being an Eastender to a West End boy when he joined Chelsea for £11m?

3   After two matches, Bolton were leading with six points and their manager said that he had been advised to get the league table framed as the club hadn't been top since 1958. Who was he?

4   In September, a *Football Focus* survey revealed that there were a record 34 players from one European country who were registered to play in the Premier League. Where were they from?

5   Which Manchester United striker became the first player to score in eight successive Premiership matches?

6   Despite going 1-0 down in Munich, England recovered to beat Germany 5-1 thanks to a hat-trick by Michael Owen. Which commentator summed up the feelings of all football fans with 'Oh, this is getting better and better and better – one, two, three for Michael Owen'?

7   In February, Arsenal beat Everton to start a run of how many consecutive wins to the end of the season and clinch them the title?

8   Who scored the winning goal for Blackburn Rovers when they beat Tottenham Hotspur 2-1 in the final of the Worthington Cup, having joined them for £8m from Manchester United?

9   Following Gerard Houllier's collapse and subsequent emergency heart surgery, who took the managerial reigns at Liverpool in his absence?

10 Who did Arsenal beat 2-0 in the FA Cup final to complete the Double?

11 Who scored the first of Tottenham Hotspur's four against Fulham and wrote himself into the record books as it was the 10,000th goal to be scored in the Premier League?

12 Which side finished second in the Scottish First Division and then went out of business and were expelled from the league 124 years after they were formed?

13 Who announced his retirement after 17 years at Southampton? He had scored 209 goals in 540 games, won eight England caps and produced several of the greatest strikes in the history of the Premiership.

14 On 20 November, who took charge of Crewe Alexandra for the 1000th time?

15 Shaun Goater was the top goal-scorer in Division One with 28 goals for which table-topping team?

153

2002–2003

1   Just before the start of the season, Rio Ferdinand moved from Leeds United to Manchester United for a record British transfer fee of £30m. Which newly appointed manager sold him?

2   Arsenal had gone a record 30 Premiership matches without defeat when they came up against Everton on 19 October and had their run ended by which 16-year-old substitute, who became the youngest ever Premiership scorer?

3   Paul Gascoigne was trying to resurrect his career, this time with a short-lived move to which country, where he joined their Division Two side, Gansu Tianma?

4   Peter Reid was sacked by which team after seven years in charge?

5   Who was cut above the left eye when Sir Alex Ferguson kicked a boot at him following Manchester United's FA Cup loss to Arsenal?

6   Liverpool finished fifth in the Premier League but lifted the League Cup when they beat Manchester United 2-0 in the final. What was the name of their goalkeeper who was named Man of the Match?

7   West Ham United were relegated despite rallying under the

caretaker managership of which *Match of the Day* pundit following Glenn Roeder's illness?

8 The most astonishing result of the season came on 29 October, when Grimsby Town won 6-5 in their Division One encounter with which team whose manager, Stan Ternent, was staggered that his side had scored five goals in an away game and still lost?

9 At the Millennium Stadium, Arsenal beat Southampton 1-0 in the FA Cup final. What was unique about the game?

10 Which club became the first team to achieve 100 years in the top division this season?

11 Who managed Portsmouth as they won the Division One title by six points from Leicester City?

12 When Thierry Henry headed one of his hat-trick in Arsenal's 3-1 win against West Ham, it was the first he had scored with his head in how many minutes of Premiership football?

13 When Manchester United claimed yet another title, Ruud van Nistelrooy, with 25, was their leading scorer. Who was the next in their list with 14 goals in the league this season?

14 The goals of Andy Liddell and Nathan Ellington propelled which side into the second tier of English football for the first time in their history?

15 At the end of the season David Seaman ended a 13-year spell at Arsenal. Who did he join on a free transfer?

154
2003–2004

1   Roman Abramovich bought Chelsea from which previous owner?

2   Which team, managed by Dave Penney, finished as Division Three champions in their first season back in the Football League?

3   Manchester United spent more than £12m buying 18-year-old Cristiano Ronaldo from which club?

4   Which side beat Bolton Wanderers 2-1 in the League Cup final to win their first trophy in their 128-year history?

5   Dave Jones was the manager of which side who were immediately relegated having won only seven games and been beaten at home 5-1 by Blackburn Wolves and 5-0 to Chelsea and gone down 5-2 to Tottenham Hotspur?

6   Who became the fifth Leeds United boss in two years but couldn't prevent them from being relegated?

7   When Manchester United won the FA Cup for the 11th time by beating Millwall 3-0, who became the first American to collect a winner's medal?

8   Who missed a drugs test and was given an eight-month ban from football?

9   Arsenal were crowned champions having won 26 games. How many league matches did they lose that season?

10 When Newcastle beat Leicester 3-1, who became the first to play in 400 Premier League games?

11 Livingston won their first major trophy when they beat Hibernian 2-0 in the final of the Scottish League Cup. What had they been called before they changed location in 1995?

12 Who, with 30 goals, was the Premier League's top scorer and became the first player to collect the PFA Player of the Year award in consecutive seasons?

13 Having spent the first half of the season in the relegation zone, which side won promotion to the Premier League under new manager Iain Dowie?

14 Which manager was sacked after six years in charge of Liverpool?

15 At the end of the season, Wimbledon announced that they were changing their name and were now to be known as what?

155
2004–2005

1   Who presented the new Sunday night show *MOTD2* on BBC Two?

2   A trio of big-name overseas managers had taken up residence in the Premiership as Rafael Benitez, Jose Mourinho and Jacques Santini all began their spells in charge at Liverpool, Chelsea and which other side respectively?

3   Arsenal equalled and then broke whose record when they extended their unbeaten league run to 43 games by beating Middlesbrough 5-3 and Blackburn 3-0, eventually peaking at 49?

4   Crystal Palace's Hungarian keeper had joined in the summer and became known for always playing in a grey tracksuit. What was his name?

5   Which Premier League club sacked their manager in August after five years in charge even though they had finished in the top five in three successive seasons?

6   Five days after the death of Brian Clough, which famous voice of football, who had commentated on Clough's last home match, retired from *Match of the Day* after 35 outstanding years behind

the microphone when he commentated on Arsenal's 1-0 win at Manchester City?

7   Who stunned the South Coast by resigning from Portsmouth and then taking the helm at Southampton?

8   Jose Mourinho's first trophy as Chelsea manager came when they beat which team 3-2 after extra time in the League Cup final?

9   In their title-winning season, how many league goals did Chelsea concede?

10 For the first time in the history of the FA Cup, the final was decided by a penalty shootout when Arsenal beat Manchester United 5-4. In which year had a final last finished 0-0?

11 Who, at 16 years and 271 days, became the latest teenager to claim the crown of being the youngest Premier League scorer when Everton beat Crystal Palace 4-0?

12 Which Arsenal player scored an own goal when he was duped by a Spanish radio station into saying that he would like to move to Real Madrid?

13 Who went onto the pitch to encourage their team with the words 'A message to the best football supporters in the world. We need a 12th man here. Where are you? Where are you? Let's be 'avin you! Come on!'

14 Which Crystal Palace striker became the first Premiership player to score more than half of his team's goals? He was responsible for 21 of their 41.

15 Who did Liverpool beat on penalties to be crowned European
    Champions having been 3-0 down at half-time in the final and
    pulling back to make it 3-3 after extra time?

156

2005–2006

1   Who became the first woman ever to present *Football Focus* during this season?

2   Liverpool began the season with the largest squad as Raphael Benitez had 42 players to chose from, including the league's tallest player, 6'7" striker Peter Crouch, who made the switch from which side for £7m?

3   Which American sports tycoon and his sons took over Manchester United in a controversial £790m buyout?

4   Chelsea paid a club record £24.4m on midfielder Michael Essien. Which national team did he represent?

5   Sunderland began their season with a defeat. Their 3-1 loss at home to Charlton was the first of how many as they embarked on a shockingly unsuccessful campaign? By contrast, they had won the equivalent number of games when coming back up as Championship champions in May.

6   Who moved from Real Madrid to Newcastle United for £17m?

7   Wayne Rooney scored twice as Manchester United beat which

side 4-0 in the League Cup final? It was United's second success in the competition and the first major final reached by their opponents, who were managed by Paul Jewell.

8   Which Frenchman was sacked as Portsmouth manager by chairman Milan Manderic after only eight months in charge?

9   Alan Shearer's goal in their 2-0 win against Portsmouth gave him a club record 201st goal to take him past whose longstanding total?

10 The Premier League was settled on 29 April when Chelsea beat Manchester United 3-0 and were crowned champions at Stamford Bridge. Who threw his medal into the crowd, was given another and lobbed that to his supporters as well?

11 Who managed Celtic to success in the Scottish Premier League and the Scottish League Cup in his first season in charge, having taken over from Martin O'Neill?

12 At the end of the season who retired as Charlton's manager after 11 years at the helm?

13 Which team left their old ground after 93 years, 13 championships, 10 FA Cups and a movie?

14 Who saved three penalties when Liverpool beat West Ham United after a shootout in the FA Cup final when the game finished 3-3 after extra time?

15 Which side did Steve Coppell manage into the Premier League for the first time in their history, having finished 16 points clear of second-placed Sheffield United?

157

2006–2007

1   Didier Drogba was the leading scorer in the Premiership with 20 goals, but which South African was in second place with 18 for Blackburn Rovers?

2   Who were the first former winners of a major trophy, the League Cup, to now be playing outside of the Football League having been relegated to the Conference?

3   Paul Robinson scored the third Premiership goal by a goalkeeper when his free kick bounced over the head of Watford's Ben Foster. Who was Robinson playing for in their 3-1 win?

4   Two Chelsea goalkeepers, Petr Cech and Carlo Cudicini, received head injuries in their match against which Premiership newcomers?

5   Which Fulham player scored the 15,000th goal in the Premier League?

6   Charlton Athletic had three different managers this season. Who only lasted a month in the hot seat in beween Iain Dowie and Alan Pardew?

7   Who became the first player since Andy Gray in 1977 to win the

PFA Player of the Year and Young Player of the Year awards in the same season?

8   Which team managed by Roy Keane, which had Niall Quinn as Chairman, won the Championship title?

9   Gavin Mahon was the captain of which bottom-placed team who were relegated from the Premiership at the end of the season?

10   Stuart Pearce replaced Peter Taylor as the manager of which team?

11   How many players were sent off when Chelsea beat Arsenal 2-1 in the Carling Cup final?

12   Which women's team won an unprecedented Quadruple of the Premier League, FA Cup, League Cup and UEFA Cup?

13   Which former champions went into administration and were relegated to the third tier of English football for the first time in their history?

14   Who scored the only goal when Chelsea completed the domestic cup Double by beating Manchester United in the FA Cup final?

15   Who resigned as manager of Sheffield United after more than seven years in charge following their relegation from the Premiership?

158

2007–2008

1   The highest-scoring match in Premier League history came when Portsmouth beat Reading 7-4. Which Zimbabwean striker scored a hat-trick for the home team?

2   Which team were relegated in bottom place with a new Premier League low of just 11 points?

3   When Martin Jol left Tottenham Hotspur he was replaced by which Spanish manager?

4   Who was Manchester United's captain as they won their tenth Premier League title?

5   The fastest goal of the Premier League season came when Geovanni scored against Wigan Athletic after just 28 seconds. Who was he playing for?

6   Who was Middlesbrough's manager when they beat Manchester City 8-1?

7   Manchester United won the Champions League after a penalty shootout with Chelsea. Edwin van der Sar saved the crucial penalty in the sudden-death stage from which unlucky Chelsea player?

8 Which Scottish side began the season in the Premier League for the first time in their history but ended it by being demoted to Division Three and then went out of business when they lost their main financial backer?

9 Martin Allen, Jon Rudkin, Steve Beaglehole, Mike Stowell, Gary Megson, Frank Burrows, Gerry Taggart and Ian Holloway all managed which Championship team during their relegation season?

10 Which manager guided Portsmouth to their first major trophy success for 58 years when they beat Cardiff City 1-0 in the FA Cup final?

11 Jonathan Woodgate scored the winning goal for which team when they beat Chelsea 2-1 in the League Cup final?

12 Who in January made a surprising return to the manager's office at Newcastle United?

13 Rangers won the Scottish Cup final 3-2 when they beat which team who were playing in the final for the first time in their history?

14 West Bromwich Albion were Championship champions, but which side came second and returned to the top division for the first time in 23 years? Their team included Steve Simonsen, Liam Lawrence and Richard Cresswell.

15 Arsenal's longest-serving player, Freddie Ljungberg joined West Ham United after nearly nine years under Arsene Wenger. Which national team did he play for 75 times?

159
2008–2009

1   As of this season, how many substitutes could each Premier League team name on the bench?

2   Which team signed Robinho from Real Madrid for a reported £32.5m?

3   Manchester United used three goalkeepers when they won their 11th Premier League title. Edwin van der Sar made 33 appearances and Tomasz Kuszczak played three games, but which future England player was between the posts during the other two games this season?

4   Who succeeded Kevin Keegan when he resigned for a second time as manager of Newcastle United?

5   Gabriel Agbonlahor scored a hat-trick inside eight minutes against Manchester City. Who was he playing for?

6   Nicolas Anelka was the Premier League's leading scorer with 19 goals. Which side did he play for?

7   Sunderland had three managers in a six-month period. Which Scotsman was in charge in between Roy Keane and Steve Bruce?

8   Which relegated team, managed by Gareth Southgate, scored only 28 goals in the Premier League?

9   Manchester United beat Tottenham Hotspur on penalties to win the Carling Cup final after the game had ended in a goalless draw, but the biggest win in the competition had come in the third round when Arsenal put six past Sheffield United. Which 19-year-old Mexican scored a hat-trick?

10 Nacho Novo scored the only goal for the Double winners Rangers as they beat Falkirk in the Scottish Cup final. What is his nationality?

11 Didier Drogba and Frank Lampard struck the winning goals for Chelsea in the FA Cup final after which Everton player had set a new record by scoring after just 25 seconds?

12 After a decade in charge of non-league Burton Albion, Nigel Clough took over as manager at his father's old club, Derby County. Which member of Brian Clough's title-winning side at the old Baseball Ground succeeded Nigel at the Pirelli Stadium?

13 Mick McCarthy took which team back into the Premier League as Championship champions?

14 Fulham ended the season in the highest league position in their history. Where did they come in the Premier League?

15 Which side won 13 and drew 17 league games but ended up with only 26 points and dropped out of the Football League when they were deducted 30 points because of financial irregularities?

160

2009–2010

1   At the start of the season, Manish Bhasin began presenting BBC One's new *Football League Show* on Saturday evenings. Who succeeded him as presenter of *Football Focus*?

2   Chelsea clinched the title when they beat which side 8-0 on the final day of the season?

3   Which former Real Madrid striker scored the winner in added time when Manchester United beat Manchester City 4-3?

4   Who replaced Owen Coyle at Burnley when he moved to Bolton Wanderers in January 2010?

5   Manchester United beat Aston Villa 2-1 in the League Cup final, but which of their regulars missed the match having broken an arm in a Premier League game against the same opponents 18 days earlier?

6   Which side were relegated from the Premier League having been docked nine points for going into administration?

7   Who scored the fastest goal of the season, in 36 seconds, for Sunderland against Tottenham Hotspur?

8   David Gold and David Sullivan bought which club in January 2010?

9   When Tottenham Hotspur beat Wigan 9-1, who became the first player to score five goals in a Premier League game since Alan Shearer in 1999?

10 Chelsea clinched the Double when Didier Drogba scored the only goal of the FA Cup final, but which Portsmouth player had earlier seen his penalty saved by Petr Cech?

11 The highest-scoring match in the history of the Scottish Premier League was between Hibernian and which other side, who came from 4-1 down, at home, to draw 6-6?

12 In March, Fulham produced one of their greatest ever results by defeating which legendary side 5-4 on aggregate to reach the quarter-finals of the Europa League?

13 Who managed Blackpool into the Premier League for the first time in their history when they beat Cardiff City 3-2 in the Championship Play-Off final?

14 Which League Two side employed Sven-Goran Erikson as Director of Football this season?

15 With a final tally of 103, Chelsea became the first team to have scored 100 goals in the top division since which 1963 side?

9
'Fergie Time'

161
2010–2011

1   Manchester United won the Premier League for the 12th time. Their biggest win of the season came in November when they beat which side 7-1?

2   The season began with a new cap on the number of players each team could include in their declared squads at the end of each transfer window. What was the maximum number they were allowed?

3   Birmingham City won their first major trophy since 1963 when they beat Arsenal 2-1 in the League Cup final. Which on-loan striker scored the winner in the 89th minute?

4   Who began the season as the new manager of Liverpool and ended it in charge of West Bromwich Albion?

5   In the second round of the FA Cup, Brighton and Hove Albion were taken to a replay by which side that were only five years old?

6   Which Bulgarian scored three hat-tricks for Manchester United in the Premier League?

7   Chesterfield won the Division Two title. What was the name of the new ground that they had moved to at the start of the season?

8   Arsenal lost a 4-0 advantage when they drew 4-4 with which side in the Premier League?

9   Bolton's captain was officially credited with having committed more fouls, 115, than any other Premier League player this season. Who was he?

10 Adel Taarabt scored 19 league goals for which Championship-winning team?

11 Which former Chelsea player managed Brighton and Hove Albion to the Division One title?

12 England's bid to host the 2018 World Cup finals ended when which other country was awarded the tournament?

13 Which club sacked Roy Keane as their manager?

14 Chelsea paid a fee that was said to be £50m for which striker?

15 Manchester City won the FA Cup final 1-0. Who were their opponents?

162

2011–2012

1   Which Scottish Premier League side were demoted to the Third Division after they went into liquidation?

2   The Premier League was decided on goal difference for the first time when Manchester City finished the season with how many more goals that Manchester United?

3   Who scored a hat-trick when Manchester United beat Arsenal 8-2?

4   In August, Cesc Fabregas rejoined which team in a £35m move from Arsenal?

5   Liverpool beat Cardiff City on penalties to win the League Cup after the final finished 2-2 at the end of extra time. Which cousin of one of the winning team was the player who missed the crucial last penalty for Cardiff?

6   What nationality is Edin Dzeko, who scored four for Manchester City in their 5-1 thrashing of Tottenham Hotspur?

7   Chelsea beat Liverpool 2-1 to win the FA Cup final. Who scored for the losing side?

8   Heart of Midlothian beat which team 5-1 in the Scottish Cup final?

9   Welshman Wayne Hennessey and David Edwards were regulars for which team who finished bottom of the Premier League?

10   With 23 goals, who was Manchester City's leading scorer in the Premier League?

11   Steve Bruce became the first managerial casualty in the Premier League when he was sacked by which club?

12   Fabrice Muamba dominated world headlines when he was brought back to life following a collapse whilst playing for Bolton Wanderers. Who were his opponents that day?

13   Reading won promotion to the Premier League when they topped the Championship table. Who was their manager?

14   Whose winning penalty in the shootout ensured that Chelsea won the Champions League final against Bayern Munich whilst also being his last ever kick for the club?

15   When Manchester City beat Manchester United 6-1 at Old Trafford, it was the first time that the losers had conceded six goals at home since which year?

163
2012–2013

1   Manchester United clinched their 13th Premier League title when they beat which team 3-0 at Old Trafford on 22 April?

2   Which side were beaten 6-0 at home by Liverpool and lost 7-3 at Arsenal?

3   With which team did David Beckham end his professional career?

4   Wigan beat Manchester City 1-0 in the FA Cup final to win a major trophy for the first time. Who was their goal-scorer?

5   Who completed the clean sweep of PFA Player and Young Player and FWA Player of the Year awards?

6   Who managed Southampton and Reading this season?

7   What nationality is Michael Laudrup who managed Swansea City to success in the League Cup final, where they beat Bradford City 5-0?

8   Who did Luis Suarez bite when Chelsea travelled to Liverpool in April?

9   Who did Harry Redknapp succeed as manager of QPR?

10   Rangers were promoted from the Scottish Third Division as champions. Who was their manager?

11   Which side won automatic promotion to the Premier League having finished in second place behind Cardiff City?

12   Which former West Ham United and QPR stalwart managed Gillingham to the Division Two title?

13   Who took charge of Manchester City for the final couple of weeks of the season when Roberto Mancini was sacked?

14   Chris Hughton managed which team to mid-table in the Premier League?

15   Sir Alex Ferguson retired as manager of Manchester United having been in charge of the club for how many games?

10
Extra Time

164

International Goalkeeping Legends

1   Captained Manchester United to their 1999 Treble and won Euro '92 with Denmark

2   Italian goalkeeper who won 58 national caps between 1987 and 1995 and spent more than a decade with Inter Milan

3   German goalkeeper who was capped 86 times and won the Bundesliga on eight occasions with Bayern Munich and the Euro '96 with his national team

4   He was in goal for France during their 1998 and 2000 successes in the World Cup and European Championship and also won two Premier League titles with Manchester United

5   Joined Liverpool in 2005 and has collected World Cup and European Championship-winner medals with Spain

6   Brazil's goalkeeper in their venerated 1970 World Cup-winning team

7   Joined Chelsea in 2004 and went a then record spell of 1,025

minutes without conceding a goal in the Premier League. He won his 100th cap for the Czech Republic in March 2013.

8 German-born goalkeeper who played on after breaking his neck during Manchester City's 1956 FA Cup final victory against Birmingham City

9 Zimbabwean-born eccentric who joined Liverpool in March 1981 and won six League titles and three FA Cups as well as once appearing in an episode of *Brookside*

10 Legendary Bayern Munich goalkeeper who spent his entire career at the club and won three consecutive European Cups with them as well as the 1974 World Cup with West Germany

11 French international who joined Tottenham Hotspur from Lyon in August 2012

12 'The Black Spider' spent his entire 20-year career with Dynamo Moscow, won 78 caps for the Soviet Union and, in 1963, became the only goalkeeper to ever be named European Player of the Year

13 Captained Italy to the 1982 World Cup at the age of 40 and won many trophies during his decade with Juventus

14 Won the European Championship with West Germany and made a notorious tackle on French defender Patrick Battiston, badly injuring him in the 1982 World Cup semi-final

15 Madrid-born goalkeeper who joined Manchester United for a reported fee of around £17m in June 2011

165

Modern Midlands Men

1   Who is the former St Mirren and Chelsea defender who was appointed manager of West Bromwich Albion in June 2012?

2   Which defender was Walsall's Player of the Year in 2010–2011 and 2011–2012?

3   Wolverhampton Wanderers were promoted back into the top flight in 2009 as Champions. Which Luton-born future Irish international was voted player of the season having played in 45 of their 46 league games?

4   Coventry City had ten managers between April 2002 and July 2013. Seven were English and two were Scottish but who was the Welsh international who spent two years at the helm?

5   In 2006, the majority shareholding in Aston Villa was purchased by which American?

6   Who was the Dublin-born captain of Birmingham City when they beat Arsenal in the 2011 League Cup final?

7   In July 2008, West Bromwich Albion sold which England U21 player to Aston Villa for a club record fee of £8.5m?

8   Jorge Leitao was top scorer for Walsall three times between 2000–2001 and 2003–2004. What was his nationality?

9   Who managed Birmingham City into the Premier League in 2002 and 2007?

10 Which former Norwegian international was sacked as Wolverhampton Wanderers manager in January 2013 after just six months in charge?

11 What is the first name of the Aston Villa goalkeeper who joined them from Manchester City in 2011 and who is known by his nickname 'Shay' Given?

12 Which West Bromwich Albion striker was born in Uzbekistan, played in Belgium and France, represents Nigeria at International level and scored 25 Premier League goals in his first two seasons after joining the club in August 2010?

13 Which former Arsenal and Aston Villa player also managed Walsall between 2004 and 2006?

14 In 2010, Birmingham City paid Valencia a club record £6m for which Serbian player?

15 Which locally born left-winger was top scorer three seasons in a row for Coventry City from 2003–2004 to 2005–2006?

166

On the Wrong End of a Premier League Thrashing

1   Manchester United beat them 9-0 in 1995

2   Newcastle United beat them 8-0 in 1999

3   Tottenham Hotspur beat them 9-1 in 2009

4   Chelsea beat them 8-0 in 2010

5   Chelsea beat them 8-0 in 2012

6   Blackburn Rovers beat them 7-0 in 1995

7   Manchester United beat them 7-0 in 1997

8   Manchester United beat them 8-1 in 1999

9   Arsenal beat them 7-0 in 2005

10 Arsenal beat them 7-0 in 2006

11 Middlesbrough beat them 8-1 in 2008

12 Chelsea beat them 7-0 in 2010

13   Manchester United beat them 8-2 in 2011

14   Chelsea beat them 7-2 in 2010

15   Tottenham Hotspur beat them 7-2 in 2000

167
Random and Difficult Timeless Facts

1   England's shortest match took place against Argentina in Buenos Aires in 1953. What caused it to be abandoned after 23 minutes?

2   The record score in a British match came in 1885 when Bon Accord lost 36-0 to which side in the Scottish Cup?

3   In 1981, which player was signed to three clubs on the same day because of technical issues when he went through Bristol City, Newcastle United and Birmingham City?

4   Which 19-year-old goalkeeper saved a penalty with his very first touch in league football after just 54 seconds of his debut for Birmingham City against Sunderland in 1980?

5   When Dixie Dean scored a record 60 goals for Everton in the 1927–1928 season, how many came from headers?

6   Which German became the first European-born foreigner to play in the Football League when he represented several clubs including Tottenham Hotspur, Burnley and Grimsby Town between 1906 and 1912?

7   Which side won the first ever Double, in 1888–1889? They didn't lose a match in the championship or concede a goal in the Cup.

8   Which player was shown a yellow card after just three seconds of Chelsea's FA Cup tie against Sheffield United in 1992?

9   Who was the first woman assistant referee to officiate in the Premier League?

10   Who scored nine goals for Tranmere Rovers when they beat Oldham Athletic 13-4 in 1935? He also missed a penalty.

11   Pat Kruse headed an own goal after just six seconds when which West Country side met Cambridge United in 1977?

12   The first Women's FA Cup final took place in 1971. Who beat Stewarton and Thistle 4-1 to begin a run of eight wins in 11 years?

13   Which Ipswich Town goalkeeper defied all odds and saved eight of the ten penalties that he faced during the 1979–1980 season?

14   Who, in 1968, became the first referee to score a goal in a professional game in Britain when he accidently deflected a Barrow cross into the Plymouth Argyle net from 15 yards. It proved to be the winner.

15   Millwall beat Fulham 1-0 in the first Football League match to be played on a Sunday. What was the year?

168
Red Card Classics

1 Frenchman dismissed for a headbutt in the 2006 World Cup final

2 England player shown the red card for back-heeling the delicate part of an over-reacting Cristiano Ronaldo during the 2006 World Cup

3 First player to be sent off in an FA Cup final, when Manchester United met Everton in 1985

4 Italian sent off for diving during their game with South Korea in the 2002 World Cup finals

5 Shown a second yellow card when he threw the ball towards the referee as England drew 0-0 with Morocco in the 1982 World Cup finals

6 Croatian who was mistakenly shown the yellow card three times by Graham Poll against Australia in 2006

7 The first man ever to be sent off whilst playing for England. It came during a European Championship semi-final against Yugoslavia in 1968.

8   Newcastle player dismissed for fighting his own teammate, Lee Bowyer, during a Premier League game against Aston Villa in 2005

9   England's goalkeeper who was sent off and gave away a penalty 14 minutes into their 2009 loss to Ukraine in a World Cup qualifier

10   Uruguayan dismissed for punching the ball off the goal line during their 2010 World Cup quarter-final against Ghana

11   Liverpool player red-carded for throwing a coin back into the crowd when they met Arsenal at Highbury in 2002

12   Aberdeen player who was shown the red card three times in the same game against Dundee United in 1997. The first was for foul play, the second for dissent and the third for kicking a corner flag whilst leaving the pitch.

13   Argentina's captain controversially sent off during their 1966 World Cup quarter-final match against England

14   Blackburn Rovers goalkeeper who was banished after just 72 seconds of their Premier League game against Leeds United in 1995 for a foul on Brian Deane

15   Sheffield United player sent off 12 seconds after coming on as a substitute when he elbowed Reading's Stephen Hunt

169
West Country Managers

1   England goalkeeper who led Plymouth Argyle in the 1990s

2   This manager had spells in charge of Bristol City and Plymouth Argyle as well as Stoke City

3   Helped Torquay United to promotion into Division Three before managing Leicester City and Manchester United. He later returned for two more spells in charge.

4   England and QPR captain who briefly managed Exeter City in the early 1980s and was twice in charge of Bristol Rovers

5   Manager who took Yeovil Town into the Football League and won the Division Two title at the second attempt

6   Three-time Crystal Palace manager who resigned from Bristol City after just a few weeks in charge in 2010

7   Bolton Wanderers, Everton, Manchester City and England midfielder who took over at Plymouth Argyle in June 2010

8   Previous clubs included Reading, Wolverhampton Wanderers and Aberdeen before he spent 2012 at Bristol Rovers

9 Managed Torquay United and Plymouth Argyle as well as QPR, Leeds United and Notts County

10 QPR and West Ham United striker who managed Torquay United for 44 months in his first spell in charge, and approximately 10 minutes in his second

11 Leeds United, Manchester United and Scotland forward who twice managed Bristol City

12 Northern Ireland's most successful manager, who was in charge of Plymouth Argyle from 1968 to 1970

13 Leeds United, Middlesbrough and England fullback who managed Bristol Rovers, Bristol City and Exeter City between 1980 and 1995

14 Welshman who took Bristol Rovers into Division One via the play-offs in 2007

15 A managerial legend who had two spells with Plymouth Argyle and also managed Yeovil Town. Having begun his career in 1963 at Bath City, he ended it thirty years later at Bristol Rovers. Elsewhere he won League Championship, FA Cup, League Cup and European Cup Winners Cup.

170
Famous Chairmen

With which clubs do you most associate these Chairmen?

1   Martin Edwards

2   Peter Swales

3   Stan Flashman

4   Peter Hill-Wood

5   Doug Ellis

6   Sir Alan Sugar

7   Sir John Hall

8   Sir Elton John

9   Sam Hammam

10 Ron Noades

11 Robert Maxwell

12 Huw Jenkins

13 Ken Bates

14 Peter Ridsdale

15 George Reynolds

171

FA Cup Finals 1871–1949

1   Which side won five of the first seven finals, including the first in 1872?

2   Between 1872 and 1892, all but two finals were played at which ground?

3   Which northern side won it five times between 1884 and 1891?

4   Who won the Cup for the first time in 1901 whilst still members of the Southern League?

5   From 1895 to 1914, which ground hosted the Cup final?

6   Which side lost four finals and won one during a seven-year spell in the first decade of the 20th century?

7   In which year did Manchester United beat Bristol City 1-0 to win the FA Cup for the first time?

8   Who, in 1923, beat West Ham United 2-0 to win the first final to be held at Wembley Stadium?

9   The first BBC radio commentary of a final came in which year,

when Cardiff City became the first Welsh side to win the Cup, beating Arsenal 1-0?

10 Alex James and Jack Lambert scored when which team beat Huddersfield Town 2-0 to claim the trophy for the first time in 1930?

11 In 1933, Dixie Dean scored one of three for which team as they beat Manchester City 3-0 to lift the trophy for the second time?

12 Who became the longest holders of the trophy when they beat Wolverhampton Wanderers 4-1 in 1939 and retained it until the war ended and the next competition was staged in 1945–1946?

13 The first post-war Cup was won 4-1 by Derby County. Which losing Charlton Athletic player achieved the distinction of becoming the first to score for both teams in a final?

14 Stan Mortensen scored one of Blackpool's two in the 1948 final but they conceded four to which team?

15 In 1949, Wolverhampton Wanderers beat Leicester City 3-1 in the final. Who was the cup-collecting winning captain?

172

FA Cup Finals 1950–1979

1   Which future Liverpool manager was dropped from their team that lost 1-0 in the 1950 final despite having scored the winning goal against Everton in the semi-final?

2   Who scored both goals when Newcastle United beat Blackpool in the 1951 final?

3   Stan Mortenson scored a hat-trick as Blackpool beat Bolton Wanderers 4-2 in the 'Matthews' final of 1953, but who scored the winner in extra time?

4   Which player scored a goal and was then carried off with a broken leg when Nottingham Forest beat Luton Town 2-1 in 1959?

5   Who managed the Tottenham side that won the Cup in 1961 and 1962?

6   Geoff Hurst and Bobby Moore had their first Cup-winning experience at Wembley when West Ham United defeated which team 3-2 in the 1964 final?

7   Which member of Everton's 1966 FA Cup-winning side would win the World Cup with England on the same ground a few weeks later?

8   Who became the first player to score in every round of the Cup when he hit the only goal of the game for West Bromwich Albion against Everton in the 1968 final?

9   Who managed Manchester City to the Cup in 1969 having previously won the competition as a player with Everton and Arsenal?

10   Chelsea took two attempts to win the 1970 Cup against Leeds United. Where was the first Cup final replay since 1912 staged?

11   In 1973, Sunderland were the surprise 1-0 winners against Leeds United after a stunning performance by their goalkeeper. What was his name?

12   Who scored two of Liverpool's goals when they beat Newcastle United 3-0 in the 1974 final?

13   Which team beat Manchester United 1-0 in the 1976 final?

14   In 1978, Roger Osborne scored the only goal of the final for Ipswich Town against which side?

15   When Arsenal beat Manchester United 3-2 in the 1979 final, three of the goals came in the last five minutes. Who scored the winner?

173

FA Cup Finals 1980–2013

1   Who headed the only goal of the match when West Ham United beat Arsenal in the 1980 final?

2   Who managed Tottenham Hotspur to successive Cup wins in 1981 and 1982?

3   Which team did Everton beat 2-0 in the 1984 Cup final?

4   Who was the manager of Coventry City when they beat Tottenham Hotspur 3-2 in the 1987 final?

5   In 1988, Wimbledon beat Liverpool 1-0 in the final. Who was the winning captain who lifted the trophy?

6   When Tottenham Hotspur beat Nottingham Forest in the 1991 final, which of their team was carried off with a self-inflicted knee injury?

7   In the 1994 final, Glenn Hoddle saw his Chelsea side lose 4-0 to which team?

8   Kenny Dalglish and Ruud Gullit took the same team to Wembley in 1998 and 1999, but both went home as losers. Who did they manage?

9   Which Frenchman scored the only goal when Arsenal beat Southampton in the 2003 final?

10   In 2004, Manchester United beat Millwall 3-0 to the disappointment of which losing player, who was hoping to win the FA Cup with a third different side?

11   Which side won the first and last finals to be staged at the Millennium Stadium, in 2001 and 2006?

12   Who scored the first Cup final goal at the new Wembley Stadium when Chelsea beat Manchester United in 2007?

13   In 2008, Portsmouth won the FA Cup for the first time since 1939. Who scored the only goal of their match against Cardiff City?

14   Who did Manchester City beat 1-0 in the 2011 final?

15   When Chelsea beat Liverpool 2-1 in the 2012 final, who became an FA Cup-winner for a record seventh time?

174

League Cup Facts

1 Aston Villa won the first competition in 1961. Who were runners-up?

2 Who became the first sponsors, in 1982?

3 In which season did it cease to be a two-leg final and start being played at Wembley?

4 Which side did Maurice Evans manage to the Cup, beating QPR 3-0 in the 1986 final?

5 Who is the only player to have won the League Cup on five occasions up to 2013?

6 In 2004, which side did Steve McClaren manage to a 2-1 win against Bolton Wanderers in the final?

7 Which team scored five goals in a fourth-round tie at home to Arsenal in 2012 but still lost because they conceded seven?

8 Who became the youngest captain in a final when he led Sunderland against Norwich City in 1985 aged 20 years, 7 months and 8 days?

9   In which season did Third Division Swindon Town beat Arsenal 3-1 in the final?

10 Which side, managed by Ray Harford, won the cup in 1988 against Arsenal and lost to Nottingham Forest in the 1989 final?

11 Who was unable to collect his medal when teammate Tony Adams broke his arm following Arsenal's 2-1 win over Sheffield Wednesday in 1993?

12 In 2013, Swansea City became the first Welsh side to win the trophy when they beat Bradford City 5-0. Who was their manager?

13 Who was in goal for Nottingham Forest in 1978 and 1979 when they beat Liverpool and Southampton in successive finals?

14 Who became the first man to win the competition as a player and manager when Manchester City beat Newcastle United 2-1 in the 1976 final?

15 Which team scored an own goal and missed a penalty when they lost the final 1-0 to Norwich City in 1985?

175
Referees

1   Name the iconic referee, famous for his appearance, who took control of many important matches in his career, including the 2002 World Cup final?

2   Who was the referee who Paulo di Canio famously pushed over in 1998?

3   Tunisian referee Ali Bin Nasser became famous at the 1986 World Cup for *not* doing what?

4   Which Englishman refereed the 2010 World Cup final?

5   On 9 February 2010, Amy Fearn was the first woman to do what?

6   Alan Shearer jokingly showed ref Matt Messias a red card for doing what?

7   Jorge Larrionda was the official for which notable incident at the 2010 World Cup?

8   Who was the Swiss referee who disallowed Sol Campbell's goal for England at Euro 2004, which would have seen them beat Portugal, and received death threats as a result?

9   Said Belqola was the first African official to do what in 1998?

10   Which Welsh referee was nicknamed 'The Book'?

11   Who showed Croatia's Josip Simunic three yellow cards before sending him off at the 2006 World Cup?

12   Which famous referee officiated at the 1950, 1954 and 1958 World Cups and was later seen on the BBC's *It's a Knockout*?

13   What did Paul Gascoigne do to upset referee Dougie Smith and get himself booked?

14   Who was the official who sent off David Beckham v Argentina at the 1998 World Cup?

15   Which English referee controversially gave two penalties in the 1974 World Cup final?

11
Penalty Shootout

176

Franz Beckenbauer

1   What was his nickname as a player?

2   In which year did he lift the World Cup as captain of West Germany?

3   Which team did he play for between 1964 and 1977?

4   How many times was he capped as a player by West Germany?

5   He won the first of his three European Cups in 1974, when Bayern Munich beat which Spanish team 4-0 in the replay of the final?

6   Having won the Bundesliga four times with Bayern Munich, he later collected the title with which other team?

7   In what year was he born?

8   In 1976, he won a third European Cup when Bayern Munich beat Saint Etienne 1-0 in the final, which was held in which Scottish stadium?

9   Which goalkeeper succeeded him as captain of Bayern Munich after he left in 1977?

10 In which year did he manage Bayern Munich to success in the UEFA Cup?

11 Which team did he play for when he won three North American Soccer League titles between 1977 and 1980?

12 He became the first man to win the World Cup as captain and manager when West Germany beat Argentina 1-0 in the final in which year?

13 Which French side did he manage for four months during their Ligue 1 title-winning season in 1990–1991?

14 In a 13-year international career he scored 14 times, but half of those goals came in which year?

15 How many times was he voted European Player of the Year?

177

David Beckham

1   How old was he when he made his Manchester United debut in 1992?

2   Where did he play on loan during the 1994–1995 season?

3   In 1996, he scored a famous goal from the halfway line against which team?

4   Which manager gave him his first cap for England?

5   Who was his best man when he married Victoria Adams in 1999?

6   In 2001, which comic character interviewed the Beckhams together on Comic Relief?

7   How many Premier League titles did he win with Manchester United?

8   In 1998, he was sent off during England's World Cup quarter-final against Argentina when he kicked which opponent whilst himself lying on the pitch?

9   How many Premier League goals did he score during his 265 appearances for Manchester United?

10 In 2006–2007, he won La Liga with which team?

11 In how many different countries did he win League titles?

12 In 2009, he played, on loan, alongside Ronaldino and Paolo Maldini at Inter Milan. Who was their coach?

13 In March 2013, he was announced as a global ambassador for the football of which nation?

14 How many times did he captain England?

15 In 2013, he joined Paris St-Germain after five years with which American side?

178

George Best

1   Where was he born?

2   Which manager signed him for Manchester United?

3   In which year did he make his league debut for Manchester United?

4   He was given the nickname 'the fifth Beatle' by the Portuguese press after he scored twice against which side in a European Cup quarter-final in 1966?

5   When Manchester United won the league title in 1966–1967, he scored ten times in the 42 games. Who was their leading scorer that season with 23 from 36 appearances?

6   He scored the second of Manchester United's goals when they beat Benfica 4-1 to lift the European Cup in 1968. At which ground was the final held?

7   In January 1970, he scored a double hat-trick as Manchester United won 8-2 in the FA Cup. Who were the losing team?

8   What is the name of his first wife, a former model he married in 1978?

9   How old was he when he retired from Manchester United in 1974?

10   In 1976, he resurrected his career alongside Rodney Marsh and Bobby Moore at which club?

11   How many caps did he win for Northern Ireland between 1964 and 1977?

12   Who wrote and recorded the tribute track 'Belfast Boy' in 1970?

13   In 1979, more than 20,000 spectators watched him make his debut for which Scottish side?

14   In which year was he named European Footballer of the Year?

15   Between 1976 and 1978, he spent the summers playing for which West Coast American side?

179

Eric Cantona

1 Which French side did he play for between 1983 and 1988?

2 He was banned from the French national side for a year after insulting their coach. What was his name?

3 Who was he playing for when his club coaches included Gerard Gili and Franz Beckenbauer?

4 Which manager signed him for Leeds United?

5 In 1995, he was banned for eight months for attacking a fan in the crowd with a kung fu kick at which ground?

6 How tall is he?

7 Who did he succeed as captain of Manchester United?

8 How many Premier League titles did he win?

9 He won 45 caps for France between 1987 and 1995. How many goals did he score?

10 In the 1994 FA Cup final, he scored two penalties as Manchester United beat which side 4-0?

11 He scored the only goal of the 1996 FA Cup final. Who was the Liverpool goalkeeper that day?

12 Between 2005 and 2011, which national team did he manage?

13 He retired from football at the end of which season?

14 He appeared as the French Ambassador alongside Cate Blanchett in which 1998 film?

15 In 2011, he joined which American side as their Director of Football?

180
Sir Bobby Charlton

1   Four of his uncles and his mother's cousin all came from a famous footballing family. What was their surname?

2   He made his England debut in which year?

3   Who was the Manchester United manager when they won the 1956–1957 League?

4   Who pulled him clear of the plane following the Munich Air Disaster in 1958?

5   He scored both of England's goals in their 2-1 win against which team in the 1966 World Cup semi-final?

6   His daughter Suzanne became famous during the 1990s. What was her job?

7   When was he named European Footballer of the Year?

8   Who was the only other Munich survivor to play alongside Charlton in Manchester United's 1968 European Cup-winning team?

9   Which side did he manage during from 1973 to 1975?

10 Who presented him with his Lifetime Achievement award at the 2008 BBC Sports Personality of the Year ceremony?

11 In which season did he collect his only FA Cup-winner's medal?

12 How many goals did he score during his 106 appearances for England?

13 In which year was he knighted?

14 Who succeeded him as captain of Manchester United?

15 How many times did he play for Manchester United?

181

Johan Cruyff

1   In which city was he born?

2   What is his real first name?

3   Which was the first side that he played for, between 1964 and 1973?

4   What phrase was used to describe Ajax's playing style?

5   How many goals did he score during his 48 appearances with the national side?

6   With which shirt number was he most associated?

7   Ajax won the European Cup three years in a row, in 1971, 1972 and 1973. Cruyff scored the only two goals of the 1972 final against which side managed by Giovanni Invernizzi?

8   How many Dutch league titles did he win during his two spells as a player with Ajax?

9   What is the name of his son, who played for Manchester United?

10 With which Spanish club did he win La Liga as both player and manager?

11 How many times was he voted European Player of the Year?

12 In 1983–1984, he won the Dutch Double with which team?

13 In which year did he captain Holland to the World Cup final?

14 After a 13-year break from management, he returned to football in 2009 and took charge of which Spanish side?

15 He had spells as a player with two NASL sides, Washington Diplomats and which other team?

182
Kenny Dalglish

1   What is his middle name?

2   How many times was he capped for Scotland?

3   As a player, he won four Scottish titles and four Scottish Cups with which side?

4   What number shirt did he wear at Liverpool?

5   Which manager gave him his Scotland debut in 1972?

6   He won the FA Cup for the first time in 1985–1986 when he was player-manager and Liverpool beat Everton 3-1 in the final. Who was his captain that day?

7   When he led Liverpool to a third League title in 1989–1990, they finished nine points ahead of which team managed by which man?

8   In 1991, he resigned as Liverpool manager following their 4-4 draw with which side?

9   How many English league titles did he win as a player and manager?

10 Who was the Chairman of Blackburn Rovers when Kenny led them to the Premier League title in 1994–1995?

11 Against which team did Dalglish score in the final game of the 1985–1986 season to ensure that Liverpool clinched their 16th League title?

12 Who did he succeed as manager of Newcastle United in January 1997?

13 In which year did Dalglish score the only goal in the European Cup final against FC Bruges?

14 In 2011, he was the caretaker manager at Liverpool and paid a reported £35m for which Newcastle United striker?

15 As a player, he won his first League Cup with Liverpool in 1980–1981. In which season did he first win it as a manager?

183
Eusebio

1   In which year was he born?

2   What was his nickname?

3   What was his real name?

4   In which country was he born?

5   How many goals did he score in his 64 games for his adopted country of Portugal?

6   Which club team did he represent between 1961 and 1975?

7   How many Primeira Liga titles did he win?

8   How many goals did he score against North Korea in the 1966 World Cup quarter-final?

9   He was a member of Benfica's 1962 European Cup-winning team. Who did they beat 5-3 in the final?

10 In the 1966 World Cup semi-final, Eusebio scored a penalty but Portugal lost 2-1 to which team?

11 He is credited with scoring 733 goals during his career. How many games did he play in?

12 In which year was he voted European Footballer of the Year?

13 Three times he was a runner-up in the European Cup. Who did Benfica lose to in his last appearance in a final in 1968?

14 He ended his career with New Jersey Americans in which year?

15 In 1966, he shared the BBC's Overseas Personality of the Year award with which other sportsman?

184

Ryan Giggs

1   Where was he born?

2   Which international schoolboy team did he captain?

3   He made his league debut for Manchester United in 1991 against which team?

4   Between 1991 and the end of the Ferguson era in 2013, how many championship medals did he win?

5   In which year was he voted BBC Sports Personality of the Year?

6   How many appearances did he make for Wales between 1991 and 2007?

7   What was the name of the six-part TV series that he made with Granada TV in 1994?

8   When he played his 759th game for Manchester United, whose appearance record did he beat?

9   He is one of four players who won the Champions League in 1999 and 2008. Giggs, Paul Scholes, Gary Neville and which other

player are in that unique group?

10 The only time that he had been sent off in his career to the end of the 2013 season came in 2001 when playing for Wales against which team?

11 Which landmark did he reach when he scored for Manchester United against Norwich City on 26 February 2012?

12 In which year did he score a Premier League goal from the penalty spot for the first time?

13 Who is the only other player to have won four FA Cups whilst playing for Manchester United to the end of the 2013 season?

14 Which team were Manchester United playing in the 1999 FA Cup semi-final when he scored possibly his greatest goal from a run inside his own half?

15 At 33 years and 80 days, who was the oldest member of the Manchester United team when he made his debut in 1991?

185

Thierry Henry

1   With which team did he make his professional debut in 1994?

2   Which side did Arsenal sign him from for £11m in 1999?

3   Whose all-time Arsenal goal-scoring record did he beat?

4   In 2001–2002, he led Arsenal to the Double and finished top club scorer with how many goals in all competitions?

5   He captained Arsenal to the 2006 Champions League final, where they lost 2-1 to which side?

6   Which shirt number did he almost always wear at Arsenal?

7   In 1998, he was a non-playing substitute when France beat Brazil 3-0 to win the World Cup final. Who was their national coach?

8   He scored 30 league goals in the season that Arsenal won the Premier League without losing a single game. What was the season?

9   Between 1997 and 2010, he was capped 123 times by France. How many goals did he score?

10   In 2003, he was named Man of the Match when Arsenal beat which Gordon Strachan-managed side 1-0 in the final?

11   He moved to Barcelona in 2007 and two years later won the Champions League final 2-0 against Manchester United under which manager?

12   In 2009, he was heavily criticised for twice controlling the ball with his hand before setting up a William Gallas goal against which team in a World Cup qualifier?

13   In which year did he briefly return to Arsenal on loan and make four further league appearances?

14   He was a member of the French side that won Euro '2000. Who did they beat 2-1 in the final?

15   In 2010, he joined which team in the MLS?

186
Frank Lampard

1 Which other West Ham United player attended the same public school as Frank, Brentwood in Essex?

2 What is the name of his football manager uncle?

3 Which year did he make his West Ham debut?

4 Which club did he join on loan in 1995–1996?

5 In the 1996–1997 season, he broke a leg against which team?

6 How much did Chelsea pay West Ham United when he moved across London in 2001?

7 In May 2013, he became Chelsea's highest ever goal-scorer. Whose record did he break?

8 He made his England debut in 1999, but in which year did he score his first international goal, against Croatia?

9 In the quarter-final of the 2006 World Cup, he was one of three players who missed a penalty during the shootout against which team?

10　In 2009, he collected his second FA Cup-winners medal when he scored the winning goal in the final against which team?

11　At the end of which season did he finish in second place behind Ronaldinho in the European Player of the Year and FIFA World Player of the Year awards?

12　He captained Chelsea when they won the 2012 Champions League final. Which team did they beat on penalties?

13　How many times did his father win the FA Cup with West Ham United?

14　Which England manager gave him his first full cap?

15　In 2013, he was captain when they beat Benfica 2-1 in the final and won the UEFA Europa League trophy. Who scored Chelsea's winning goal?

187
Denis Law

1   In which city was he born in 1940?

2   Which future Premier League star was named after Law but with a double 'n' in Dennis as the national authorities wanted to ensure it was not too similar to Denise?

3   Where did he begin his professional career in 1956?

4   What was his then British record transfer fee when he joined Manchester City in 1960?

5   In 1961, he scored six goals in an FA Cup tie against Luton Town. Why were they struck from the records?

6   Which Italian team did he play for in 1961–1962?

7   He player 55 times for Scotland. How many goals did he score?

8   His only FA Cup-winners medal came in 1963 when he scored the opening goal in Manchester United's 3-1 win against which team in the final?

9   In which year was he named European Footballer of the Year, having scored 46 goals in 41 games for Manchester United?

10 He won the Division One title twice. The first was in 1965; when was the second?

11 What caused him to miss the 1967–1968 European Cup semi-finals and final?

12 In 1973, he was given a free transfer to Manchester City by which Manchester United manager?

13 He scored a record 237 goals in how many games for Manchester United?

14 In 1963, he scored for which team against England at Wembley in the FA Centenary match?

15 His final touch in league football came when he backheeled a goal for Manchester City against which team?

188

Diego Maradona

1   In which year was he born?

2   Which professional team did he make his debut for at the age of 15?

3   When did he make his debut for Argentina?

4   How much was his world record transfer fee when he moved from Boca Juniors to Barcelona in 1982?

5   Which former Argentina manager was also his manager during part of his time at Barcelona?

6   In which year did he captain Argentina to victory in the World Cup final?

7   In 1984, he was transferred for another world record fee. Which club bought him for £6.9m?

8   How long was his ban from football that was imposed in 1991 for failing a drugs test?

9   His only major European trophy was the 1989 UEFA Cup when

he scored in the final for Napoli against which West German side that was managed by Arie Haan?

10   When did he make his last appearance for Argentina?

11   Who was England's goalkeeper when Maradona scored twice during their 1986 World Cup quarter-final?

12   In 1990, he was in the Argentinian side that lost 1-0 in the World Cup final to which team?

13   Which team was he managing when he told the media in a live press conference to 'suck it and keep on sucking it'?

14   Which Dubai-based team did he manage in 2011–2012?

15   Which player did Maradona say 'should go back to the museum'?

189

Lionel Messi

1 In which year was he born?

2 By what first name is he better known?

3 Which youth team did he play for before joining Barcelona in 2003?

4 Who was the manager of Barcelona when he made his senior debut at the age of 17 years and 114 days?

5 At what age did he become the all-time highest scorer for Barcelona?

6 In which year did he score his first goal for Argentina, in a friendly against Croatia?

7 On March 30 2013, he became the first player to score in how many consecutive La Liga matches, which included every other team in the league?

8 Which internationally respected magazine named him in the top 100 most influential people in the world in 2011 and 2012?

9   In 2011, he scored one of Barcelona's three against which team in the Champions League final to give him a third winner's medal in the competition?

10 In March 2013, a Japanese jeweller recreated which part of his body in pure gold with a sale value of $5.25m?

11 How many goals did he score in his 60 appearances for Barcelona in the 2011–2012 season?

12 What number has he worn since Ronaldinho left the club?

13 Argentina lost 4-0 in the 2010 World Cup quarter-finals to which team?

14 In which year did he win an Olympic Gold medal with Argentina?

15 By the end of the 2012–2013 season, how many La Liga titles had he won?

190

Bobby Moore

1   Where was he born?

2   Which year was he born?

3   In 1958, he made his debut for West Ham United under which manager?

4   He made his England debut in ahead of the 1962 World Cup finals in a warm-up friendly against which country?

5   How old was he when he was appointed England captain?

6   In 1964, he lifted the FA Cup after West Ham United beat which team 3-2 in the final?

7   In 1965, West Ham United beat Munich 1860 2-0 in the European Cup Winner's Cup final. Where was it held?

8   How many goals did he score for England?

9   In 1966, he led England to the World Cup when they beat West Germany 4-3 in the final. Who captained the opposition that day?

10   After winning the World Cup in 1966, Bobby and his teammates celebrated at the club of which well-known entertainer?

11   What was he falsely accused of stealing in Bogota during the build-up to the 1970 World Cup finals?

12   England went out of the 1970 World Cup when they were beaten by West Germany in the quarter-finals. But the most iconic image was of Moore swapping shirts with which player at the end of their group game against Brazil?

13   How many caps did he win for England?

14   His final professional appearance at Wembley came for Fulham in the FA Cup final when they lost 2-0 to West Ham United. What was the year?

15   When he died of cancer at the age of 51, he was a regular football co-commentator with which radio station?

191
Pele

1   What is Pele's real name?

2   How old was Pele when he played in the winning Brazilian side at
    the 1958 World Cup finals in Sweden?

3   Which club side did Pele play for between 1956 and 1974?

4   In the 1962 World Cup finals, Pele missed most of the tournament
    having been injured against which team?

5   What was significant about the penalty goal that Pele scored for
    Santos against Vasco da Gama on 19 November 1969?

6   How many Brazilian caps did he win?

7   How many goals did he score for Brazil?

8   In which year was Pele awarded an honorary knighthood by Queen
    Elizabeth II?

9   Which American soccer team did he play for in 1975–1977?

10 In the final of the 1970 World Cup, Pele's pass set up which other player to score Brazil's fourth goal against Italy?

11 Which shirt number did Pele wear throughout his career?

12 Which British university awarded Pele an honorary degree in 2012?

13 Pele was a member of how many World Cup-winning Brazilian sides?

14 Pele's final international appearance for Brazil came in a 2-2 draw with Yugoslavia in which year?

15 The cast of which film included Pele, Phill Jupitas, Martin Bashir and Bradley Walsh?

192
Ronaldo

1   What is his full name?

2   In which year was he born?

3   How many times was he a member of a World Cup-winning squad?

4   With which Brazilian club did he begin his career in 1993?

5   Which Dutch side did he play for between 1994 and 1996?

6   How many international goals did he score in his 98 games for Brazil?

7   How many times was he voted FIFA Player of the year?

8   During 1996–1997, he scored 47 goals in 49 games, including the winner in the European Cup Winner's Cup, for which Spanish club?

9   What name did he wear on his back when Brazil won Bronze at the 1996 Olympic Games? Ronaldo was already taken by Ronaldo Guiro.

10 Which Italian side signed him for a world record £19m in 1997?

11 Having moved to Real Madrid in 2002, he scored a hat-trick against which British club to knock them out of the 2003 Champions League at the quarter-final stage?

12 Ronaldo's appearance in the 1998 World Cup final made worldwide headlines. Why?

13 What was unusual about his hat-trick against Argentina in a qualifying match for the 2006 World Cup?

14 After an injury-hit season with Real Madrid, he ended his career back in Brazil with 29 goals in 52 games for which side?

15 Ronaldo holds the record for the number of goals scored at World Cup final tournaments. How many did he score and whose record did he break?

193
Cristiano Ronaldo

1   On which island was Cristiano Ronaldo born?

2   At the age of 15, he was diagnosed with a medical condition that threatened to end his career. What was it?

3   At both World Cup 2010 and Euro 2012, Ronaldo's Portugal lost in the knockout stages to which nation?

4   About whom did Ronaldo say, 'You cannot compare a Ferrari with a Porsche because it's a different engine. You cannot compare them'?

5   For which Portuguese club did Ronaldo make his league debut?

6   When he moved from Manchester United to Real Madrid, he became the most expensive footballer in history. What was the reported transfer fee?

7   He scored his first international goal in the opening match of which major tournament?

8   Which Real Madrid legend presented Ronaldo with his shirt on arrival at the club?

9   Ronaldo was sent off in the Manchester 'derby' of January 2006 for kicking which former United player?

10 How many Premier League titles did he win with Man Utd?

11 Ronaldo was seen by TV cameras making what gesture after Man Utd teammate Wayne Rooney was sent off in a European Championship quarter-final?

12 True or false: in the 2008 Champions League final, Ronaldo scored in the penalty shootout v Chelsea?

13 Ronaldo won his 100th international cap for Portugal against which British team in 2012?

14 Of whom did Ronaldo say, 'He's been my father in sport'?

15 What is the name of the fashion boutiques he owns in Portugal?

194

Ian Rush

1 Which was his first league side?

2 Which manager paid £300,000 to take him to Liverpool?

3 He ended his Anfield career as their all-time record goal-scorer. What was his Liverpool total?

4 His first goal for Liverpool came in the European Cup as Liverpool beat which Finnish side 7-0 at Anfield?

5 His first trophy came when he scored one of Liverpool's three in the 1982 League Cup final against which team?

6 1983–1984 was his most prolific season for Liverpool. How many goals did he score in his 65 appearances?

7 Which Italian side did he join for the 1987–1988 season?

8 How many League titles did he win with Liverpool?

9 In 2010, a Chester art installation of what animal was named after him, complete with moustache and Chester football kit?

10 In 1989, he scored twice against which side when Liverpool won the FA Cup final 3-2?

11 He scored 28 goals in his 73 games for Wales but only one hat-trick. Who was it against?

12 He joined Leeds United on a free transfer in 1996. Who was the Liverpool manager at the time?

13 At the age of 37, he joined which Welsh side in 1998?

14 He finished his career overseas with a club called Olympic. In which city were they based?

15 He was briefly manager of which League Two side?

195
Alan Shearer

1   In which year did he make his debut for Southampton?

2   In his first full game against Arsenal he became, at 17 years and 240 days, the youngest First Division player to score a hat-trick since which player?

3   Which Southampton manager sold him to Blackburn Rovers in 1992?

4   Who was his striking partner at Blackburn Rovers when their combined nickname was the SAS?

5   Which season did Blackburn Rovers win the Premier League?

6   How many goals did he score in his 35 Premier League games in 1995–1996?

7   Who were England's opponents when he scored on his international debut in 1992?

8   How many goals did he score in his 63 appearances for England?

9   What was his reported transfer fee when he joined Newcastle United in 1996?

10 In August 1999, which manager controversially dropped him ahead of Newcastle United's match against Sunderland?

11 He retired in 2006, having become Newcastle's record scorer with 206 goals for the club. Whose record did he beat?

12 Who was the manager of Newcastle United at the time of his retirement?

13 In 2008, he helped raise more than £250,000 for which charity by cycling from Newcastle to London?

14 In 2009, he briefly became acting manager of Newcastle United because of the illness of which full-time manager of the club?

15 How many times did he captain England?

196
Peter Shilton

1   In which year was he born?

2   In May 1966, he made his league debut for which club?

3   How many full England caps did he win?

4   Against which side did he score a goal in 1967, when the ball bounced over the head of his opposite number, Campbell Forsyth?

5   In which year did he make his only FA Cup final appearance?

6   Which England manager gave him his first cap?

7   When he joined Stoke City in 1974 it was for a then world record fee for a goalkeeper. How much were Leicester reported to have received?

8   With which side did he twice with the European Cup?

9   Which player scored two against Shilton in the 1986 World Cup quarter-final?

10 After five years at Southampton, he spent a further five with which Midlands team?

11 In which season did he collect a Division One championship medal?

12 With which team did he play his 1,249th and final game in 1997 before retiring at the age of 47?

13 Which side did he manage between 1992 and 1995?

14 How many times did he captain England?

15 Which goalkeeping legend did he replace at Leicester City and Stoke City?

12
Post-Match Analysis

197

Alan Hansen

1 Which Scottish side did he play for between 1973 and 1977?

2 When did he make his debut as a regular *Match of the Day* pundit?

3 What was his fee when he moved to Liverpool in 1977?

4 How many Division One titles did he win with Liverpool?

5 At the start of which season did he warn that Manchester United would not be able to 'win anything with kids'?

6 In which feature film did he make a brief appearance?

7 How many times did he play for Scotland?

8 Which manager appointed him Liverpool captain?

9 For which other sport has he occasionally made TV appearances as a pundit?

10 How many goals did he score in his 620 games for Liverpool?

11 Who was his regular co-pundit when he first appeared on *Match of the Day*?

12 He appeared in all three of Scotland's matches in which World Cup finals?

13 He won the European Cup on three occasions, the last coming in 1984 when Liverpool beat which side on penalties?

14 In which season did he lead Liverpool to his final league title, finishing nine points clear of Aston Villa?

15 He won the FA Cup twice. Who were the opposition on both occasions?

198

Mark Lawrenson

1   Who was manager of Preston North End when he made his debut at the age of 17?

2   In the summer of 1977, Alan Mullery signed him to which club?

3   What was his club record fee when Liverpool bought him in 1981?

4   Two players scored their first goals for Liverpool when they came on as late substitutes during their 7-0 win against Finnish side Oulun Pallseura in 1981. Lawrenson was one; who was the other?

5   He made 39 appearances for which international team?

6   For many year he worked alongside which commentator on the BBC's major live games?

7   In 2002, he shaved off his moustache on *Football Focus* having lost a wager that which side would be relegated from the Premier League?

8   How old was he when he retired from playing with Liverpool?

9   Who was the Oxford United chairman when he briefly managed them in 1988?

10   How many Division One titles did he win with Liverpool?

11   How many appearances did he make for Liverpool?

12   In 1989, he spent a season playing for which side in the American Soccer League?

13   He spent September 1989 to November 1990 as manager of which Division Four side?

14   From 1999 to 2004, he was the resident sidekick to which *Football Focus* presenter?

15   In 1996, he was appointed defensive coach at which club?

199
Voices of Football on BBC Radio

1   Born in Northern Ireland in 1952, his first FA Cup final commentary came in 1986 (AG)

2   Liverpool-born football and athletics commentator for BBC Radio, who has also worked with ITV and Sky (AP)

3   Blackpool-supporting football and rugby league commentator for Radio 5 Live (DO)

4   As well as football, he has commentated many times on the Tour de France for Radio 5 Live (SB)

5   Began with BBC Leeds before moving to Radio 5 Live and then ITV Sport (PD)

6   Former Capital Radio voice of football, who joined Radio 5 Live in 2002 and is known for his exuberant style (JP)

7   Born in Glasgow in 1937 and for many decades the BBC's main commentator on Scottish football (AM)

8   Joined BBC Radio Derby in 1973 and was appointed Chief Football Correspondent in 2004 (MI)

9   After a career that included spells with Fulham and Reading, he
    became one of BBC Radio's main football commentators in the
    1960s and early 1970s (ME)

10 Irishman whose first football commentary for Radio 5 Live came
    in 2002 (CM)

11 Welsh-born BBC broadcaster who was heard at almost every
    major sporting event during the 1970s and 1980s (PJ)

12 Pioneering BBC Radio commentator who covered every FA Cup
    final from 1946 to 1963 (RG)

13 The BBC's football correspondent from 1968 to 1991, with a
    distinctive West County accent (BB)

14 Northumberland-born football and golf commentator who made
    his FA Cup final debut for Radio 5 Live in 2010 (JM)

15 Actor who began reading the Saturday evening football scores on
    Sports Report in 1973 (JAG)

200

Footballers and Sports Personality of the Year

1 Which footballer was placed second in the 1958 and 1959 polls?

2 In which year was Sven-Goran Eriksson awarded Coach of the Year?

3 In 1966, Bobby Moore was voted Sports Personality of the Year and Geoff Hurst was placed third. Which sporting star split the two World Cup winners?

4 The 1990 Sports Personality of the Year, Paul Gascoigne, also recorded a single with Lindisfarne that reached number 2 in the UK singles chart that year. What was the exact title of the song?

5 2002 was the most recent year that a footballer won the award for Overseas Sports Personality of the Year. Who was the player?

6 Which football manager won Coach of the Year in 2002 and 2004?

7 In which year did Celtic become the only Scottish Club to date to win Team of the Year?

8   Which club was David Beckham playing for when he won Sports Personality of the Year?

9   Which footballer was voted into second place behind Princess Anne in 1971?

10   Which is the only football club to win the Team of the Year award three times up to the end of 2012?

11   In which year did Michael Owen win the Sports Personality of the Year award?

12   Which was the first football club to win Team of the Year?

13   In 2009, Ryan Giggs was voted Sports Personality of the Year. In which year had he made his league debut for Manchester United?

14   How many English-born managers have won Coach of the Year up to the end of 2012?

15   Only one goalkeeper has ever appeared in the top three of the main award – who was it?

THE
ANSWERS

1
Pre-Match Warm-up

1 Quick Fire

1 Sir Alex Ferguson
2 Bristol Rovers
3 Match of the Day
4 1966
5 Celtic
6 1992–1993
7 Tottenham Hotspur
8 David Beckham
9 Melchester Rovers
10 Brazilian
11 Roman Abramovich
12 South Africa
13 Liverpool
14 Diego Maradona
15 Manchester City

2 Name the Country

1 Netherlands
2 Germany
3 Italy
4 Portugal
5 Ukraine
6 Hungary
7 Greece
8 Turkey
9 France
10 Spain

11 Belgium

12 Republic of Ireland

13 Bulgaria

14 Norway

15 Switzerland

3 Which City?

1 Glasgow

2 Liverpool

3 Birmingham

4 Istanbul

5 Brussels

6 Barcelona

7 Lisbon

8 Stoke-on-Trent (Burslem)

9 Florence

10 Rotterdam

11 Turin

12 Gelsenkirchen

13 Rome

14 Genoa

15 Buenos Aires

4 Leading Goal-Scorers 2012–2013

1 Robin Van Persie (26)

2 Edin Dzeko (14)

3 Frank Lampard (15)

4 Santi Cazorla (12)

5 Gareth Bale (21)

6 Marouane Fellaini (11)

7 Luis Suarez (23)

8 Romelu Lukaku (17)

9   Michu (18)

10 Kevin Nolan (10)

11 Grant Holt (8)

12 Dimitar Berbatov (15)

13 Jon Walters (8)

14 Rickie Lambert (15)

15 Christian Benteke (19)

5 True or False

1   False

2   True

3   False. It was written by Rogers and Hammerstein for *Carousel*.

4   False. It was at the end of the 1998 World Cup.

5   True

6   True

7   True

8   False

9   True

10 True

11 False

12 False

13 True

14 True

15 False

6 More True or False

1   True

2   True

3   False. It was 49.

4   False

5   False

6   True

7   True

8   False

9   True

10 True

11 True

12 True – Hazell

13 False. He was approached by Labour.

14 True

15 False

2
Welcome to the BBC

7 Gary Lineker

1   Winston
2   1978–1979
3   Scotland
4   5
5   Terry Venables
6   *Football Focus*
7   Bobby Charlton
8   Nagoya Grampus Eight
9   1999
10 *An Evening with Gary Lineker*
11 10
12 Everton
13 Tottenham Hotspur
14 Alan Smith
15 Sport Relief

8 Jimmy Hill

1   1928
2   1949
3   Fulham
4   £20 a week
5   Arthur Cox
6   Brentwich United
7   Brian Moore
8   Dickie
9   Highbury – Arsenal were playing Liverpool when linesman Dennis Drewitt pulled a muscle.

10 David Coleman

11 Loftus Road, the ground of QPR

12 Trevor Francis

13 1987–1988

14 *Jimmy Hill's Sunday Supplement*

15 Coventry City

9 BBC TV Football Presenters

1　Ray Stubbs

2　Walley Barnes

3　Harry Gration

4　Bob Wilson

5　Sam Leitch

6　Adrian Chiles

7　Dan Walker

8　Barry Davies

9　Celina Hinchcliffe

10 Steve Rider

11 Mark Pougatch

12 Frank Bough

13 Manish Bhasin

14 Jake Humphrey

15 Gabby Logan

10 Football on BBC TV – The Early Years

1　1937

2　George Allison

3　20 miles

4　He commentated on the first live post-war match, Barnet v Wealdstone.

5　Peter Dimmock

6　Kenneth Wolstenholme

7   William Hartnell
8   £20,000
9   Liverpool 3 - 2 Arsenal
10 David Attenborough
11 1967
12 £6
13 Barry Stoller
14 Jimmy Hill moving from ITV to the BBC
15 1974–1975

11 Football on the Box

1   *Match of the Day*
2   *Football Focus*
3   *Sportsnight with Coleman*
4   *The Big Match*
5   *Sportsview*
6   *Football Italia*
7   *Row Z*
8   *The Saint and Greavsie*
9   *Soccer AM*
10 *Sportscene*
11 *MOTD2*
12 *Fantasy Football League*
13 *Football Fever*
14 *The Football League Show*
15 *Saturday Sport Special*

12 BBC TV Voices of Football

1   Tony Gubba
2   Len Martin
3   Gavin Peacock
4   Gerald Sinstadt

5   Mark Bright
6   Sir Trevor Brooking
7   Jon Champion
8   Tim Gudgin
9   Terry Venables
10 Garry Richardson
11 Guy Mowbray
12 Clive Tyldesley
13 Damian Johnson
14 Garth Crooks
15 Lee Dixon

13 John Motson and Barry Davies

1   Cranbrook School in Kent
2   9 (6 finals)
3   1966
4   2008
5   1994
6   Hereford United
7   2
8   Brian Clough
9   12
10 Barnet
11 Tottenham Hotspur
12 3 hours before kick-off
13 Dentistry
14 Wycombe Wanderers
15 Francis Lee

14 Kenneth Wolstenholme

1   1920
2   The RAF

3 Bootham Crescent
4 *Sportsview*
5 Hugh Johns
6 23
7 Bolton Wanderers
8 Panathinaikos
9 Serie A
10 £60
11 *Lenin of the Rovers*
12 David Coleman
13 Alan Ball
14 Nick Hancock
15 *50 Sporting Years... And It's Still Not All Over*

3
Fans Arrive

15 Former Ground Names

1　Sunderland
2　Leicester City
3　Wimbledon
4　Shrewsbury Town
5　Bolton Wanderers
6　Manchester City
7　Scunthorpe United
8　Derby County
9　Coventry City
10　Colchester United
11　Reading
12　Middlesbrough
13　Walsall
14　Hartlepool United
15　Southampton

16 More Former Ground Names

1　Highbury
2　The New Den
3　Burnden Park
4　Huddersfield Town
5　Norwich City, Carrow Road
6　Wycombe Wanderers
7　Doncaster Rovers
8　Vetch Field
9　Saltergate
10　Withdean Stadium

11 Trent Bridge
12 Darlington
13 Hull City
14 Springfield Park
15 Victoria Ground

17 English League Stadiums with a capacity below 30,000

1   Carlisle United
2   West Bromwich Albion
3   Rotherham United
4   Hull City
5   Barnsley
6   Bradford City
7   Stoke City
8   Doncaster Rovers
9   Tranmere Rovers
10 Gillingham
11 Walsall
12 Cheltenham Town
13 Burnley
14 Blackpool
15 Oxford United

18 Scottish Football Grounds

1   Kilmarnock
2   Hibernian
3   Heart of Midlothian
4   Aberdeen
5   Rangers
6   Queen's Park
7   Dundee United
8   Motherwell

9   Airdrie United

10 Queen of the South

11 Stranraer

12 Dunfermline

13 Dundee

14 Forfar Athletic

15 East Fife

19 A European Tour

1   Nou Camp

2   Stadio Giuseppe Meazza (nicknamed San Siro)

3   Allianz Arena

4   Estadio da Dragao

5   Estadio Santiago Bernabeu

6   Stadio Olimpico, Rome

7   Red Star Stadium

8   Signal Iduna Park (Westfalenstadion)

9   Parc des Princes

10 St Jacob-Park

11 Luzhniki Stadium

12 Philips Stadion

13 Juventus Stadium

14 Donbass Arena

15 Vicente Calderon Stadium

4
Meet the Teams

20 Arsenal

1 1996
2 Michael Thomas
3 David O'Leary
4 Herbert Chapman
5 Sylvain Wiltord
6 The Invincibles
7 Shenley Training Ground, London Colney
8 Scotland
9 Southampton
10 Stewart Houston
11 Cesc Fabregas
12 Bertie Mee
13 Pat Rice
14 European Cup Winner's Cup
15 Manchester City

21 Aston Villa

1 Birmingham
2 Peter Withe
3 2006
4 River Plate
5 Chelsea
6 Christian Benteke
7 Manchester United
8 John Gregory
9 7
10 A lion

11 Atkinson (Ron and Dalian)

12 Jimmy Rimmer

13 Everton

14 Paul Lambert

15 Scottish

22 Birmingham City

1   Lee Clark

2   Small Heath Alliance

3   Everton

4   St Andrews

5   1956

6   Gil Merrick

7   Kevin Phillips

8   Football League Trophy

9   Nikola Zigic

10 Arsenal

11 Trevor Francis

12 Wigan Athletic

13 Barry Fry

14 1988–1999

15 Steve Bruce

23 Blackburn Rovers

1   1875

2   Scott Dann

3   1913–1914

4   Kenny Dalglish

5   Ewood Park

6   Manchester United

7   2008

8   Matt Jansen

9   Ray Harford
10 1928
11 The Full Members Cup
12 Venky's London Limited
13 Alan Shearer
14 Chelsea
15 Simon Garner

24 Celtic

1   Celtic Park
2   Tony Mowbray
3   The Old Firm
4   Motherwell
5   1966–1967
6   Aberdeen
7   Slovakian
8   Billy McNeill
9   Henrik Larsson
10 Ronnie Simpson
11 Gary Hooper
12 8 out of the 9 scored
13 Martin O'Neill
14 The Bhoys
15 1965

25 Chelsea

1   1905
2   Ted Drake
3   Ron Harris
4   43
5   2009–2010
6   Wolverhampton Wanderers

7 Peter Cech

8 The head of a Chelsea Pensioner

9 Jose Mourinho

10 Bayern Munich

11 193

12 Bobby Campbell

13 Manchester City

14 The 1965 League Cup

15 Juan Mata

26 Everton

1 St Domingo's FC

2 Goodison Park

3 Rapid Vienna

4 Dixie Dean

5 David Moyes

6 Neville Southall

7 Manchester City

8 1969–1970

9 Howard Kendall

10 Wimbledon

11 Brian Labone

12 Manchester United

13 Marouane Fellaini

14 159

15 Alex Young

27 Huddersfield Town

1 West Yorkshire

2 19th

3 3

4 John Smith's Stadium (Galpharm Stadium)

5 Billy Smith
6 Terry Poole
7 Bristol Rovers
8 Mark Robins
9 Malcolm Macdonald
10 Ray Wilson
11 1922
12 Tom Johnston
13 Andy Booth
14 2
15 Jordan Rhodes

28 Leeds United

1 1919
2 Dennis Wise
3 10
4 Arsenal
5 5
6 Norwich City
7 Jack Charlton
8 Valencia
9 Ken Bates
10 Republic of Ireland
11 Jimmy Armfield
12 1991–1992
13 Elland Road
14 Rio Ferdinand
15 Brian McDermott

29 Liverpool

1 Brendan Rogers
2 9

3 Anfield

4 1965

5 5

6 Ian Callaghan

7 Kenny Dalglish

8 1996

9 Jerome Sinclair

10 You'll Never Walk Alone

11 Real Madrid

12 1994–1995 League Cup

13 Luis Suarez

14 Phil Neal

15 Graeme Souness

30 Manchester City

1 City of Manchester Stadium

2 1937

3 Joe Hart

4 Tony Book

5 Sergio Aguero

6 Newcastle United

7 1998

8 AC Milan

9 Joe Mercer

10 1981

11 Thailand

12 23

13 1976

14 AC Milan

15 QPR

31 Manchester United

1 1966–1967
2 Paul Scholes
3 Newton Heath LYR FC
4 Ron Atkinson
5 Everton
6 Jimmy Greenhoff
7 Cristiano Ronaldo
8 Bobby Charlton
9 Bryan Robson
10 1998–1999
11 Gary Birtles
12 1958
13 Glazer
14 Aston Villa
15 Denmark

32 Middlesbrough

1 Steve Gibson
2 North Yorkshire
3 Aston Villa
4 Anglo-Scottish Cup
5 Jack Charlton
6 2004
7 George Camsell
8 Chelsea
9 Stuart Boam
10 Bryan Robson
11 Afonso Alves
12 Tony Mowbray
13 Brighton and Hove Albion
14 Wilf Mannion

15 Australian

33 Newcastle United

1   St James' Park
2   The Texaco Cup
3   Paul Gascoigne
4   Kevin Keegan
5   A magpie
6   Manchester City
7   Shay Given
8   Greek
9   Len Shackleton
10 1926–1927
11 Demba Ba
12 Ujpesti Dozsa
13 Osvaldo Ardiles
14 Alan Shearer
15 Chris Hughton

34 Norwich City

1   1902
2   Martin Peters
3   Carrow Road
4   Ken Brown
5   Stephen Fry
6   Kevin Keelan
7   Grant Holt
8   1992–1993
9   Irish
10 Sunderland
11 Ron Ashman
12 Tottenham Hotspur

13 Nigel Worthington
14 Norfolk
15 Chris Hughton

35 Rangers

1   Glasgow
2   114
3   1972
4   Mark Hateley
5   Nacho Novo
6   Bill Struth
7   Barry Ferguson
8   9
9   Jimmy Smith
10 Lionel Charbonnier
11 Chelsea
12 Third
13 Walter Smith
14 Ibrox Park
15 Ally McCoist

36 Reading

1   1920
2   Ted Drake
3   2006–2007
4   1899 Hoffenheim
5   Madejski Stadium
6   Shaka Hislop
7   Jimmy Quinn
8   Trevor Senior
9   The Full Members Cup
10 Martin Hicks

11 1927

12 Brendan Rogers

13 Steve Death

14 Manchester United

15 Steve Coppell

37 Southampton

1 Hampshire

2 Lawrie McMenemy

3 27

4 Mick Channon

5 1983–1984

6 Gordon Strachan

7 Mauricio Pochettino

8 The Saints

9 Martin Chivers

10 Carlisle United

11 8

12 Rupert Lowe

13 Norwegian

14 2008–2009

15 Burnley

38 Tottenham Hotspur

1 Northumberland Park

2 Keith Burkinshaw

3 A cockerel

4 Welsh

5 Real Madrid

6 Crewe Alexandra

7 Steve Perryman

8 Teddy Sheringham

9   Derby County
10 Erik Thorstvedt
11 1950–1951
12 1987
13 Andre Villas-Boas
14 Gerry Francis
15 27

39 West Ham United

1   The Boleyn Ground
2   Alvin Martin
3   1965
4   Ted Fenton
5   Thames Ironworks FC
6   Frank Lampard
7   Vic Watson
8   Phil Parkes
9   Sam Allardyce
10 1985–1986
11 Joe Cole
12 Wolverhampton Wanderers
13 Ron Greenwood
14 Trevor Brooking
15 Lucas Neill

40 Wigan Athletic

1   1960
2   1932
3   Steve Bruce
4   2006
5   Tottenham Hotspur
6   Estudiantes

7 Shaun Maloney

8 The Football League Trophy

9 Swansea City

10 Kevin Langley

11 Antonio Valencia

12 Paul Jewell

13 2005–2006

14 Emile Heskey

15 The DW Stadium

41 Wolverhampton Wanderers

1 Stan Cullis

2 The UEFA Cup

3 Bill Slater

4 Steve Bull

5 Sunderland

6 Emlyn Hughes

7 2008–2009

8 Molineux

9 Manchester City

10 1891

11 Billy Wright

12 Norwegian

13 Graham Turner

14 Sir Jack Hayward

15 John Richards

5
The Manager's Team Talk

42 Sir Matt Busby

1 Bellshill, Scotland
2 Manchester City
3 1933–1934
4 George Patterson
5 1
6 1945
7 5
8 Johnny Carey
9 The GB Olympic Team
10 The Busby Babes
11 Red Star Belgrade
12 Alex Stepney
13 1968
14 Wilf McGuinness
15 This is Your Life

43 Brian Clough

1 Middlesbrough
2 251
3 29
4 Peter Taylor
5 1971–1972
6 Brighton and Hove Albion
7 Michael Sheen
8 44
9 Allan Brown
10 Kenny Burns

11 Herbert Chapman
12 Birmingham City
13 Malmo FF
14 John Robertson
15 1992–1993

44 Sir Alex Ferguson

1 Glasgow
2 Queen's Park
3 1974
4 4
5 Darren Ferguson
6 Les Sealey
7 Barcelona
8 1992–1993
9 Roy Keane
10 Ole Gunnar Solskjaar
11 Steve McLaren
12 Moscow
13 Steve Bruce
14 Cristiano Ronaldo
15 1999

45 Jose Mourinho

1 Bobby Robson
2 Benfica
3 AS Monaco
4 Claudio Ranieri
5 41
6 Olympique de Marseille
7 £75,000
8 Frank Lampard

9   Manchester United

10 Steve Clarke

11 Manchester City

12 Diego Milito

13 That he was being handcuffed

14 150

15 Real Madrid

46 Bill Nicholson

1   Scarborough

2   Tottenham Hotspur

3   1950–1951

4   1

5   Walter Winterbottom

6   1958

7   Bobby Smith

8   Danny Blanchflower

9   Atletico Madrid

10 Martin Chivers

11 Wolverhampton Wanderers

12 1974

13 Pat Jennings

14 Glory, Glory, my life with Spurs

15 Terry Neill

47 Bob Paisley

1   Bishop Auckland

2   Anti-tank gunner

3   Liverpool

4   1974

5   West Ham United

6   Club Bruges

7   Emlyn Hughes
8   6
9   1974–1975
10 Alan Kennedy
11 Middlesbrough
12 David Fairclough
13 Vancouver Whitecaps
14 Ian Rush
15 Joe Fagan

48 Sir Alf Ramsey

1   Southampton
2   32
3   Ipswich Town
4   The Wingless Wonders
5   France
6   Jimmy Greaves
7   USA
8   Uruguay
9   Geoff Hurst
10 Alan Ball
11 Peter Bonetti
12 Sir Harold Thompson
13 69
14 Birmingham City
15 54

49 Don Revie

1   Leicester City
2   1956
3   Jack Taylor
4   6

5   Billy Bremner

6   5

7   Allan Clarke

8   Peter Lorimer

9   Southampton

10 AC Milan

11 1973–1974

12 Joe Mercer

13 Malcolm MacDonald

14 Brian Clough

15 United Arab Emirates

50 Sir Bobby Robson

1   County Durham

2   Electrician

3   Fulham

4   West Bromwich Albion

5   20

6   Scotland

7   Mick Mills

8   Kevin Keegan

9   Peter Shilton

10 PSV Eindhoven

11 Barcelona

12 Porto

13 Freddie Shepherd

14 Republic of Ireland

15 2002

51 Bill Shankly

1   All four of them

2   A miner

3 Carlisle United

4 £5

5 Huddersfield Town

6 1959

7 The Boot Room

8 1963–1964

9 Leeds United

10 Roger Hunt

11 This is Anfield

12 Borussia Monchengladbach

13 Chris Lawler

14 1974

15 'You'll Never Walk Alone'

52 Jock Stein

1 A miner

2 John

3 Llanelli Town

4 An ankle injury

5 Dunfermline Athletic

6 10

7 1965

8 Charlie Gallagher

9 1967

10 Stevie Chalmers

11 Feyenoord

12 44

13 61

14 New Zealand

15 Wales

53 Arsene Wenger

1   1949
2   AS Monaco
3   Japan
4   Bruce Rioch
5   1997–1998
6   Galatasaray
7   Sylvain Wiltord
8   An asteroid
9   Jose Mourinho
10 49 games
11 Jens Lehmann
12 Cesc Fabregas
13 Le Professeur
14 Hertfordshire
15 Sol Campbell

6
First Half

54 Desmond Lynam

1   Ennis, County Clare
2   Sports Report
3   Frank Bough
4   1988
5   Brighton and Hove Albion
6   Richard Whiteley
7   If
8   Boxing
9   Steve Rider
10 Gerald Williams
11 How do they do that?
12 Insurance
13 16
14 The Premiership
15 I should have been at work

55 World Cup 1930–1962

1   Uruguay
2   The lowest crowd in World Cup finals history. Officially given as 2,459, but the actual figure in attendance was estimated at around 300.
3   Czechoslovakia
4   All 16 competing teams kicked off their first-round matches at the same time.
5   It was the first and only occasion in World Cup history where Germany was eliminated in the first round and also failed to reach the last eight.

6 Paris

7 USA

8 Uruguay

9 Switzerland

10 Hungary

11 13

12 Pele

13 The Battle of Santiago

14 Sir Bobby Robson

15 Vava

56 World Cup 1966

1 Pickles

2 Old Trafford, Goodison Park, Villa Park, Hillsborough, Roker Park and Ayresome Park

3 Pak Doo-Ik

4 The owners of Wembley Stadium had a greyhound meeting scheduled on the same Friday and refused to move it.

5 Antonio Rattin

6 World Cup Willie

7 Roger Hunt

8 Portugal

9 Lev Yashin

10 Franz Beckenbauer

11 Eusebio

12 Gordon Banks, Ray Wilson, Jack Charlton, Bobby Moore, George Cohen, Alan Ball, Nobby Stiles, Martin Peters, Roger Hunt, Bobby Charlton and Geoff Hurst

13 Soviet Union

14 Ipswich Town

15 Queen Elizabeth II

57 World Cup 1970

1 Mexico
2 He was alleged to have stolen a bracelet, but all charges were later dropped.
3 He was the first substitute used in finals history, coming on for the Soviet Union v Mexico in the opening match.
4 Gerd Muller
5 Gordon Banks
6 Mexico '70 was the first to be broadcast in colour.
7 Allan Clarke
8 Jairzinho
9 Red and Yellow cards
10 Mário Zagallo
11 Estadio Azteca (Aztec Stadium)
12 Peter Bonetti
13 He played on with his arm in a sling after West Germany had used both substitutes.
14 Carlos Alberto
15 Having won the World Cup three times, Brazil were given permanent possession of it by FIFA.

58 World Cup 1974

1 He designed the new FIFA World Cup Trophy which was awarded for the first time in 1974.
2 Haiti
3 Scotland
4 He was the first player to be sent off with a red card in a World Cup finals match
5 Yugoslavia
6 Total Football
7 East Germany 1 West Germany 0
8 Sweden

9   Grzegorz Lato

10 Fourth

11 It was the first time a World Cup-winner had played for a club outside his home country. Netzer played for Real Madrid.

12 Olympic Stadium, Munich

13 Jack Taylor

14 Johan Neeskens and Paul Breitner

15 Franz Beckenbauer

59 World Cup 1978

1   Argentina hosted the event despite having suffered a military coup only two years previously, which meant some nations questioned their participation.

2   Cesar Luis Menotti

3   Willie Johnston

4   Iran or Tunisia

5   Clive Thomas

6   Archie Gemmill

7   France and Hungary arrived at the stadium for their group match with very similar kits, so the officials ordered France to wear the shirts of the local team.

8   Austria

9   Arie Haan

10 Peru

11 The penalty shootout

12 Mario Kempes (6 goals)

13 Dick Nanninga

14 Osvaldo Ardiles

15 Daniel Bertoni

60 World Cup 1982

1   24

2   The Falklands War, given Argentina's presence in the tournament
3   Algeria
4   West Germany and Austria played out a 1-0 victory for the Germans ensuring both teams qualified for the next stage, so depriving Algeria. Subsequently FIFA decided to play all final group games simultaneously.
5   El Salvador
6   Bryan Robson
7   The youngest player to appear at the finals, aged 17 years and 41 days
8   David Narey
9   Valencia
10 0-0
11 Paulo Rossi
12 Harald Schumacher
13 Santiago Bernabéu Stadium, Madrid
14 Marco Tardelli
15 Dino Zoff (Aged 40)

61 World Cup 1986

1   Colombia
2   Sir Alex Ferguson
3   Pat Jennings
4   The Mexican Wave
5   Denmark
6   Morocco
7   Algeria
8   Gary Lineker
9   Belgium
10 Peter Shilton
11 Peter Beardsley, Peter Reid, Terry Butcher and Terry Fenwick
12 France

13 Carlos Billardo and Franz Beckenbauer

14 Napoli

15 Jorge Burruchaga

62 World Cup 1990

1   Sir Bobby Robson

2   Salvatore Schillaci

3   Cameroon

4   Republic of Ireland, the Netherlands and Egypt

5   Andreas Brehme from the penalty spot in the 85th minute

6   Stuart Pearce and Chris Waddle

7   Yugoslavia

8   Costa Rica

9   Cagliari (Sardinia) and Palermo (Sicily)

10   They got there without winning a match (three draws followed by a penalty shootout win).

11   He became the first player to be sent off in a World Cup final.

12   Stuart McCall and Maurice Johnston

13   It was the first goal Italy had conceded in the tournament (in their sixth match)

14   Jack Charlton

15   Franz Beckenbauer

63 World Cup 1994

1   The World Cup was decided by penalty kicks (Brazil won 3-2).

2   Highest average attendance at the finals matches – 69,000

3   He was expelled after failing a drugs test

4   Andrés Escobar

5   Bulgaria

6   Dunga

7   He scored a record five goals in one match v Cameroon.

8   All four teams finished level on four points with a goal difference of 0.

9 Ray Houghton

10 Saudi Arabia

11 Roger Milla, aged 42

12 'Rocking the baby' in celebration of the birth of Bebeto's new born son, Mattheus

13 It was the first match to be played indoors in World Cup history.

14 Jack Charlton and John Aldridge

15 Wear coloured jerseys

64 World Cup 1998

1 John Collins

2 Lens

3 Davor Suker (Croatia)

4 Paul Durkin (England) and Hugh Dallas (Scotland)

5 Michael Laudrup

6 Iran won 2-1.

7 Romania

8 Alan Shearer, Paul Merson and Michael Owen

9 David Beckham

10 He scored the 'golden goal' in extra time to end the match and send France through.

11 Stade de France

12 Denis Bergkamp

13 Ronaldo. He was omitted from the original starting line-up, only to be reinstated 45 minutes prior to kick-off.

14 Croatia

15 Zinedine Zidane (2) and Emmanuel Petit

65 World Cup 2002

1 Japan and South Korea

2 Senegal

3 Brazil and Spain

4   Roy Keane returned home following a quarrel with manager, Mick McCarthy.

5   He controversially disallowed two Spain 'goals' in their quarter-final defeat to hosts, South Korea.

6   Bora Milutinovic (who coached China in 2002)

7   Turkey

8   David Beckham with a penalty in a 1-0 victory

9   Ronaldinho

10 Germany and Spain

11 Michael Ballack

12 He scored the fastest ever goal in World Cup finals history, 10.8 seconds for Turkey v South Korea.

13 Pierluigi Collina

14 Four times – 1966, 1982, 1986 and 2002

15 Ronaldo

66 World Cup 2006

1   Germany and Costa Rica, with Germany winning 4-2

2   Trinidad and Tobago

3   Sweden

4   Germany, Brazil, Argentina, England, France, Italy, France, Spain and Mexico

5   Switzerland

6   Ghana

7   Serbia and Montenegro

8   Portugal and the Netherlands

9   Graham Poll

10 Leipzig

11 Owen Hargreaves

12 Germany's Miroslav Klose with five goals

13 Zinedine Zidane for headbutting Marco Materazzi

14 David Trezeguet

15 Fabio Cannavaro

67 World Cup 2010

1 Leopard
2 Soccer City and Ellis Park
3 New Zealand, who had three draws in the group stages and were eliminated
4 France
5 Clint Dempsey
6 Jermain Defoe
7 Serbia
8 Barcelona with 13 players
9 Luis Saurez
10 Manuel Neuer
11 Thomas Muller, David Villa, Wesley Sneider and Diego Forlan
12 The vuvuzela
13 Theirs was the first squad to include three siblings – Jerry, Johnny and Wilson Palacios.
14 Howard Webb
15 Andres Iniesta

68 Which Nationality?

1 Oman
2 Bermuda
3 Costa Rica
4 New Zealand
5 South Africa
6 Benin
7 Mexico
8 Trinidad and Tobago
9 Togo
10 Belgium

11 Uruguay

12 Georgia

13 Portugal

14 Argentina

15 Liberia

69 Spanish Players in Britain

1   Ivan Campo

2   Cesc Fabregas

3   Villarreal

4   Michu

5   21

6   Juan Mata

7   Roberto Martinez

8   Liverpool and Chelsea

9   David de Gea

10 Xabi Alonso

11 £50m

12 Aston Villa

13 Nayim

14 Mikel Arteta

15 Newcastle United

70 Italian Players in Britain

1   Fabrizio Ravanelli

2   Why Always Me

3   Chelsea and Tottenham

4   Benito Carbone

5   Roberto di Matteo

6   Sheffield Wednesday, West Ham and Charlton

7   Massimo Taibi

8   Fabio Borini

9   Marco Materazzi
10 Gianfranco Zola
11 Real Madrid
12 Leicester City
13 Attilo Lombardo
14 Blackburn Rovers
15 Gianluca Vialli

71 German Players in Britain

1   Michael Ballack
2   Thomas Hitzlsperger
3   A dive to the ground
4   Chelsea, Middlesbrough and Stoke City
5   Brentford
6   Dietmar Hamann (England 0 Germany 1)
7   Alavés
8   Steffen Freund
9   Jens Lehmann
10 Lewis Holtby
11 Hamburg
12 Owen Hargreaves
13 Bert Trautmann
14 Christian Ziege
15 Lukas Podolski

72 French Players in Britain

1   Djibril Cissé
2   Arsenal, Liverpool, Man City, Bolton, Chelsea and West Bromwich Albion
3   Fabien Barthez and Laurent Blanc
4   Patrick Vieira and Emmanuel Petit
5   Olivier Dacourt

6 15
7 Newcastle Utd, Fulham, Man Utd, Everton, Tottenham and Sunderland
8 £25m
9 Chelsea, Arsenal and Tottenham
10 Lille
11 Marcel Desailly
12 Portsmouth and Everton
13 Eight (2003–2011)
14 Patrice Evra
15 Kevin Keegan

73 Scandinavian Players in Britain
1 Sami Hyypia
2 Bolton Wanderers and West Ham Utd
3 Ron Atkinson in 1984
4 Jan Molby
5 Aston Villa, Tottenham, Liverpool and Wimbledon
6 Seb Larsson
7 Fulham
8 Peter and Kasper Schmeichel
9 Thomas Sorensen
10 Olof Mellberg
11 Barcelona
12 Shefki Kuqi
13 Henning Berg with Blackburn and Man Utd
14 Thomas Gravesen
15 Thomas Brolin

74 Eastern European Players in Britain
1 Georgiou Kinkladze
2 Tottenham, Man Utd and Fulham

3 Luka Modric
4 Slaven Bilic
5 Rennes
6 Stiliyan Petrov
7 Milan Baros
8 Barnsley
9 Bradford City
10 Andrei Kanchelskis
11 Branislav Ivanovic
12 Nemanja Vidic
13 Temuri Ketsbaia
14 Jerzy Dudek
15 AC Milan

75 South American Players in Britain

1 QPR
2 He jumped into the crowd to punch a fan who had been abusing him.
3 West Ham Utd
4 Uruguay
5 David Luiz
6 1978 with Argentina
7 Faustino Asprilla
8 Manchester United and Chelsea
9 Carlos Tevez
10 Peru
11 Ajax Amsterdam
12 Antonio Valencia
13 Gilberto Silva
14 Deportivo La Coruna
15 Rafael and Fabio

76 The Far East, Australia and Britain

1   Harry Kewell
2   Borussia Dortmund
3   Park Ji-Sung
4   Mark Bosnich
5   Arsenal, Fulham, West Brom and Cardiff City
6   Kevin Muscat
7   Tim Cahill
8   Craig Moore
9   Millwall, Blackburn Rovers, West Ham and Everton
10 Mark Schwarzer
11 China
12 Manchester City and Leicester City
13 Brett Emerton
14 Middlesbrough
15 Mark Viduka

77 American Players in Britain

1   Tim Howard
2   Clint Dempsey
3   Rangers, Sunderland and Man City
4   Brad Guzan
5   Landon Donovan
6   Brad Freidel
7   Roy Wegerle
8   Carlos Bocanegra
9   Brian McBride
10 Kasey Keller
11 Cobi Jones
12 Man Utd, Charlton Athletic, West Ham and Birmingham City
13 John Harkes
14 Football League Championship

15 Jay DeMerit

78 African Players in Britain

1 Chelsea and Manchester City
2 Ivory Coast
3 Nwankwo Kanu
4 Tony Yeboah
5 Kolo and Yaya
6 1984 (when winning on penalties v Roma)
7 Lauren
8 Bolton Wanderers and Charlton Athletic
9 Anzhi Makhachkala
10 Zaire (now the Democratic Republic of Congo)
11 Michael Essien
12 Emmanuel Adebayor
13 Papa Bouba Diop (Senegal)
14 Jay Jay Okocha
15 Steven Pienaar

79 Euros up to 1992

1 1960
2 Henri Delauney
3 Soviet Union and Yugoslavia
4 Spain
5 Third
6 Gerd Muller
7 Antonin Panenka
8 Italy (1-0)
9 Horst Hrubesch
10 Michel Platini with nine goals
11 Parc des Princes, Paris
12 Ray Houghton

13 Marco van Basten
14 CIS. Scotland beat them 3-0.
15 Denmark

80 Euro '96

1   Wembley, Old Trafford, Villa Park, Anfield, Elland Road, Hillsborough, City Ground and St James' Park
2   'Football Comes Home'.
3   The Provisional IRA claimed responsibility for detonating a bomb in the city centre which injured over 200 people and caused widespread damage.
4   'The Dentist's Chair' following photos that appeared in the press of the England team on a night out on their pre-tournament tour of Hong Kong
5   Shearer (2), Sheringham (2)
6   Patrick Kluivert scored a late consolation goal for the Netherlands v England and that took them through instead of Scotland.
7   Spain, Bulgaria and Rumania
8   Germany won 2-0
9   Portugal
10 David Seaman
11 Gareth Southgate
12 France and the Czech Republic
13 The golden goal (by Germany's Oliver Bierhoff)
14 Alan Shearer
15 Jurgen Klinsmann

81 Euro 2000–2012

1   Belgium and the Netherlands
2   Portugal
3   Abel Xavier
4   David Trezeguet

5 Switzerland and Croatia

6 Darius Vassell

7 Greece

8 Angelos Charisteas

9 Austria and Switzerland

10 Russia

11 Germany in the Ernst Happel Stadium, Vienna

12 Ukraine v France

13 Kiev

14 Mario Balotelli

15 They were the first international team to win three consecutive major tournaments (Euro 2008, World Cup 2010 and Euro 2012).

82 UEFA Champions League Finals

1 Marseille

2 Ajax

3 Gianluca Vialli

4 Andy Cole

5 Real Madrid

6 Bayer Leverkuson

7 AS Monaco

8 Rafael Benitez

9 Sol Campbell

10 Filippo Inzaghi

11 Moscow

12 Edwin van der Sar

13 None

14 Wembley Stadium

15 Jose Bosingwa

83 European Cup Finals

1 1956

2   Alfredo Di Stefano

3   All of them

4   Paddy Crerand

5   Ajax

6   Leeds United

7   1977

8   Peter Shilton

9   Phil Thompson

10 Tony Barton

11 Juventus

12 Porto

13 AC Milan

14 Red Star Belgrade

15 Barcelona

84 European Cup Winners Cup 1961–1999

1   Barcelona

2   Rangers

3   Tottenham Hotspur

4   Jim Standen

5   Peter Osgood

6   Ian Bowyer

7   Real Madrid

8   Rangers

9   Don Revie

10 West Ham United

11 Howard Kendall

12 Aberdeen

13 Arsenal

14 Gianfranco Zola

15 Lazio

85 UEFA Cup Finals

1   Alan Mullery
2   The first leg was abandoned after 27 minutes because of a waterlogged pitch and was replayed the next day.
3   Bill Nicholson
4   Kevin Keegan
5   Dutch
6   Tottenham Hotspur
7   Real Madrid
8   Italy
9   Bayern Munich
10 Inter Milan
11 David Seaman
12 Alaves
13 Mark Schwarzer
14 Fulham
15 Amsterdam

86 Women's Football

1   Sweden
2   Arsenal Ladies
3   Kelly Smith
4   Marta
5   Germany and USA
6   Birgit Prinz
7   Wolfsburg
8   Spain
9   FA Women's Super League
10 Mia Hamm and Abby Wambach
11 The English Football Association
12 Everton
13 Germany

14 The 1999 World Cup final in which the USA beat China beat on penalties

15 The UEFA Women's Cup (now called the UEFA Women's Champions League)

87 Other Tournaments

1 The Maracana Stadium, Rio de Janeiro
2 The winners of the Premier League and the winners of the FA Cup
3 FA Trophy
4 2000
5 Uruguay
6 Lazio
7 Corinthinians
8 Africa Cup of Nations. He scored the only goal in the final v Burkino Faso.
9 The Welsh Premier League
10 FA Vase
11 Celtic (36 victories up to 2013)
12 Le Tournoi
13 Tahiti
14 Atletico Madrid
15 Associate Members Cup

88 England Managers

1 Manchester United
2 1961–1962
3 Joe Mercer
4 29
5 Viv Anderson
6 Glenn Hoddle
7 Elton John
8 James Hazell

9   John Gorman

10 Hamburger SV

11 David Beckham

12 Lazio

13 Scott Carson

14 Bobby Moore

15 Finland

89 England Captains

1   Cuthbert Ottaway (v Scotland 30/11/1872)

2   Billy Wright and Bobby Moore (90 games)

3   Bryan Robson

4   Emlyn Hughes

5   48

6   Ron Flowers

7   Eddie (Edris) Hapgood, give a Nazi salute

8   Tony Adams

9   Johnny Haynes

10 Peter Shilton

11 It was the first full England international at the 'new' Wembley

12 Jimmy Armfield

13 Scunthorpe United

14 Ray Wilkins (v Morocco in 1986)

15 Alan Shearer

90 English Legends

1   Tom Finney

2   Frank Swift

3   Vivian Woodward

4   Ted Drake

5   Duncan Edwards

6   Stan Mortensen

7 Tommy Lawton

8 Johnny Haynes

9 Raich Carter

10 Eddie Hapgood

11 Billy Wright

12 Wilf Mannion

13 Stanley Matthews

14 Cliff Bastin

15 Stephen Bloomer

91 Scotland National Managers

1 Andrew Beattie

2 71

3 Celtic

4 Ally MacLeod

5 Andy Roxburgh

6 Dawson Walker

7 Willie Ormond

8 9

9 1980

10 USA

11 Birmingham City

12 Ipswich Town

13 Bertie Vogts, West Germany 1974

14 Ferguson

15 Bobby Brown

92 Scotland Captains (by initials)

1 George Young

2 Billy Bremner

3 Gary McAllister

4 Barry Ferguson

5 Graeme Souness
6 Roy Aitken
7 Archie Gemmill
8 Colin Hendry
9 Paul Lambert
10 John Greig
11 Danny McGrain
12 Tommy Docherty
13 Alex McLeish
14 Kenny Dalglish
15 Frank McLintock

93 Great Scots

1 Dave Mackay
2 Jimmy Johnstone
3 Denis Law
4 David Cooper
5 John Robertson
6 Ally McCoist
7 Gordon Strachan
8 Ian St John
9 Alan Hansen
10 Alex James
11 Sandy Jardine
12 Hughie Gallacher
13 Billy McNeil
14 Andy Goram
15 Jim Baxter

94 Northern Ireland Managers

1 Billy Bingham
2 Lawrie Sanchez

3   Peter Doherty
4   Norwich City
5   1976
6   Danny Blanchflower
7   34
8   David Healy
9   Bertie Peacock
10 Dave Clements
11 Ecuador
12 Everton
13 England 8 - 3 Northern Ireland
14 Bryan Hamilton
15 1996

95 Northern Ireland Legends

1   Sammy Nelson
2   Gerry Armstrong
3   Martin O'Neill
4   Mal Donaghy
5   Iain Dowie
6   Chris Nicholl
7   Terry Neill
8   Maik Taylor
9   David Healy
10 Keith Gillespie
11 Jim Magilton
12 Pat Jennings
13 David McCreery
14 Jimmy Nicholl
15 Allan Hunter

96 Wales National Managers

1 Walley Barnes
2 27th
3 Tottenham Hotspur
4 1958
5 7
6 Bobby Gould
7 Terry Yorath
8 Swansea City
9 Craig Bellamy
10 Larissa
11 Mike Smith
12 Northampton Town
13 John Toshack, against Scotland in 1979
14 Trevor Morris
15 Mike England

97 Welsh Wizards

1 Ian Rush
2 Leighton James
3 Ryan Giggs
4 Peter Nicholas
5 Dean Saunders
6 Mark Hughes
7 John Charles
8 Andy Melville
9 Joey Jones
10 Ivor Allchurch
11 Kevin Radcliffe
12 Robert Earnshaw
13 Dai Davies
14 Clayton Blackmore

15 Craig Bellamy

98 Republic of Ireland Players

1   Robbie Keane
2   Kevin Kilbane
3   Steve Staunton
4   Niall Quinn
5   Tony Cascarino
6   Paul McGrath
7   John O'Shea
8   Packie Bonner
9   Ray Houghton
10 Richard Dunne
11 Kevin Moran
12 Frank Stapleton
13 Roy Keane
14 Andy Townsend
15 Don Givens

7
Half-Time Entertaiment

99 Football and the UK singles chart
1 Del Amitri
2 'Diamond Lights'
3 Lonnie Donegan
4 'Smokie'
5 'Back Home' by the 1970 England World Cup Squad
6 Keith Allen
7 1981
8 Everton
9 'Three Lions' by Baddiel and Skinner and The Lightning Seeds
10 Number 68
11 Brian Moore
12 Middlesbrough
13 Manchester United and with Status Quo with 'Come On You
   Reds' in 1994
14 Yeovil Town with 'Yeovil True'
15 'Blue Is The Colour' by Chelsea

100 Football on Film
1 Colm Meaney
2 *Escape to Victory*
3 Arsenal
4 *Bend It like Beckham*
5 *The Ball of Fortune*
6 Jackie Collins
7 *When Saturday Comes*
8 Ken Loach
9 *The Love Match*

10 Brian Glover

11 Hull City

12 George Allison

13 Clare Grogan

14 Mike Bassett

15 *Those Glory Glory Days*

101 Great Football Books

1   Hunter Davies

2   Nick Hornby

3   Eamon Dunphy

4   David Peace

5   Arthur Hopcroft

6   Simon Kuper

7   David Winner

8   Brian Clough

9   Desmond Morris

10 David McVay

11 Ronald Reng

12 Rogan Taylor and Andrew Ward

13 Tony Adams

14 Pete Davies

15 Brian Glanville

102 1970s Entertainers

1   Stan Bowles

2   Frank Worthington

3   Rodney Marsh

4   Tony Currie

5   Keith Weller

6   Duncan McKenzie

7   Liam Brady

8   Alan Hudson

9   Trevor Francis

10 Terry Mancini

11 Derek Dougan

12 Francis Lee

13 Peter Osgood

14 Trevor Brooking

15 Charlie George

103 Celebrity Supporters 1

1   Crewe Alexandra

2   Chelsea

3   Sunderland

4   Huddersfield Town

5   West Bromwich Albion

6   Swansea City

7   Liverpool

8   Manchester United

9   Newcastle United

10 Arsenal

11 Fulham

12 Brighton and Hove Albion

13 Celtic

14 West Ham United

15 Southend United

104 Celebrity Supporters 2

1   Fulham

2   Port Vale

3   Tottenham Hotspur

4   Sheffield United

5   Swindon Town

6 Manchester City

7 Norwich City

8 Arsenal

9 Middlesbrough

10 QPR

11 Barnsley

12 Bristol City

13 Birmingham City

14 Blackburn Rovers

15 Crystal Palace

105 Match of the Day – True or False

1 True

2 False

3 True

4 True

5 False

6 True

7 True

8 False

9 True

10 True

11 True

12 False

13 True

14 False

15 False

106 Quotes of the 1970s

1 Alan Ball (1970)

2 Rodney Marsh (1971)

3 Pat Saward, Brighton manager (1972)

4   Barry Davies (1972)

5   Terry Venables (1973)

6   Bill Shankly (1973)

7   Bob Stokoe (1973)

8   Eric Morecambe (1974)

9   Malcolm Allison (1975)

10 David Coleman (1976)

11 Malcolm Macdonald (1976)

12 Brian Clough (1977)

13 Tommy Docherty (1977)

14 John Toshack (1978)

15 Don Revie (1979)

107 British Goalkeepers

1   Dave Beasant

2   Jim Leighton

3   Jack Kelsey

4   Gordon Banks

5   Peter Shilton

6   Neville Southall

7   Joe Hart

8   Pat Jennings

9   Ray Clemence

10 David Seaman

11 Nigel Spink

12 David James

13 William 'Fatty' Foulke

14 Paul Robinson

15 Ron Springett

108 British Transfer Records

1   Alf Common

2   Sunderland
3   Notts County
4   £100,000
5   Martin Peters
6   Hamburg
7   Brian Clough
8   £300,000
9   7
10 €100m (around £85m)
11 Dennis Bergkamp
12 Stan Collymore
13 Bournemouth
14 Jose Mourinho
15 24

109 Club Nicknames 1 (England)

1   Southend United
2   The Shrimps
3   The stadium was built on a cherry tree orchard
4   Tamworth, named after a local pub
5   The Monkey Hangers
6   Sheffield Wednesday
7   Bury (JT Ingham in 1892 during the club's Lancashire Senior Cup success)
8   Charlton Athletic
9   The Tangerines
10 Huddersfield Town 'The Terriers'
11 Millwall v Hull City
12 The Bantams
13 Crystal Palace, 'The Eagles'
14 The Bees
15 Northampton Town, due to the local shoemaking industry

110 Club Nicknames 2 (Scotland, Wales and Northern Ireland)

1   Celtic
2   The Jags
3   Berwick Rangers
4   The Gers
5   Airbus UK Broughton
6   River Bann (The Bannsiders)
7   Bangor
8   Hamilton Academical
9   The Dons
10 St Mirren
11 The Bluebirds
12 Glentoran v Crusaders
13 Hearts
14 Diamonds
15 The Ironsides

111 Club Nicknames (Overseas)

1   St Etienne
2   The Peasants (Boeren)
3   Real Madrid
4   Lions (Aslanlar)
5   The Red Devils (Manchester United)
6   AC Milan
7   Napoli
8   Chievo
9   The Canaries
10 Juventus
11 Corinthians
12 False – Santos are known as The Fish.
13 Paris St Germain

14 Bayern Munich

15 The Miners

112 Footballing Brians

1 Brian Moore

2 Brian Clough

3 Brian Kilcline

4 Brian Little

5 Brian Kidd

6 Brian McDermott

7 Brian Talbot

8 Bryan Robson

9 Brian Laws

10 Brian Horton

11 Brian Howard

12 Brian Flynn

13 Brian Laudrup

14 Brian Hall

15 Brian Greenhoff

113 Mascots

1 Aberdeen

2 Manchester United

3 Swansea City

4 Fulham

5 Arsenal

6 Celtic

7 West Ham United

8 Bristol City

9 Hartlepool

10 Rangers

11 Leeds United

12 Southend United

13 Millwall

14 Walsall

15 Plymouth Argyle

8

Second Half: Match of the Day Memories

114 David Coleman

1 1926
2 The Stockport Express
3 *Grandstand*
4 Princess Anne
5 6
6 *Sportsnight with Coleman*
7 1960
8 Athletics
9 The Beatles
10 1973
11 'Colemanballs'
12 *A Question of Sport*
13 Sydney 2000
14 The Grand National
15 None

115 1964–1965

1 John White
2 Alan Ball
3 Wolverhampton Wanderers
4 Leicester City
5 Danny Blanchflower
6 50
7 Birmingham City
8 It was the day of Sir Winston Churchill's state funeral.
9 Munich 1860
10 Bill Shankly

11 434
12 Leeds United
13 Newcastle United
14 Andy McEvoy
15 57

116 1965–1966

1 Manchester United
2 Tony Hateley
3 Liverpool
4 Mixed breed Collie
5 Blackburn Rovers
6 Bobby Charlton
7 Northampton Town
8 Joe Mercer
9 Geoff Hurst
10 Wolverhampton Wanderers.
11 Derek Temple
12 West Bromwich Albion
13 He became the first substitute to be used in the Football League.
14 9
15 Martin Peters

117 1966–1967

1 Chelsea
2 David Herd
3 Everton
4 Southampton
5 Alec Stock
6 Lisbon
7 Bobby Tambling
8 Dave Mackay

9   Vancouver Royals
10 Nottingham Forest
11 Scotland
12 Hartlepool United
13 Coventry City
14 Stoke City
15 Tony Adams

118 1967–1968

1   David Coleman
2   Alex Stepney
3   West Bromwich Albion
4   Dave Sexton
5   Sheffield United
6   Francis Lee
7   Leeds United
8   Benfica
9   £125,000
10 West Bromwich Albion
11 Malcolm Allison
12 Dunfermline Athletic
13 George Best
14 Ipswich Town
15 The Rover's Return pub side who appeared in a match in
    Coronation Street.

119 1968–1969

1   Clarke
2   Sunderland
3   13
4   Swindon Town
5   Neil Young

6 Cyprus
7 Ian St. John
8 Derby County
9 Billy Bremner
10 Fulham
11 On The Ball
12 Newcastle United
13 Wilf McGuinness
14 50p
15 AC Milan

120 1969–1970
1 David Coleman
2 Sandy Brown
3 Jimmy Greaves
4 Celtic
5 Barry Endean
6 Harry Catterick
7 Fourth
8 Manchester City
9 Aston Villa
10 Anderlecht
11 Ron Harris
12 David Vine
13 Swansea
14 Cambridge United
15 Bobby Charlton

121 1970–1971
1 Bertie Mee
2 Willie Carr
3 Bournemouth and Boscombe Athletic

4   Real Madrid
5   Martin Chivers
6   Colchester United
7   Blackpool
8   Mick Jones
9   Frank McLintock
10   Eddie Kelly
11   Scunthorpe United
12   Frank O'Farrell
13   Leeds United
14   Tony Brown
15   Leicester City

122 1971–1972

1   John Motson
2   Luxembourg
3   Peter Lorimer
4   Derby County
5   Stoke City
6   Ron Saunders
7   Ricky George
8   The Watney Cup
9   Hibernian
10   UEFA Cup
11   George Best
12   Arsenal
13   Willie Johnston
14   Francis Lee
15   On holiday in the Isles of Scilly

123 1972–1973

1   Martin Peters

2 Emlyn Hughes
3 Tommy Docherty
4 Queens Park Rangers
5 Ralph Coates
6 Jim Montgomery
7 Retired
8 Borussia Moenchengladbach
9 Malcolm Allison
10 USSR
11 Hereford United
12 6th place
13 Ajax
14 West Bromwich Albion
15 'Pop' Robson

124 1973–1974
1 Jimmy Hill
2 David Harvey
3 Arsenal
4 Chelsea
5 29
6 The Welsh FA Cup
7 Jan Tomaszewski
8 Denis Law
9 113
10 Mick Channon
11 Sam Longson
12 Carlisle United
13 6
14 Wolverhampton Wanderers
15 Brendan Foster

125 1974–1975

1 Bob Paisley

2 44

3 Dave Mackay

4 5-4

5 Aston Villa

6 Alan Taylor

7 Football Focus

8 Rangers

9 Bayern Munich

10 7th

11 Stockport County

12 Mick Walsh

13 5

14 Huddersfield Town

15 Bill Nicholson

126 1975–1976

1 QPR

2 Mike Doyle

3 Five Million

4 John Toshack

5 Birmingham City

6 One

7 Jock Wallace

8 Bobby Stokes

9 Terry Neill

10 Bayern Munich

11 Steve Heighway

12 Ten

13 31

14 Sunderland

15 11th in Division Two

127 1976–1977
1   Brighton and Hove Albion
2   Aberdeen
3   David Wagstaff
4   Gordon Lee
5   Genesis
6   Manchester City
7   John Yates
8   Old Trafford
9   Manchester United
10 £500,000
11 Keith Burkinshaw
12 Andy Gray
13 Sammy Chung
14 3-1
15 Crystal Palace

128 1977–1978
1   Leeds United
2   Nottingham Forest
3   Ian Moores
4   Blythe Spartans
5   Chelsea
6   John Robertson
7   Ipswich Town
8   Ron Greenwood
9   Wembley Stadium
10 Herbert Chapman (Huddersfield Town and Arsenal)
11 They were all penalties
12 Wigan Athletic

13 Bob Latchford
14 Its 500th edition
15 20

129 1978–1979

1   Club Atletico Huracan
2   Chelsea
3   Czechoslovakia
4   David Mills
5   15
6   Brian Talbot
7   Clive Allen
8   Tiger and Scorcher
9   Billy McNeill
10 Assistant Manager, Peter Taylor
11 Alan Sunderland
12 Kevin Keegan
13 Brighton and Hove Albion
14 42
15 Chester City

130 1979–1980

1   Manchester City
2   Billy Bonds
3   Justin Fashanu
4   Newport County
5   Burnley
6   Desmond Lynam
7   SV Hamburg
8   60
9   Peter Shilton
10 Derby County

11 Dave Sexton

12 Secretary of the Football League

13 Aberdeen

14 Glenn Hoddle

15 David Johnson

131 1980–1981

1 Sunday afternoons

2 Crystal Palace

3 Tottenham Hotspur

4 14

5 Ipswich Town

6 West Ham United

7 Geoff Hurst

8 Southampton

9 Tommy Hutchison

10 Frans Thijssen, Ipswich Town

11 Clive Allen

12 Ron Atkinson

13 Swansea City

14 Ron Saunders

15 Southend United

132 1981–1982

1 Swansea City

2 Jimmy Hill

3 West Bromwich Albion

4 2

5 Ipswich Town

6 Kevin Keegan

7 The Milk Cup

8 Peter Withe

9 QPR
10 QPR
11 Cyrille Regis
12 Preston North End
13 Watford
14 *Boys from the Blackstuff*
15 Bobby Robson

133 1982–1983

1 Newcastle United
2 Ian Rush
3 Bob Paisley
4 Raddy Antic
5 Thames Valley Royals
6 Watford
7 Aberdeen
8 John Benson
9 Gordon Smith
10 Dundee United
11 Gary Lineker
12 Joe Fagan
13 Mark Chamberlain
14 Frank Stapleton
15 Wimbledon

134 1983–1984

1 Tottenham Hotspur
2 Alan Kennedy
3 Charlie Nicholas
4 Coventry City
5 Tony Woodcock
6 Everton

7   33

8   Tony Parks

9   Harry Rednapp

10 Elton John

11 Alex Ferguson

12 Kenny Dalglish

13 45

14 Chelsea

15 Runners-up in Division One

135 1984–1985

1   AC Milan

2   1912

3   Everton

4   Danish

5   Newcastle United

6   Kevin Ratcliffe

7   Stoke City

8   Peter Shreeves

9   John Aldridge

10 Kevin Moran

11 20 – 0

12 Norwich City

13 Kerry Dixon

14 George Graham

15 David Platt

136 1985–1986

1   Manchester United

2   Ian Wright

3   Alvin Martin

4   Oxford United

5 Kenny Dalglish

6 9

7 Craig Johnston

8 Wales

9 Swansea City

10 Graeme Souness

11 46

12 Gary Lineker

13 Ipswich Town

14 Don Howe

15 Barcelona

137 1986–1987

1 Ron Atkinson

2 Clive Allen

3 John Lukic

4 144

5 Luton Town

6 Athletic Bilbao

7 Gary Mabbutt

8 Charlton Athletic

9 Ruud Gullit

10 Sunderland

11 1959

12 Aston Villa

13 Matt Le Tissier

14 9

15 AS Monaco

138 1987–1988

1 Liverpool

2 Oxford United

3 Gillingham
4 Nigel Clough
5 Manchester United
6 Steve Bull
7 Chelsea
8 Stein
9 John Aldridge
10 Swindon Town
11 Frank McAvennie
12 Jimmy Hill
13 Neil McNab
14 Middlesbrough
15 Terry Venables

139 1988–1989
1 Desmond Lynam
2 Tottenham Hotspur
3 Tony Cottee
4 Jan Molby
5 9
6 Michael Thomas
7 Aberdeen
8 Sutton United
9 Wallace
10 West Ham United
11 Ronnie Whelan
12 Crystal Palace
13 Mo Johnston
14 George Graham
15 Leeds United

140 1989–1990

1   1925
2   Perry Suckling
3   Gary Lineker
4   Swindon Town
5   Derby County
6   Michael Knighton
7   Alan Ball
8   Oldham Athletic
9   PSV Eindhoven
10 Rangers
11 Ron Atkinson
12 Lee Martin
13 Aston Villa
14 Mick Quinn
15 Real Sociedad

141 1990–1991

1   Neville Southall
2   BBC Radio 5
3   12
4   Graham Taylor
5   Third
6   Gary Charles
7   18
8   John Sheridan
9   Johan Cruyff
10 Chelmsford
11 Everton
12 1953
13 Teddy Sheringham
14 Howard Kendall

15 Ryan Giggs

142 1991–1992

1   The FA Premier League

2   Barnet

3   Kevin Keegan

4   Aldershot

5   Arsenal

6   Kenny Dalglish

7   Hibernian

8   Lennie Lawrence

9   Nimes

10 Brian McClair

11 Luton Town

12 Des Walker

13 Sunderland

14 Japan

15 Trevor Francis

143 1992–1993

1   Alan Hansen

2   Green

3   Eric Cantona

4   3

5   Ronnie Rosenthal

6   Sheffield United

7   Southampton

8   Brian Kidd

9   David O'Leary

10 Brian Clough

11 Andy Linighan

12 90

13 Alan Sugar
14 Rangers
15 Roger Hunt

144 1993–1994

1   Swindon Town
2   Roy Evans
3   Renato Pagliari
4   Andy Cole
5   Endsleigh
6   Dean Saunders
7   Parma
8   Mike Walker
9   Chelsea
10 San Marino
11 Tim Flowers
12 Crystal Palace
13 Efan Ekoku
14 Manchester City
15 Dundee United

145 1994–1995

1   Jurgen Klinsmann
2   Jack Walker
3   Ipswich Town
4   Robbie Fowler
5   Nine months
6   Nottingham Forest
7   Nayim
8   Bolton Wanderers
9   Paul Merson
10 Joe Royle

11 Bryan Robson

12 Coventry City

13 Alan Shearer

14 Tony Yeboah

15 Chelsea

146 1995–1996

1   Alan Hansen

2   Mark McGhee

3   Newcastle United

4   Southampton

5   Nottingham Forest

6   Brian Little

7   Chris Kamara

8   Armani

9   Steve Lomas

10 1958

11 He became the first player to score 100 Premier League goals

12 Paul Gascoigne

13 Jean-Marc Bosman

14 Juninho

15 Tranmere Rovers

147 1996–1997

1   Gary Lineker

2   61 weeks

3   £15m

4   Neil Sullivan

5   Middlesbrough

6   Barnsley

7   Chesterfield

8   Kenny Dalglish

9   Roberto Di Matteo
10 Leeds United
11 Kilmarnock
12 Bury
13 Fenerbahce
14 Leicester City
15 Terry Venables

148 1997–1998
1   Teddy Sheringham
2   Ian Wright
3   Barnsley
4   David Pleat
5   Everton
6   Christian Gross
7   Chelsea
8   Michael Owen
9   Newcastle United
10 285
11 Macclesfield Town
12 Kevin Keegan
13 Manchester City
14 Pride Park
15 Bolton Wanderers

149 1998–1999
1   Charlton Athletic
2   David O'Leary
3   Robbie Fowler
4   Ole Gunnar Solskjaer
5   Barcelona
6   Tottenham Hotspur

7   Jimmy Glass
8   Ruud Gullit
9   Howard Wilkinson
10 Arsenal
11 Wimbledon
12 Tony Parkes
13 Dick Advocaat
14 Roy Keane
15 Bradford City

150 1999–2000
1   Gary Lineker
2   World Club Competition
3   PSV Eindhoven
4   Leeds United
5   Steffen Iversen
6   Real Madrid
7   18
8   The Worthington Cup
9   Wimbledon
10 Robbie Keane
11 Celtic
12 David Moyes
13 Chelsea
14 1923
15 Kevin Phillips

151 2000–2001
1   Claudio Ranieri
2   Sheffield Wednesday
3   Mark Viduka
4   Stoke City

5 Germany
6 Delfi Geli
7 Gerard Houllier
8 Everton
9 Marcus Stewart
10 22
11 Coventry City
12 Ruud van Nistelrooy
13 Rushton and Diamonds
14 Teddy Sheringham
15 Jean Tigana

152 2001–2002
1 Fabien Barthez
2 Frank Lampard
3 Sam Allardyce
4 France
5 Ruud Van Nistelrooy
6 John Motson
7 13
8 Andy Cole
9 Phil Thompson
10 Chelsea
11 Les Ferdinand
12 Airdreonians
13 Matthew Le Tissier
14 Dario Gradi
15 Manchester City

153 2002–2003
1 Terry Venables
2 Wayne Rooney

3 China

4 Sunderland

5 David Beckham

6 Jerzy Dudek

7 Trevor Brooking

8 Burnley

9 It was the first to be played indoors when the roof was closed.

10 Everton

11 Harry Rednapp

12 9,639

13 Paul Scholes

14 Wigan Athletic

15 Manchester City

154 2003–2004

1 Ken Bates

2 Doncaster Rovers

3 Sporting Lisbon

4 Middlesbrough

5 Wolverhampton Wanderers

6 Kevin Blackwell

7 Tim Howard

8 Rio Ferdinand

9 None

10 Gary Speed

11 Meadowbank Thistle

12 Thierry Henry

13 Crystal Palace

14 Gerard Houllier

15 Milton Keynes Dons

155 2004–2005

1   Adrian Chiles
2   Tottenham Hotspur
3   Nottingham Forest
4   Gabor Kiraly
5   Newcastle United, Sir Bobby Robson
6   Barry Davies
7   Harry Redknapp
8   Liverpool
9   15
10 1912
11 James Vaughan
12 Jose Reyes
13 Delia Smith
14 Andy Johnson
15 AC Milan

156 2005–2006

1   Celina Hinchcliffe
2   Southampton
3   Malcolm Glazer
4   Ghana
5   29
6   Michael Owen
7   Wigan
8   Alain Perrin
9   Jackie Milburn
10 Jose Mourinho
11 Gordon Strachan
12 Alan Curbishley
13 Arsenal
14 Pepe Reina

15 Reading

157 2006–2007
1 Benni McCarthy
2 Oxford United
3 Tottenham Hotspur
4 Reading
5 Moritz Volz
6 Les Reed
7 Cristiano Ronaldo
8 Sunderland
9 Watford
10 England U21's
11 3
12 Arsenal Ladies
13 Leeds United
14 Didier Drogba
15 Neil Warnock

158 2007–2008
1 Benjamin 'Benjani' Mwaruwari
2 Derby County
3 Juande Ramos
4 Gary Neville
5 Manchester City
6 Gareth Southgate
7 Nicolas Anelka
8 Gretna
9 Leicester City
10 Harry Redknapp
11 Tottenham Hotspur
12 Kevin Keegan

13 Queen of the South
14 Stoke City
15 Sweden

159 2008–2009

1 7
2 Manchester City
3 Ben Foster
4 Joe Kinnear
5 Aston Villa
6 Chelsea
7 Ricky Sbragia
8 Middlesbrough
9 Carlos Vela
10 Spanish
11 Louis Saha
12 Roy McFarland
13 Wolverhampton Wanderers
14 7th
15 Luton Town

160 2009–2010

1 Dan Walker
2 Wigan Athletic
3 Michael Owen
4 Brian Laws
5 Ryan Giggs
6 Portsmouth
7 Darren Bent
8 West Ham United
9 Jermain Defoe
10 Kevin-Prince Boateng

11 Motherwell
12 Juventus
13 Ian Holloway
14 Notts County
15 Tottenham Hotspur

9
'Fergie Time'

161 2010–2011

1 Blackburn Rovers

2 25

3 Obafemi Martins

4 Roy Hodgson

5 FC United of Manchester

6 Dimitar Berbatov

7 Proact Stadium

8 Newcastle United

9 Kevin Davies

10 QPR

11 Gus Poyet

12 Russia

13 Ipswich Town

14 Fernando Torres

15 Stoke City

162 2011–2012

1 Rangers

2 8

3 Wayne Rooney

4 Barcelona

5 Anthony Gerrard

6 Bosnian

7 Andy Carroll

8 Hibernian

9 Wolverhampton Wanderers

10 Sergio Aguero

11 Sunderland

12 Tottenham Hotspur

13 Brian McDermott

14 Didier Drogba

15 1930

163 2012–2013

1   Aston Villa

2   Newcastle United

3   Paris Saint – Germain

4   Ben Watson

5   Gareth Bale

6   Nigel Adkins

7   Danish

8   Branislav Ivanovic

9   Mark Hughes

10 Ally McCoist

11 Hull City

12 Martin Allen

13 Brian Kidd

14 Norwich City

15 1500

10
Extra Time

164 International Goalkeeping Legends
1   Peter Schmeichel
2   Walter Zenga
3   Oliver Kahn
4   Fabien Barthez
5   Pepe Reina
6   'Felix' Mielli Venerando
7   Peter Cech
8   Bert Trautmann
9   Bruce Grobbelaar
10 Sepp Maier
11 Hugo Lloris
12 Lev Yashin
13 Dino Zoff
14 Harald Schumacher
15 David de Gea

165 Modern Midlands Men
1   Steve Clarke
2   Andy Butler
3   Kevin Foley
4   Chris Coleman
5   Randy Lerner
6   Stephen Carr
7   Curtis Davies
8   Portuguese
9   Steve Bruce
10 Stale Solbakken

11 Seamus

12 Peter Osaze Odemwingle

13 Paul Merson

14 Nikola Zigic

15 Gary McSheffrey

166 The Wrong End of a Premier League Thrashing

1 Ipswich Town

2 Sheffield Wednesday

3 Wigan Athletic

4 Wigan Athletic

5 Aston Villa

6 Nottingham Forest

7 Barnsley

8 Nottingham Forest

9 Everton

10 Middlesbrough

11 Manchester City

12 Stoke City

13 Arsenal

14 Sunderland

15 Southampton

167 Random and Difficult Timeless Facts

1 A monsoon

2 Arbroath

3 Mick Harford

4 Tony Coton

5 40

6 Max Seeburg

7 Preston North End

8 Vinnie Jones

9   Wendy Toms
10 Robert 'Bunny' Bell
11 Torquay United
12 Southampton
13 Paul Cooper
14 Ivan Robinson
15 1974

168 Red Card Classics

1   Zinedine Zidane
2   Wayne Rooney
3   Kevin Moran
4   Francesco Totti
5   Ray Wilkins
6   Josep Simunic
7   Alan Mullery
8   Kieron Dyer
9   Rob Green
10 Luis Suarez
11 Jamie Carragher
12 Dean Windass
13 Antonio Rattin
14 Tim Flowers
15 Keith Gillespie

169 West Country Managers

1   Peter Shilton
2   Tony Pulis
3   Frank O'Farrell
4   Gerry Francis
5   Gary Johnson
6   Steve Coppell

7   Peter Reid

8   Mark McGhee

9   Neil Warnock

10 Leroy Rosenior

11 Joe Jordon

12 Billy Bingham

13 Terry Cooper

14 Paul Trollope

15 Malcolm Allison

170 Famous Chairmen

1   Manchester United

2   Manchester City

3   Barnet

4   Arsenal

5   Aston Villa

6   Tottenham Hotspur

7   Newcastle United

8   Watford

9   Wimbledon

10 Crystal Palace

11 Oxford United

12 Swansea City

13 Chelsea

14 Leeds United

15 Darlington

171 FA Cup Finals 1871–1949

1   Wanderers

2   Kennington Oval

3   Blackburn Rovers

4   Tottenham Hotspur

5 Crystal Palace
6 Newcastle United
7 1909
8 Bolton Wanderers
9 1927
10 Arsenal
11 Everton
12 Portsmouth
13 Bert Turner
14 Manchester United
15 Billy Wright

172 FA Cup Finals 1950–1979

1 Bob Paisley
2 Jackie Milburn
3 Bill Perry
4 Roy Dwight
5 Bill Nicholson
6 Preston North End
7 Ray Wilson
8 Jeff Astle
9 Joe Mercer
10 Old Trafford
11 Jim Montgomery
12 Kevin Keegan
13 Southampton
14 Arsenal
15 Alan Sunderland

173 FA Cup Finals 1980–2013

1 Trevor Brooking
2 Keith Burkinshaw

3　Watford
4　John Sillett
5　Dave Beasant
6　Paul Gascoigne
7　Manchester United
8　Newcastle United
9　Robert Pires
10 Dennis Wise
11 Liverpool
12 Didier Drogba
13 Nwankwo Kanu
14 Stoke City
15 Ashley Cole

174 League Cup Facts

1　Rotherham United
2　The Milk Marketing Board
3　1967
4　Oxford United
5　Ian Rush
6　Middlesbrough
7　Reading
8　Barry Venison
9　1969
10 Luton Town
11 Steve Morrow
12 Michael Laudrup
13 Steve Sutton
14 Tony Book
15 Sunderland

175 Referees

1 Pierluigi Collina
2 Paul Alcock
3 Spotting Diego Maradona's 'Hand of God' goal v England
4 Howard Webb
5 Take full control of an English Football League match. She took over the Coventry v Nottm Forest fixture for the final 20 minutes after starting referee Tony Bates got injured.
6 Accidentally knocking Robbie Savage to the floor when signalling for a free kick
7 Frank Lampard's disallowed over the line 'goal' v Germany
8 Urs Meier
9 Referee the World Cup Final
10 Clive Thomas
11 Graham Poll
12 Arthur Ellis
13 'Booking' the official when returning his dropped cards
14 Kim Milton Nielsen
15 Jack Taylor

11
Penalty Shootout

176 Franz Beckenbauer

1 Der Kaiser
2 1974
3 Bayern Munich
4 103
5 Atletico Madrid
6 SV Hamburg
7 1945
8 Hampden Park
9 Sepp Maier
10 1996
11 New York Cosmos
12 1990
13 Marseille
14 1966
15 Twice

177 David Beckham

1 17
2 Preston North End
3 Wimbledon
4 Glenn Hoddle
5 Gary Neville
6 Ali G
7 6
8 Diego Simeone
9 62
10 Real Madrid

11 4

12 Carlo Ancelotti

13 China

14 59

15 LA Galaxy

178 George Best

1 Belfast

2 Matt Busby

3 1963

4 Benfica

5 Denis Law

6 Wembley Stadium

7 Northampton Town

8 Angie

9 27

10 Fulham

11 37

12 Don Fardon

13 Hibernian

14 1968

15 Los Angeles Aztecs

179 Eric Cantona

1 Auxerre

2 Henri Michel

3 Marseille

4 Howard Wilkinson

5 Selhurst Park

6 6'2" or 188 cms

7 Steve Bruce

8 4

MATCH OF THE DAY QUIZ BOOK

9   20
10 Chelsea
11 David James
12 The French Beach Football Team
13 1996–1997
14 Elizabeth
15 New York Cosmos

180 Sir Bobby Charlton

1   Milburn
2   1958
3   Matt Busby
4   Harry Gregg
5   Portugal
6   A weather presenter on the BBC
7   1966
8   Bill Foulkes
9   Preston North End
10 His brother Jack
11 1962–1963
12 49
13 1994
14 Martin Buchan
15 758

181 Johan Cruyff

1   Amsterdam
2   Hendrik
3   Ajax
4   Total Football
5   33
6   14

7   Inter Milan

8   8

9   Jordi

10 Barcelona

11 3

12 Feyenoord

13 1974

14 Catalonia

15 Los Angeles Aztecs

182 Kenny Dalglish

1   Mathieson

2   102

3   Celtic

4   7

5   Tommy Docherty

6   Alan Hansen

7   Aston Villa and Graham Taylor

8   Everton

9   9

10 Jack Walker

11 Chelsea

12 Kevin Keegan

13 1978

14 Andy Carroll

15 2011–2012

183 Eusebio

1   1942

2   The Black Pearl

3   Eusebio da Silva Ferreira

4   Mozambique

5   41
6   Benfica
7   11
8   4
9   Real Madrid
10 England
11 745
12 1965
13 Manchester United
14 1979
15 Sir Garry Sobers

184 Ryan Giggs

1   Cardiff
2   England
3   Everton
4   13
5   2009
6   64
7   Ryan Giggs' Soccer Skills
8   Sir Bobby Charlton
9   Wes Brown
10 Norway
11 It was his 900th appearance for Manchester United
12 2010
13 Roy Keane
14 Arsenal
15 Mal Donaghy

185 Thierry Henry

1   Monaco
2   Juventus

3   Ian Wright

4   32

5   Barcelona

6   14

7   Aime Jacquet

8   2003–2004

9   51

10 Southampton

11 Josep Guardiola

12 Republic of Ireland

13 2012

14 Italy

15 New York Red Bulls

186 Frank Lampard

1   Stewart Robson

2   Harry Redknapp

3   1995

4   Swansea City

5   Aston Villa

6   £11m

7   Bobby Tambling

8   2003

9   Portugal

10 Everton

11 2005–2006

12 Bayern Munich

13 2

14 Kevin Keegan

15 Branislav Ivanovic

187 Denis Law

1 Aberdeen
2 Dennis Bergkamp
3 Huddersfield Town
4 £55,000
5 The match was abandoned because of a waterlogged pitch
6 Torino
7 30
8 Leicester City
9 1964
10 1967
11 A knee injury
12 Tommy Docherty
13 404
14 The Rest of the World
15 Manchester United

188 Diego Maradona

1 1960
2 Argentinos Juniors
3 1977
4 £5m
5 Cesar Luis Menotti
6 1986
7 Napoli
8 15 months
9 Stuttgart
10 1994
11 Peter Shilton
12 West Germany
13 Argentina
14 Al-Wasl

15 Pele

189 Lionel Messi

1   1987
2   Leo
3   Newell's Old Boys
4   Frank Rijkaard
5   24
6   2006
7   19
8   TIME
9   Manchester United
10 His left foot
11 73
12 10
13 Germany
14 2008
15 6

190 Bobby Moore

1   Barking, Essex
2   1941
3   Ted Fenton
4   Peru
5   22
6   Preston North End
7   Wembley Stadium
8   2
9   Uwe Seeler
10 Danny La Rue
11 A bracelet
12 Pele

13 106
14 1975
15 Capital Gold

191 Pele

1   Edson Arantes do Nascimento
2   17
3   Santos
4   Czechoslovakia
5   It was his 1,000th senior goal
6   92
7   77
8   1997
9   New York Cosmos
10 Carlos Alberto
11 10
12 Edinburgh University
13 3
14 1971
15 Mike Bassett, England Manager

192 Ronaldo

1   Ronaldo Luis Nazario de Lima
2   1976
3   2 (1994 and 2002)
4   Cruzeiro
5   PSV Eindhoven
6   62
7   3
8   Barcelona
9   Ronaldinho
10 Inter Milan

11 Manchester United

12 He was omitted from the team sheet issued before kickoff apparently due to illness. Ronaldo's name then appeared on a resubmitted list and he was allowed to play.

13 They were all penalties

14 Corinthians

15 15, Gerd Muller

193 Cristiano Ronaldo

1   Madeira

2   Tachycardia, a racing heart

3   Spain

4   Lionel Messi

5   Sporting Lisbon

6   £80m

7   Euro 2004

8   Alfredo Di Stefano

9   Andrew Cole

10 3

11 Winking towards the Portuguese bench

12 False, he missed United's 3rd kick

13 Northern Ireland

14 Sir Alex Ferguson

15 CR7

194 Ian Rush

1   Chester City

2   Bob Paisley

3   346

4   Oulun Palloseura

5   Tottenham Hotspur

6   47

7   Juventus

8   5

9   A Rhino

10 Everton

11 Faroe Islands

12 Roy Evans

13 Wrexham

14 Sydney

15 Chester City

195 Alan Shearer

1   1988

2   Jimmy Greaves

3   Ian Branfoot

4   Chris Sutton

5   1994–1995

6   31

7   France

8   30

9   £15m

10 Ruud Gullit

11 Jackie Milburn

12 Glenn Roeder

13 Sport Relief

14 Joe Kinnear

15 34

196 Peter Shilton

1   1949

2   Leicester City

3   125

4   Southampton

5   1969
6   Sir Alf Ramsey
7   £325,000
8   Nottingham Forest
9   Diego Maradona
10 Derby County
11 1977–1978
12 Leyton Orient
13 Plymouth Argyle
14 15
15 Gordon Banks

12
Post-Match Analysis

197 Alan Hansen

1 Partick Thistle
2 1992
3 £110,000
4 8
5 1995–1996
6 *Bend It like Beckham*
7 26
8 Kenny Dalglish
9 Golf
10 14
11 Trevor Brooking
12 Spain, 1982
13 Roma
14 1989–1990
15 Everton

198 Mark Lawrenson

1 Bobby Charlton
2 Brighton and Hove Albion
3 £900,000
4 Ian Rush
5 Republic of Ireland
6 John Motson
7 Bolton Wanderers
8 30
9 Kevin Maxwell
10 5

11 356

12 Tampa Bay Rowdies

13 Peterborough United

14 Ray Stubbs

15 Newcastle United

199 Voices of Football on BBC Radio

1 Alan Green

2 Alan Parry

3 David Oates

4 Simon Brotherton

5 Peter Drury

6 Jonathan Pearce

7 Archie Macpherson

8 Mike Ingham

9 Maurice Edelston

10 Conor McNamara

11 Peter Jones

12 Raymond Glendenning

13 Bryon Butler

14 John Murray

15 James Alexander Gordon

200 Footballers and Sports Personality of the Year

1 Bobby Charlton of Manchester United

2 2001

3 World Speedway Champion, Barry Briggs

4 Fog on the Tyne (Revisited)

5 Ronaldo, Brazil

6 Arsene Wenger, Arsenal

7 1967

8 Manchester United; he won in 2001

9   George Best, Manchester United
10 Liverpool in 1977, 1986 and 2001
11 1998
12 Tottenham Hotspur in 1961
13 1991
14 None
15 In 1972, Gordon Banks was voted into second place behind Mary Peters